D1156268

A FACTS ON FILE PUBLICATION

DISARMAMENT
& NUCLEAR TESTS

1964-69

INTERIM
HISTORY

Bridge Between Today's News and Tomorrow's History

DISARMAMENT
& NUCLEAR TESTS
1964-69

INTERIM
HISTORY

DISARMAMENT
& NUCLEAR TESTS

1964-69

Edited by Vojtech Mastny
Assistant Professor of History
Columbia University (New York)

FACTS ON FILE, INC.   NEW YORK

DISARMAMENT & NUCLEAR TESTS 1964-69

Copyright, 1970, by Facts on File, Inc.

Library of Congress Catalog Card Number: 72-122210

ISBN 0-87196-154-7

9 8 7 6 5 4 3 2 1

CONTENTS

1966

1967

BACKGROUND

I N THE PERIOD FROM THE ESTABLISHMENT of the U. S. nuclear monopoly —after the first explosion of an A-bomb at Alamogordo, N.M. July 16, 1945—to the partial test ban treaty of Aug. 5, 1963, disarmament negotiations made only limited progress. They were hampered by the Soviet effort to catch up with the U.S. in nuclear armaments and by the concomitant tensions between the Western and the Eastern blocs. The first Soviet explosions of an A-bomb in Aug. 1949 and of an H-bomb in Aug. 1953 were decisive steps toward a nuclear "balance of terror."

The inconclusive results of the major confrontations between the West and the East—the 2d Berlin crisis of June-Oct. 1961 and the Cuban missile crisis of Oct. 1962—promoted in the early 1960s a mutual desire to reduce tensions, including those resulting from the accelerating armaments race. Both the U.S. and the USSR had improved their systems of delivery vehicles, shifting their reliance from strategic bombers to missiles. At the same time the gradual disintegration of the blocs and the independent nuclear programs of France and Communist China complicated the problem of disarmament, transforming it from a bilateral into a multilateral one. France and Communist China condemned the disarmament efforts of countries—the U.S., USSR and Britain—that they suspected of trying to perpetuate a nuclear monopoly as instrument of political blackmail. But because of the vast disproportion in the size of armaments between the 2 superpowers and all other countries, the relationship between the U.S. and the USSR continued to dominate the disarmament discussions.

Starting in 1946, disarmament discussions were conducted in several international bodies: the UN Atomic Energy Commission (founded Jan. 24, 1946), the UN Commission for Conventional Armaments (founded Feb. 13, 1947), the Committee of 12 (established Dec. 13, 1950 to prepare a merger of the above 2 commissions), the UN Disarmament Commission (established Jan. 11, 1952, as a result of their merger), the Subcommittee of 5 (formed Apr. 19, 1954 by the UN Disarmament Commission), the International Atomic Energy Agency (established Oct. 26, 1956 and concentrating upon the peaceful uses of atomic energy), test-ban talks groups (which began negotiations in Geneva Oct. 31, 1958 and then continued intermittently through technical experts until the limited nuclear test ban treaty was signed in Moscow Aug. 5, 1963), the UN Committee on Peaceful Uses of Outer Space (established Dec. 12, 1959), the 10-Member Disarmament Committee (created Sept. 7, 1959 outside of UN and disbanded June 28, 1960), the 18-Nation Disarmament Committee (created Dec. 13, 1961). Small negotiating bodies proved to be more productive than larger ones, and by 1964 the 18-Nation Disarmament Committee, meeting in Geneva, had become established as the most important forum for negotiations.

This volume records the developments involving disarmament and nuclear tests during the period 1964-9. It supplements a previous INTERIM HISTORY book entitled DISARMAMENT & NUCLEAR TESTS 1960-63. As with its predecessor volume and most other INTERIM HISTORY books, its contents are largely adapted from material that appeared in FACTS ON FILE during the period covered. As in all INTERIM HISTORY books, great pains were taken to present all pertinent material—much of it quite controversial—without bias.

Glossary of Acronyms

Listed below are definitions of many of the shortened names and word forms used in this book:
ABM—anti-ballistic missile system
AEC—Atomic Energy Commission (U.S.)
BMEWS—Ballistic Missile Early Warning System (U.S.)
CBW—chemical and biological warfare
ENDC—18-Nation Disarmament Committee (UN)
Euratom—European Atomic Energy Community
FOBS—fractional orbital bombardment system
IAEA—International Atomic Energy Agency (UN)
ICBM—intercontenental ballistic missile
IRBM—intermediate-range ballistic missile
ISS—Institute for Strategic Studies (London)
kiloton—energy (produced by a nuclear explosion) equivalent to that produced by the explosion of 1,000 tons of TNT
megaton—energy (produced by a nuclear explosion) equivalent to that produced by the explosion of one million tons of TNT
MIRV—multiple independently targed re-entry vehicle
NATO—North Atlantic Treaty Organization
SAC—Strategic Air Command (U.S.)
SALT—strategic arms limitation talks
TV—television
UAR—United Arab Republic (Egypt)
UK—United Kingdom of Great Britain & Northern Ireland (Britain)
UN—United Nations
U.S.—United States of America
USSR—Union of Soviet Socialist Republics (Soviet Union, Russia)

1964

The Geneva 18-Nation Disarmament Committee met in 2 sessions during 1964—from Jan. 21 to Apr. 23 and from June 3 to Sept. 17. The most important proposals discussed though not accepted during these meetings were Pres. Lyndon B. Johnson's nuclear weapons "freeze" plan of Jan. 21 and a Jan. 28 Soviet proposal to scrap bomber aircraft. The USSR and U.S. Apr. 20 pledged unilaterally to cut the production of fissionable materials for nuclear weapons production but did not specify any controls of these pledges. Disarmament was an important issue in the U.S. Presidential campaign, during which Republican candidate Barry Goldwater criticized the 1963 test ban treaty for allegedly endangering U.S. national security. Communist China became the world's 5th nuclear power by exploding an atomic device Oct. 16.

PRE-GENEVA INITIATIVES

New Year's Messages

Soviet Premier Nikita S. Khrushchev and Soviet Pres. Leonid I. Brezhnev had cabled Pres. Johnson Dec. 30, 1963 to express their personal and official New Year's greetings. Their message, received at the President's office in Austin, Tex., cited the 1963 Moscow agreement curtailing nuclear weapons tests as an example of the "further significant successes" they hoped for in 1964. The Soviet leaders stressed their belief that "cooperation of governments in resolving urgent international questions ... is entirely possible."

Pres. Johnson replied Jan. 1 that his "highest purpose" would be the preservation and strengthening of peace in the new year. He added: "The time for simply talking about peace, however, has passed—1964 should be a year in which we take further steps toward that goal." "In our hands have been placed the ... hope of millions; it is my fervent hope that we are good stewards of that trust." Mr. Johnson's message was amplified by a White House spokesman who, in a release to newsmen Jan. 1 of Presidentially-authorized remarks, said that Mr. Johnson was prepared to launch an "unrelenting peace offensive" to lessen cold war tensions. The President was described as acutely aware of the fact that the U.S. and USSR had the power to totally destroy each other. Mr. Johnson was reported to feel that a new "hard-line" U.S. policy might best be based on a readiness to seek new East-West negotiations without forgetting past Soviet tactics and actions.

The President's views were echoed by U.S. State Secy. Dean Rusk Jan. 2 at a New Year's press conference in Washington. Rusk, declaring that "peace remains the most urgent business of mankind," said that the U.S. was ready to re-examine with the USSR the entire range of East-West problems. He made it clear, however, that he foresaw no "large or dramatic" agreements between the 2 powers but, rather, that he hoped for a series of pragmatic agreements to avoid trouble. Rusk added that the most dangerous problems facing the 2 sides were those created by Communist China, Cuba and North Vietnam.

Khrushchev Proposes Pact Renouncing War

The first diplomatic initiative of 1964 was taken by the USSR Jan. 2 in an appeal to all governments of the world to join in a treaty renouncing war as a means of settling territorial disputes. The Soviet appeal was made in a personal message from Khrushchev to the heads of state or government of every country with which the USSR maintained diplomatic relations. The message, dated Dec. 31, 1963, was delivered in world capitals Jan. 2 and was made public by the USSR Jan. 3.

According to the English text transmitted by the Soviet press agency Novosti, the Khrushchev appeal included these statements: "The Soviet government, guided by the interests of stengthening peace and preventing war, is submitting the following proposal to the consideration of the governments of all states: to conclude an international agreement (or treaty) on the renunciation by states of the use of force for the solution of territorial disputes or questions of frontiers. In our opinion, such an agreement should include the following principal propositions:

"First, a solemn undertaking by the state parties to the agreement not to resort to force to alter the existing state frontiers;

"2d, recognition that the territory of states should not, even temporarily, be the object of any invasion, attack, military occupation or any other forcible measures directly or indirectly undertaken by other states for whatever political, economic, strategic, frontier, or any other considerations;

"3d, a firm declaration that neither differences in social or state systems, nor denial of recognition or the absence of diplomatic relations, nor any other pretexts can serve as a justification for the violation by one state of the territorial integrity of another;

"4th, an undertaking to settle all territorial disputes exclusively by peaceful means, such as negotiations, mediation, conciliatory procedure, and also other means...in accordance with the charter of the United Nations."

Khrushchev's message indicated, however, that the USSR considered several of the world's current problems to be special cases not coming within the provisions of the proposed treaty. Citing the cases of Taiwan (Formosa) and West Irian (Netherlands New Guinea), it said: "Taiwan's unlawful occupation by American troops should be terminated. The island is an inalienable part of the People's Republic of China.... Take, for instance, such a recent case as West Irian's reunification with Indonesia. The demands of the liberated states for the return of territories that are still under the colonial yoke or under foreign occupation are unquestionably just... In this event the oppressed peoples have no other choice but to take up arms themselves." The message also singled out Germany, Korea and Vietnam as special cases that could be dealt with best by withdrawal of U.S. military forces.

2 other major problems taken up by the Khrushchev message were foreign military bases and the current instability along Asian frontiers: "War bases, established in foreign territories alienated from other states, should be liquidated.... The peoples of the Asian continent face great tasks [to eliminate]...age-old poverty and want. This calls...above all for peace and tranquility on the borders."

Khrushchev's appeal concluded with a pledge that the USSR would do everything possible to bring about an antiwar treaty, in the hope that it would lead to general disarmament and assure world peace.

Western Responses

In reply to the Khrushchev message, the U.S. State Department said Jan. 3 that the Soviet proposal would be studied carefully even though it was a "disappointing" response to Pres. Johnson's efforts to find an understanding with the Soviet Union. The department's statement was issued after State Secy. Rusk had conferred by phone with Pres. Johnson on the matter. It avoided an open rejection of the Khrushchev suggestion, although it made clear that the U.S. considered his message "not an objective statement of the problem of territorial disputes." The U.S., it said, would examine the Soviet appeal in the hope that elements of it might be developed into "constructive steps... in easing tensions." Administration sources made it clear to newsmen, however, that the Khrushchev plan was unacceptable because it amounted to a request that the West unilaterally renounce force, liquidate its military bases and peacefully withdraw from most of the areas that were the subject of dispute with the Soviet bloc. Khrushchev, in contrast, was said to have been explicit in claiming for the Soviet bloc the right to support "just" liberation and anticolonial movements with military force if necessary. The Johnson Administration was said to feel that the Khrushchev proposal was essentially intended as a propaganda venture and that a too-hasty rejection of it would bring discredit on the U.S.

Pres. Johnson spoke on disarmament in his State-of-the-Union message, delivered Jan. 8 before a joint session of Congress. He said: "Our ultimate goal is a world without war, a world made safe for diversity, in which all men, goods and ideas can freely move across every border and every boundary. We must advance toward this goal in 1964 in ... different ways." "We must" maintain U.S. defense and use it, "as John Kennedy used it in the Cuban crisis and for the test-ban treaty, to demonstrate both the futility of nuclear war and the possibilities for lasting peace." The U.S. must also "take new steps" toward control and eventual abolition of arms and "develop with our allies new means of bridging the gap between the East and the West, facing dangers boldly wherever danger exists, but being equally bold in our search for new agreements which can enlarge the hopes of all while violating the interests of none." "In short, ... we must be constantly prepared for the worst and constantly acting for the best.... We intend to bury no one, and we do not intend to be buried. We can fight, if we must, as we have fought before, but we pray that we will never have to fight again." In the message, Pres. Johnson announced reductions in the U.S. military budget. Disclosing that the U.S. was cutting production of material for nuclear weapons by 25%, Mr. Johnson called on "our adversaries to do the same."

The Soviet government welcomed with reserve the cautious military budget reduction foreseen by Pres. Johnson. The position taken by most of the Soviet press was that Mr. Johnson had made clear the

American intention to maintain strong defenses but that, in disclosing U.S. plans to make some cuts in military expenditures and to close some redundant bases, he had made at least a token response to Khrushchev's 1963 challenge for reciprocal cuts in Soviet and Western military spending. Western news agencies in Moscow reported Jan. 9 that the Soviet press and radio had limited its comment to the portion of Mr. Johnson's address that referred to curtailment of conventional forces. Only *Krasnaya Zvezda (Red Star)*, the Defense Ministry newspaper, was said to have mentioned the President's announcement that the U.S. planned to reduce production of fission materials for nuclear weapons and his challenge to the USSR to follow suit. The full text of Mr. Johnson's address was published without comment Jan. 11 by *Izvestia*, the government newspaper.

Replying Jan. 18 to the Russian proposal for a world treaty outlawing territorial aggression, the U.S. accepted the central idea but appended to the proposal suggestions for strengthening and broadening the proposed treaty to cover the forms of aggression utilized by the Soviet bloc in the years since World War II. The American counter-proposals were made in a message from Pres. Johnson to Khrushchev, which was delivered to Soviet Amb.-to-U.S. Anatoly F. Dobrynin by State Secy. Rusk. The note was made public in Washington Jan. 20. The President's message specifically rejected portions of the Soviet proposal that had been tailored to meet the USSR's strategic and political goals, particularly suggestions that Taiwan come under Communist Chinese control, West Germany be subjected to special restrictions and the U.S. liquidate its system of foreign military bases. Mr. Johnson called on Khrushchev to stop "emphasizing our well-known disagreements" and instead join the U.S. in supporting, at the impending Geneva disarmament conference, proposals to reduce the risk of nuclear war.

In his response to Khrushchev's general appeal for the banning of territorial war, Mr. Johnson made a series of proposals that he termed "even broader and stronger than your own." They were directed at outlawing the particular types of aggression involved in Communist-led subversion and guerrilla warfare and that might be involved in a Communist attempt to suppress Western rights of occupation in and access to Berlin. Mr. Johnson proposed:

"First, all governments or regimes shall abstain from the direct or indirect threat or use of force to change:

"International boundaries;

"Other territorial or ... dividing lines established or confirmed by international agreement or practice;

"The dispositions of truce or military armistice agreements; or

"Arrangements or procedures concerning access to or passage across or the administration of those areas where international agreement or practice has established or confirmed such arrangements or procedures.

"Nor shall any government or regime use or threaten force to enlarge the territory under its control or administration by overthrowing or displacing established authorities.

"2d, these limitations shall apply regardless of the direct or indirect form which such threat or use of force might take, whether in the form of aggression, subversion or clandestine supply of arms, regardless of . . . any question of recognition, diplomatic relations, or difference of political systems.

"3d, the parties to any serious dispute, in adhering to these principles, shall seek a solution by peaceful means—resorting to negotiation, mediation, conciliation, arbitration, judicial settlement, action by a regional or appropriate United Nations agency or other peaceful means of their own choice.

"4th, these obligations, if they are to continue, would have to be quite generally observed. Any departure would require reappraisal; and the inherent right of self-defense which is recognized in Article 51 of the United Nations Charter would, in any event, remain fully operative."

British Prime Min. Sir Alec Douglas-Home replied Jan. 24 to Khrushchev's proposal for a world agreement outlawing war as a means of settling territorial disputes. Douglas-Home's note, made public Jan. 25, said that Britain would "welcome any measures aimed at effectively outlawing the use of force" but that Britain was convinced that in many cases, as in the Communist efforts to win control of Laos and South Vietnam, infiltration and subversion were as great a danger to peace as overt aggression. Douglas-Home called on Khrushchev to drop "outworn" propaganda views on alleged Western colonialism and militarism and to clarify his position on the specific measures he envisaged.

FIRST PERIOD OF GENEVA TALKS

The 1964 session of the UN 18-Nation Disarmament Committee (ENDC) opened in Geneva Jan. 21. The session, the 157th held by the committee since its inception in Mar. 1962, was not attended by France; the French boycott of the Geneva conference had effectively reduced the committee to 17 members ever since the talks began. The 17 participating nations were: West—U.S., Britain, Italy, Canada. Soviet bloc—USSR, Poland, Czechoslovakia, Rumania, Bulgaria. Neutrals—India, Mexico, Sweden, United Arab Republic, Burma, Ethiopia, Brazil, Nigeria.

U.S. Proposes A-Weapon 'Freeze'

In a personal message from Pres. Johnson to the opening session of the conference, the U.S. offered to join the Soviet Union in East-West negotiations to "freeze" the numbers and types of nuclear-armed strategic weapons possessed by both nations and their allies. The "freeze" presumably would apply to all nuclear delivery systems—long-range bombers, fixed-site missiles and Polaris submarines—capable of being used for strategic purposes.

The President's message was read at the Geneva meeting by William C. Foster, director of the U.S. Arms Control & Disarmament Agency and chief U.S. representative at the opening session. Semyon K. Tsarapkin, the chief Soviet negotiator, also addressed the opening session, but he read from a prepared text and made no apparent response to the U.S. proposal. (Tsarapkin's address listed the following subjects as those which the USSR wanted discussed at the 1964 sessions: the reduction of Western and Soviet forces in Germany coupled with the creation of a network of inspection posts to guard both sides against a surprise attack from German territory; the transformation of Germany into a zone free of nuclear weapons; the reduction of military budgets; the signing of a mutual non-aggression pact by the NATO and Warsaw Treaty powers.)

Mr. Johnson's message declared that there was "only one item on the agenda of this conference ... and that one item is peace." Citing the successes of the Geneva meetings held in 1963—the U.S.-Soviet "hot line" agreement, the Moscow treaty curbing nuclear tests and the UN declaration banning nuclear weapons from space, the President said that "this conference has led to more concrete and effective results than any disarmament conference in modern history." He pledged that the U.S. would do its share to "mark 1964 as the year the world turned for all time away from the horrors of war and constructed new bulwarks of peace." "Specifically," the President said, "this nation now proposes 5 major types of potential agreement:

"First, ... in consultation with our allies, we will be prepared to discuss means of prohibiting the threat or use of force, directly or indirectly—whether by aggression, subversion, or the clandestine supply of arms—to change boundaries or demarcation lines; to interfere with access to territory; or to extend control or administration over territory by displacing established authorities.

"2d, while we continue our efforts to achieve general and complete disarmament under effective international control, we must first endeavor to halt further increases in strategic armaments now. The United States, the Soviet Union and their respective allies should agree to explore a verified freeze of the number and characteristics of strategic nuclear offensive and defense vehicles. For our part, we are convinced that the security of all nations can be safeguarded within the scope of such an agreement and that this initial measure preventing the further expansion of the deadly and costly arms race will open the path to reductions in all types of forces from present levels.

"3d, in this same spirit of early action, the United States believes that a verified agreement to halt all production of fissionable materials for weapons use would be a major contribution to world peace. Moreover, while we seek agreement on this measure, the U.S. is willing to achieve prompt reductions through both sides closing comparable production facilities on a plant-by-plant basis, with mutual inspection. We have started in this direction—we hope the Soviet Union will do the same—and we are prepared to accept appropriate international verification of the reactor shut-down already scheduled in our country.

"4th, we must further reduce the danger of war by accident, miscalculation or surprise attack. In consultation with our allies, we will be prepared to discuss proposals for creating a system of observation posts as a move in this direction.

"5th, and finally, to stop the spread of nuclear weapons to nations not now controlling them, let us agree: (a) That nuclear weapons not be transferred into the national control of states which do not now control them, and that all transfers of nuclear materials for peaceful purposes take place under effective international safeguards; (b) that the major nuclear powers accept in an increasing number of their peaceful nuclear activities the same inspection they recommended for other states; and (c) on the banning of all nuclear weapons tests under effective verification and control."

(The proposal advanced by Mr. Johnson for control of nuclear weapons delivery systems was not new. It had been proposed previously by several leaders, particularly French Pres. Charles de Gaulle, who had urged the control and destruction of all bombers and strategic missiles and had ordered the French boycott of the Geneva meetings on the ground that none of the participants had advanced realistic proposals for disarmament. De Gaulle's proposal, advanced in 1962, had been rejected by Khrushchev.)

(Washington officials reported Jan. 21 that the U.S. had completed the first Western disarmament inspection of Soviet scientific posts in Antarctica. The U.S. inspection, carried out by a team headed by John C. Guthrie, director of the State Department's Soviet Affairs Office, was said to have found no evidence that the Soviet posts were being used for unauthorized military or nuclear purposes. The U.S. team was reported to have visited the USSR's Vostok and Smirny bases as well as the Scott Station operated by the New Zealand government. The inspections were the first to be carried out under a 12-power treaty, signed in 1959, banning military activities in the Antarctic.)

USSR Proposes Bomber-Burning

At the meeting of the Geneva disarmament conference held Jan. 28, the Soviet Union called on the nations of the world to join in destroying all their bomber aircraft even in advance of an agreement on general disarmament. The Russian proposal was made in a memo presented by Soviet negotiator Semyon Tsarapkin, who noted that although the manned bomber was rapidly becoming obsolete, it remained a major weapon capable of use for offensive strikes over long distances and its elimination would enhance the security of all nations. Tsarapkin, meeting with newsmen later Jan. 28, stressed that the Soviet proposal was based on the destruction of "all" bombers and not just those considered obsolete and expendable by the governments possessing them.

William C. Foster, chief U.S. representative at the Geneva talks, told newsmen Jan. 28 that the Russian proposal was acceptable "in principle" to the U.S. Foster indicated that the U.S. had suggested privately to the USSR in 1963 that the 2 governments discuss the mutual scrapping of certain types of bombers. Washington officials confirmed the same day that the U.S. had proposed the destruction of B-47 and Badger aircraft, comparable jet bombers that were being retired as obsolete by both nations.

Another proposal made in the Soviet memo was greeted with interest by the other delegations in Geneva: a suggestion that the recently-announced reductions in the U.S. and Soviet military budgets be followed up with a further cut of 10% to 15% in military expenditures. The memo also repeated Soviet proposals for (a) the liquidation of all foreign military bases, (b) the signing of an East-West nonaggression pact, (c) inspection to guard against surprise attack in central Europe, (d) measures to halt the spread of nuclear weapons.

(Tsarapkin had warned at a Geneva news conference Jan. 23 that the U.S.-sponsored plan for a multilateral Western nuclear force would have to be "swept away" before there could be any agreement curbing the spread of atomic weapons. He made clear the Soviet view that a Western nuclear force would put such weapons in the hands of nations not currently possessing them even if none of these nations legally had the authority to launch them. Tsarapkin declared that if West German "militarists" were able to obtain nuclear weapons through the proposed Western force, "they would not hestitate to unleash atomic war.")

U.S. & Soviet Proposals Discussed

The U.S. proposal for the "freezing" of nuclear-armed strategic weapons was explained to the conference in detail Jan. 31 by Foster, who said the U.S. plan had been intended to apply primarily to "long-range weapons of the greatest effectiveness" in order to "halt the race for more and better strategic nuclear vehicles." Foster stressed, however, that, if implemented, the freeze would have to apply to all long-range missiles and bomber aircraft and to anti-missile missile systems. Clarifying the latter point, Foster said that "a freeze on strategic delivery systems without a freeze on anti-missile systems would be destabilizing and therefore unacceptable."

Soviet plans for a disarmament time-table that would permit the major powers to retain a limited and balanced "nuclear umbrella" until the final stage of disarmament were revived by Tsarapkin Feb. 4. Tsarapkin, elaborating on proposals advanced in 1963 by Soviet Foreign Min. Andrei A. Gromyko, said that the USSR would accept a disarmament program that permitted the U.S. and USSR to keep specified numbers of operational missiles on their own territories until general disarmament was near. (The U.S. had refused to discuss the elimination of strategic missiles in the first stage of disarmament on the ground that this would mean a military disadvantage for the West.) Tsarapkin insisted, however, that all foreign-based missiles would have to be withdrawn by the great powers in the first stage of disarmament.

The U.S. called on the USSR Feb. 6 to join in a pledge to refrain from giving nuclear weapons or the technical information needed for their manufacture to nations not currently possessing them. Foster said that "the spread of nuclear weapons...to non-nuclear nations constitutes a grave threat to the security and peace of all nations." He added that the U.S. was prepared to join with the USSR in private negotiations on a declaration in which the 2 nations would commit themselves to prevent the further spread of nuclear weaponry. U.S. proposals for a reduction in the output of fissile materials for weapons purposes were reiterated by Foster Feb. 13. Foster declared that the U.S. was prepared to act quickly on its past offer to transfer to peaceful usage 60,000 kilograms (132,000 pounds) of fissile materials produced for use in weapons. The U.S. offer was conditional on the USSR's reciprocal transfer of 40,000 kilograms (88,000 pounds) of weapons-grade fission materials to peaceful use.

Tsarapkin declared Feb. 18 that the U.S. plan for freezing strategic weapons at current levels was unacceptable to the USSR because it did not remove the threat of nuclear war at an early stage of disarmament. He insisted that the Soviet proposal for the early elimination of all but a limited number of strategic missiles would accomplish this and, at the same time, would fulfill Western demands for the retention of retaliatory missile power until Soviet-bloc armed forces had been reduced to a level at which they no longer could be used to launch an attack on the West. Tsarapkin demanded, however, that the West accept the Soviet proposal "in principle" before beginning detailed scrutiny of its provisions.

British Foreign Secy. R. A. Butler took charge of Britain's delegation in Geneva Feb. 24. In his first address at the conference, Butler called on the USSR Feb. 25 to cooperate in supporting UN peace-keeping operations before the conclusion of a world disarmament agreement. Butler asserted that the UN would be in a better position to intervene in explosive situations if it were able to draw on its experience in the Congo and Middle East and plan new peace-keeping operations with the support of the major powers.

Foster left the Geneva talks Feb. 27 to return to his post in Washington. In a final statement at the conference that day, he warned that the U.S. would be forced to continue perfecting its defenses unless an agreement was reached on a "verified" disarmament pact. He said the U.S. had more than doubled its complement of strategic missiles during the conference's first 2 years and would increase its missile strength 750% by 1965 if it carried out current military construction programs. Adrian S. Fisher, deputy director of the Arms Control & Disarmament Agency, replaced Foster as U.S. delegation chief.

Fisher, in his first major statement at the conference, announced Mar. 5 that the U.S. was opening one of its largest nuclear reactors to inspection by the UN International Atomic Energy Agency. He said that the IAEA would be invited to send inspectors to the nuclear reactor and plant of the Yankee Atomic Electric Co., in Rowe, Mass. The Yankee reactor, built by a consortium of 12 private New England utility companies at a cost of $57 million, had produced more than a billion kilowatt-hours of electricity in 1963. Fisher said that if the USSR felt able to open one of its power reactors to inspection, the U.S. would be prepared to discuss extension of the program to other reactors on a reciprocal basis. He stressed that the Yankee reactor would be kept open to the IAEA even if the USSR failed to reciprocate. Tsarapkin replied only that the question of international control over nuclear power plants was a "very difficult subject."

(3 smaller U.S. reactors already had been opened to IAEA inspection. They were 2 research reactors located at Brookhaven, N.Y. and a power reactor at Picqua, O.)

Tsarapkin Mar. 12 again denounced the U.S.' proposal for a strategic weapons "freeze" as an attempt to subject Soviet defenses to legalized "espionage" while retaining Western missile forces intact. He said that a "potential aggressor" could take advantage of the U.S. plan to "verify" his targets and then launch a sudden attack with the strategic forces remaining at his disposal. He rejected Fisher's contention that in a world of rapidly mounting strategic armaments the "freeze" would constitute a real measure of disarmament. (Soviet Foreign Min. Gromyko Mar. 3 had denounced the U.S. for allegedly having forced the Geneva conference to discuss plans that were intended to step up the arms race rather than lead to disarmament. Gromyko, in an interview published prominently by the Soviet government newspaper *Izvestia,* charged that the U.S.' obstructive tactics had impaired the usefulness of the Geneva talks. He dismissed the U.S. disarmament plan as an attempt to "establish international control over the most secret weapons" while avoiding serious disarmament measures.)

Fisher Mar. 17 outlined the reasons for the U.S.' rejection of the Soviet plan for the scrapping of all but a limited number of strategic missiles in the first stage of disarmament. He said that (a) it would produce "radical shifts" in the current East-West military balance; (b) it did not provide for verification to assure that additional missiles were retained by a party to the treaty; (c) it was linked to a demand for the dismantling of all foreign bases, including those Western bases that had become an integral part of the East-West military balance. He made it clear that the USSR's acceptance of U.S. demands for retention of a nuclear umbrella until the final stage of disarmament did not make up for the other questionable provisions of the Soviet disarmament plan.

Gomulka Plan

The Polish government called Feb. 29 for a treaty "freezing" the current levels of nuclear armaments on the territories of East and West Germany, Poland and Czechoslovakia. The proposal was made in a memo handed to the Warsaw ambassadors of East Germany and Czechoslovakia and of the U.S., Britain, USSR and the other countries who had armed forces contingents on the territories designated. Based on disarmament ideas advanced by Polish CP First Secy. Wladyslaw Gomulka in Dec. 1963, it was labeled an extension rather than a successor to the 1957 "Rapacki plan," in which Polish Foreign Min.

Adam Rapacki had proposed the complete banning of nuclear weapons from Central Europe. Rapacki, making public the new "Gomulka plan" at a Warsaw news conference Mar. 5, said that it had been put forward in an effort "to stabilize the situation in Central Europe and to put developments in that area on a path that would lessen tensions and make disarmament possible." *Major points of the Gomulka plan:*

●All nuclear and thermonuclear armaments would be frozen at existing levels on the territories, the territorial waters and in the airspace of the 4 countries designated. The freeze would be extended to new areas "through the accession of other European states" to the agreement.

●"Parties maintaining armed forces in the area... would undertake obligations not to produce, not to introduce or import, not to transfer to other parties... in the area the nuclear and thermonuclear weapons."

●"The supervision and control [of the accord] could be exercised by mixed commissions composed of representatives of the Warsaw Pact and of the North Atlantic Treaty Organization on a parity basis." The system of supervision and safeguards could include inspection of all Central European facilities for nuclear production and of "frontier railway, road, waterway junctions, sea and airports."

Rapacki, answering reporters' questions about the plan, confirmed that its provisions for inspection by mixed NATO-Warsaw Pact commissions had been designed to meet Western objections to direct contact with representatives of the East German government. Rapacki refused to say whether the supervision commissions would be given complete freedom of movement throughout the 4 countries. He refused to say what effect the plan was intended to have on the current U.S. proposals for establishment, with West German participation, of a unified Western nuclear striking fleet. (Polish Amb.-to-UN Bohdan Lewandowski told newsmen in New York Mar. 5 that the Gomulka plan would not bar West Germany from participating in the nuclear fleet but would bar the fleet from West German territorial waters.)

Stalemate in Geneva

The U.S. delegation to the UN 18-nation Disarmament Committee, meeting in Geneva, announced Mar. 19 that the U.S. was prepared to destroy 480 operational B-47 jet bombers if the USSR would destroy an equal number of TU-16 "Badger" bombers, considered the equivalent of the B-47 in size, range and speed. U.S. delegation chief Fisher, declared that the resultant "bomber bonfire" could serve as a "graphic example of armament reduction to the entire world." Fisher said that the U.S. was prepared to destroy B-47s from its "operational inventory" at the rate of 20 a month for the next 2 years and, in addition, was ready to match the USSR in destroying further agreed numbers of the equivalent planes that the 2 nations maintained "stored... for emergency mobilization."

Soviet chief delegate Tsarapkin rejected the U.S. proposal Mar. 19 as an attempt to pass off the retirement of obsolete aircraft as disarmament. He called on Fisher to reply to the recent Soviet call for the destruction of all bomber planes everywhere. Fisher answered that the Soviet proposal was certain to be rejected by nations dependent principally on bombers for their defense. The U.S. plan, he said, could be applied directly by the 2 great powers and would "assure that the bombers destroyed could not be transferred to the armament inventories of other nations."

Indian delegate Vishnu C. Trivedi Mar. 24 announced his country's support "in principle" of the Soviet plan's provisions for the destruction of all but a limited number of missiles in the first stage of disarmament. Trivedi, who indorsed the idea that a limited number of atomic-armed missiles be left to the U.S. and USSR as a "nuclear umbrella" against surprise attack, called on the West to accept the Soviet plan so that negotiations on the missile question could proceed. The USSR had refused to submit the proposal in detail until the other participants accepted the plan in principle. Trivedi's position was welcomed by Tsarapkin but was criticized by Western delegates for its acceptance of a plan whose contents were unknown.

A British plan for the establishment of military observation posts throughout Europe, Russia, Britain and America was presented at the conference Mar. 26. Submitted by British delegate Peter J. M. Thomas, the proposal called for the posts to be manned by NATO and Warsaw Treaty organization personnel responsible for guarding against surprise or accidental attack. The British suggested that the posts be manned on an "adversary basis"—with those in Communist territory staffed with Western personnel and *vice versa.* Thomas said that the existence of a system of such posts would dispel the fear and distrust that were "the root of many of our problems."

The Soviet delegation denounced the British proposal Mar. 26 as another attempt to establish controls without disarmament. Tsarapkin said that, without a reduction of troop levels in Europe and the banning of nuclear weapons from both parts of Germany, inspection posts would breed rather than lessen distrust.

U.S. delegate Fisher announced Apr. 1 that Soviet demands for the elimination of most strategic missiles in the projected first stage of general disarmament were not acceptable to the U.S. Fisher rejected the Indian suggestion that the U.S. accept the proposal in principle while negotiations continued on parts of the plan on which the East and West differed, particularly in the West's demand that any disarmament pact leave it a "missile umbrella" with which it could protect itself against attack by Soviet-bloc conventional forces during the early stages of disarmament.

British delegate Thomas charged Apr. 7 that the USSR's proposals at the conference had been unrealistic in that they provided for too-rapid disarmament in the first stage of implementation of a treaty. Thomas, noting that the USSR had called for the first-stage destruction of nearly all nuclear armaments and of 30% of the great powers' conventional arms within 18 months, declared that such a range of disarmament actions would be "too large for adequate verification in the short time allowed" and that participating states would lack confidence that other states had carried out the agreement faithfully.

Discussing Soviet proposals for a 10%-15% reduction of all states' military budgets, Fisher said at the conference Apr. 9 that the USSR's published military budget consisted in 1964 of "some 16 words and one sum" and did not truly reflect Soviet military activities. Fisher noted that the published USSR military budget had declined by 15% in 1955-1960, during a period when Russia was known to have carried out intensive nuclear armament. He added: "Suppose that the reduction from 1955 to 1960 had been by agreement, on our innocent assumption that it would result in some comparable measure of disarmament.... How wrong we would have been proven 5 years later."

United Arab Republic delegate Abdel Fattah Hassan called on the U.S. Apr. 9 to abandon its plan for a shipborne Western nuclear striking force if the USSR agreed in return to accept Pres. Johnson's proposal for a freeze of nuclear-armed strategic missile forces. Neither the U.S. nor the Soviet delegations commented on the suggestion at the conference, but Tsarapkin called on Hassan privately Apr. 10 to express the USSR's interest in the proposal.

Pres. Johnson's Jan. 21 proposal for a freeze of nuclear armed missile and bomber forces was presented at the conference Apr. 16, Fisher said that the freeze was intended to be applied to: (1) all ground-launched surface-to-surface missiles with a range of more than 1,000 kilometers (621 miles); (2) all sea-launched missiles, including those of the Polaris type, with a range of more than 100 kilometers (62 miles); (3) all strategic bombers weighing more than 27-1/2 tons and air-to-surface missiles with a range of 100 kilometers or more. Verification would be assured by a variety of measures, among them permanent international inspection of all strategic airfields, missile launching sites and missiles research and production centers. Missile tests and training exercises would be permitted under the surveillance of international observers. Worn or damaged missiles would be replaceable on an inspected one-for-one basis, but no improvement of missiles or of launching systems would be permitted. Fisher contended that the proposed freeze would "keep many hundreds of the deadliest weapons ever devised by man out of the arsenals of the future and would halt all progress on even more deadly ones now being developed."

Tsarapkin rejected the plan on the grounds that it would not "get rid of one missile or bomber" and would require inspection measures that would open the USSR's strategic forces to Western military espionage.

The discussion of the U.S. proposal was the last major activity of the Geneva conferees before they agreed Apr. 23 to recess.

U.S. & SOVIET ARMAMENTS

Both Nations Pledge A-Arms Cuts

Soviet and American pledges of cutbacks in the production of fissionable materials for nuclear weapons were announced Apr. 20 in statements made simultaneously by U.S. Pres. Johnson in New York and Soviet Premier Khrushchev in Moscow. Britain associated itself with the U.S.-Soviet action in a statement made the following day by Prime Min. Douglas-Home. The pledges were made unilaterally by each government and were not subject to verification. The announcements stressed that the pledges did not constitute a substantive disarmament measure but were considered a demonstration of the 3 governments' hopes for such measures in the future. France, the world's 4th nuclear power, refused to join in the promised cutbacks.

White House sources reported Apr. 20 that the pledges had been arranged in a recent series of private communications between Pres. Johnson and Khrushchev. Mr. Johnson was said to have initiated the exchange after the Administration had decided, on the basis of AEC-Defense Department assessments, that the U.S.' nuclear arsenal had reached a level that justified a reduction in future weapons production. Khrushchev's assent to a similar cutback in Soviet output of weapons-grade fissile material was said to have been communicated to Mr. Johnson Apr. 17 by Soviet Amb.-to-U.S. Anatoly F. Dobrynin.

The U.S. announcement was made by Pres. Johnson in an address in New York at a meeting of the Associated Press. The President, declaring that "our relationship with the Soviet Union" was at "the center of our concern for peace," said: "Today . . . there are new pressures and new realities which make it permissible to hope that the pursuit of peace is in the interests of the Soviet Union as it is in ours." The U.S.' restraint "may be convincing the Soviet leaders of the reality that we in America seek neither war not the destruction of the Soviet Union." "Our own position is clear. We will . . . pursue any agreement, we will take any action which might lessen the chance of war without sacrificing the interests of our allies or our own ability to defend the alliance against attack. In other words, our guard is up but our hand is out.... I have ordered a further substantial reduction in our production of enriched uranium to be carried out over a 4-year period. When added to previous reductions, this will mean an over-all decrease in the production of plutonium by 20% and of enriched uranium by 40%.... This is not disarmament. This is not a declaration of peace. But it is a hopeful sign and it is a step forward which... we can take in the hope that the world may yet one day live without the fear of war."

The Soviet announcement was made in a statement issued by Khrushchev, broadcast by Moscow radio and distributed by Tass simultaneously with Mr. Johnson's speech. Khrushchev said: "A moment has now come when the possibility emerged of taking steps toward a reduction of the fissionable materials for military purposes. The Soviet government has examined... to what limit our country can go in this direction, given the present balance of nuclear power in the world arena, without in any way weakening the defenses of the Soviet Union and the firmness of the nuclear rocket shield reliably safeguarding the security of all countries of the Socialist community." The USSR had reached the following decisions: "(1) To discontinue now the construction of 2 new big atomic reactors for the production of plutonium. (2) In the next several years to reduce substantially the production of uranium-235 for nuclear weapons. (3) Accordingly, to allocate more fissionable materials for peaceful uses—in atomic power stations, in industry, agriculture, in medicine, in the implementation of major scientific, technical projects, including the distillation of sea water."

The British announcement was made by Douglas-Home Apr. 21 in a statement to the House of Commons. Douglas-Home asserted that Britain had reduced its acquisition of fissile materials "to the minimum necessary to maintain our independent nuclear deterrent and to meet all our defense requirements for the foreseeable future." He said that Britain's production of plutonium for weapons was to be "gradually terminated" and that none of the plutonium that Britain supplied to the U.S. in return for enriched uranium would be used for weapons by either country. Douglas-Home acknowledged that the U.S.-British-Soviet action was not a genuine measure of disarmament, but he asserted that it was "a welcome psychological step on the road to peace."

Nuclear Forces Compared

An official U.S. estimate of the relative strength of U.S. and Soviet nuclear power was published Apr. 14 by the U.S. Defense Department. The nuclear assessment was made public in response to Sen. Barry Goldwater's (R., Ariz.) charges that Defense Secy. Robert S. McNamara had weakened the defenses of the U.S. by overdependence on strategic missiles to the detriment of manned aircraft and naval vessels.

The Defense Department statement, reportedly issued with White House authorization, said: McNamara and other Administration officials had "stated on several occasions that our strategic nuclear forces are so large and so powerful as to be capable of absorbing a full first strike directed against them and surviving with sufficient power to completely destroy the aggressor. Questions have been raised, however, regarding the magnitude of our superiority." This superiority was great and continuing to grow. The information in the statement had been released "so that there may be no misunderstanding on this point." *The statement gave this assessment of U.S. and Soviet strength:*

Strategic air forces—The U.S. Air Force currently maintained 540 long-range nuclear bombers on alert. The Soviet Air Force could muster no more than 120 heavy bombers and 150 medium bombers capable of reaching U.S. territory and returning home; their range limited them to objectives in Alaska and the Pacific Northwest.

Inter-continental missiles—Approximately 750 inter-continental ballistic missiles (ICBMs) were in place at U.S. Air Force launching sites and were operational. The USSR was believed to have approximately 188 operational ICBMs.

Polaris missiles—192 Polaris missiles already were deployed aboard operational U.S. nuclear submarines. Each of these missiles (16 carried by each sub) was capable of reaching targets 1,500 miles from its underwater launching point. The USSR had "substantially fewer" submarine-borne missiles, none of which were believed capable of underwater launching. The Soviet missiles were believed to have ranges of 500 miles or less.

"The statement said that much of the U.S.' military superiority was due to the progress achieved since the Kennedy Administration came into office in Jan. 1961. Since then, it said, the number of nuclear warheads in the U.S.' strategic alert forces had been increased by 100%, the number of tactical warheads assigned to NATO forces in Europe had been increased by 60%. U.S. tactical air strength was 35% greater, and U.S. airlift capacity had been increased by 75%.

U.S. Preparedness Stressed

In an address before the graduating class of the U.S. Coast Guard Academy in New London, Conn., Pres. Johnson asserted June 3 that the military strength of the U.S. was greater than that of "any adversary or combination of adversaries" and exceeded "the combined might of all the nations in the history of the world." "We, as well as our adversaries, must stand in awe before the power our craft has created and our wisdom must labor to control," he said. "This staggering strength" was built "not to destroy but to save, not to put an end to civilization but rather to try to put an end to conflict"; "those who would answer every problem with nuclear weapons, display not bravery but bravado, not wisdom but a wanton disregard for the survival of the world and the future of the race."

The President identified these 5 areas in which U.S. strength was increasing, and he gave these examples of this growth:

(1) *Ability to deter atomic destruction*—Nuclear power on alert had been increased 2-1/2 times; the U.S. had more than 1,000 fully armed ICBM and Polaris missiles "ready for retaliation" and more than 1,100 strategic bombers, "many of which are equipped with air-to-surface and decoy missiles."

(2) *Ability "to fight less than all-out war"*—The number of combat-ready divisions had been increased 45% airlift capacity had been increased 75%, supporting tactical aircraft 30%, the number of tactical nuclear warheads in Europe 60%; 6 divisions plus supporting units "can be moved into action in a few weeks."

(3) *Struggle against subversion*—Specialized forces had been increased 8 times since 1961; the Army had 6 special-action forces on call around the world "to assist our friendly nations"; the Navy and Air Force had several thousand men similarly trained, and "behind these groups are 5 brigade-size backup forces ready to move into instant action"; "we now have 344 teams at work in 49 countries to train the local military...."

(4) *Development of new weapons.*

(5) *Ability of the American fighting man*—52% of enlisted men were under 25 and high school graduates; 65% of commissioned officers were college graduates.

At a Democratic Party dinner in San Francisco June 19, Pres. Johnson, pledged an "offensive in the pursuit of peace" based on a position of U.S. military might that "makes it possible to seek agreement without fearing loss of liberty." He said: "We have used that strength not to intimidate others, but to show others that we cannot be intimidated—not to incite our enemies but to indicate our intention to defend freedom wherever necessary."

The U.S. Atomic Energy Commission indicated Nov. 9 that while adhering to the 1963 nuclear test-ban treaty, it was maintaining a "readiness capability" to carry out atmospheric tests if any signer should violate the treaty. The commission's financial report noted government appropriations of almost $36 billion for military and peaceful nuclear energy development since atomic development was first started in 1940. The report attributed steadily rising atomic costs (weapons development and fabrication expenses rose 15% to $805 million in fiscal 1964) mainly to "costs related to the safeguard commitments in connection with the test ban treaty, including increased underground testing, maintenance of weapons laboratories, and developing a readiness capability for the conduct of atmospheric tests."

U.S. Presidential Campaign

Republican Criticism & Positions

Campaigning for the GOP Presidential nomination, Sen. Barry Goldwater made these criticisms of the Administration's disarmament policy:

Mar. 19—The Administration was ineffectually opposing "Soviet brinkmanship" with "American back-downmanship."

Mar. 20—Defense Secy. McNamara "and the State Department are engaged in unilateral disarmament at the expense of peace ... freedom." "I want to protect you against the soft-headed people who believe in coexistence with communism." The U.S. proposal for reciprocal bomber-burning "make[s] me sick to my stomach because it brings war that much closer." Soviet missiles were "a little more reliable than ours" since they had been tested for "re-entry with warheads" and in a "nuclear environment."

Mar. 25 (in Detroit)—Defense Secy. McNamara "was turning the profession of arms into a 2d-class craft" and was narrowing U.S. military response to "withdrawal or nuclear holocaust."

Apr. 1 (in San Francisco)—The Johnson Administration was convinced that the Soviet Union "has tacitly accepted the establishment of American strategic superiority," but "the Soviet has not accepted our superiority. They fear it . . ., and they are trying to overcome it."

The Critical Issues Council of the Republican Citizens Committee Apr. 21 issued a report on "The Atlantic Alliance and United States Security." It asserted that decision must be reached on the "fundamental question" of "who controls" the NATO nuclear-deterrent force. It said control of this force should be given to a small multinational group responsible to the 15-nation NATO council. The report called for larger conventional forces in Europe and increased European contributions to the conventional forces. Gen. Lauris Norstad, ex-NATO commander, who headed the task force that wrote the report, said at a news conference Apr. 21 that a distinction must be made between NATO nuclear weapons and the U.S.' own nuclear striking force. He called attention to the report's assertion that the U.S. must recognize the necessity of European participation in planning Western defense and that the European nations must understand the need for swift U.S. action in emergency.

In a letter sent to Goldwater July 12, Republican Gov. William W. Scranton of Pennsylvaina called the Senator's conservative views a "crazy-quilt collection of absurd and dangerous positions" and charged: "You have too often casually prescribed nuclear war as a solution to a troubled world"; "Goldwaterism has come to stand for nuclear irresponsibility." (Scranton had attacked Goldwater July 9 for "reckless comments . . . in the area of war and peace." Referring to a Goldwater interview published in a West German news magazine, *Der Spiegel,* Scranton denounced Goldwater's view that "others" in addition to the President should be allowed to "decide when nuclear destruction shall be released." In the *Der Spiegel* interview, Goldwater, when asked if he stood by his 1960 suggestion for using of nuclear weapons to help possible Eastern European uprisings, replied: "If that became necessary, if that were the only way, yes.")

The 1964 Republican platform adopted at the GOP National Convention in San Francisco July 14, largely reflected Goldwater's views. It proclaimed in regard to disarmament and nuclear weapons:

Losing a critical lead—This Administration has delayed research and development in advanced weapons systems and thus confronted the American people with the fearsome possibility—that Soviet advances, in the decade of the 1970's, may surpass America's present lead. Its misuse of cost effectiveness has stifled the creativity of the nation's military, scientific and industrial communities.

It has failed to originate a single new major strategic weapons system after inheriting from a Republican Administration the most powerful military force of all time. . . .

It has endangered security by downgrading efforts to prepare defenses against enemy ballistic missiles. It has retarded our own military development for near and outer space, while the enemy's development moves on.

Invitations to Disaster. This Administration has adopted policies which will lead to a potentially fatal parity of power with Communism instead of continued military superiority for the United States.

It has permitted disarmament negotiations to proceed without adequate consideration of military judgment—a procedure which tends to bring about, in effect, a unilateral curtailment of American arms....

It has failed to take minimum safeguards against possible consequences of the limited nuclear test ban treaty....

Reducing the risks of war—A dynamic strategy aimed at victory—pressing always for initiatives for freedom, rejecting always appeasement and withdrawal—reduces the risk of nuclear war.... It is accommodation, not opposition, that encourages a hostile nation to remain hostile and to remain aggressive.

The road to peace is a road not of fawning amiability but of strength and respect....

Freedom's Shield—and Sword—Finally, Republicans pledge to keep the nation's sword sharp, ready, and dependable.

We will maintain a superior, not merely equal, military capability as long as the Communist drive for world domination continues....

Republicans will never unilaterally disarm America. We will demand that any arms-reduction plan worthy of consideration guarantee reliable inspection. We will demand that any such plan assure this nation of sufficient strength, step by step, to forestall and defend against possible violations.

We will take every step necessary to carry forward the vital military research and development programs. We will pursue these programs as absolutely necessary to assure our nation of superior strength in the 1970s....

We will fully implement such safeguards as our security requires under the limited nuclear-test-ban treaty....

We will end 2d best weapons policies. We will end the false economies which place price ahead of the performance upon which American lives may depend.... We will prepare a practical civil-defense program....

We Republicans, with the help of Almighty God, will keep those who would bury America aware that this nation has the strength and also the will to defend its every interest....

Democratic Convention

In the keynote address to the Democratic National Convention, delivered in Atlantic City, N.J. Aug. 24, Sen. John O. Pastore (R.I.) urged that the nation keep a "safe" trigger-finger on the atomic bomb, and he asserted that both the Republican Party and its Presidential candidate, Sen. Goldwater, had been "captured" by extremists. Pastore recalled that during the Cuban missile crisis of 1962, "when the world stood still and all of us held our breath, ... there stood John Kennedy— 10 feet tall ... and for the first time ... we saw Nikita Khrushchev pick up his marbles and go home." "And when I hear anyone speak glibly and loosely about whose finger should be on the trigger of the atomic bomb," Pastore said, "I become concerned..., for in an all-out atomic war, there won't be any winner, and surely weapons of this magnitude should be used only as a last resort. And then solely and strictly on the decision of the President.... For the challenge of our time is to maintain peace with honor and to avert a thermo-nuclear holocaust.... The sanity of America is the security of the world."

The 1964 Democratic platform proclaimed in regard to disarmament and nuclear weapons:

... By the end of 1960, military strategy was being shaped by the dictates of arbitrary budget ceilings instead of the real needs of national security. There were, for example, too few ground and air forces to fight limited war, although such wars were a means to continued Communist expansion. Since then, and at the lowest possible cost, we have created a balanced, versatile, powerful defense establishment, capable of countering aggression across the entire spectrum of conflict, from nuclear confrontation to guerrilla subversion. We have increased our intercontinental ballistic missiles and Polaris missiles from fewer than 100 to more than 1,000, more than 4 times the force of the Soviet Union. We have increased the number of combat ready divisions from 11 to 16.

Until such time as there can be an enforceable treaty providing for inspected and verified disarmament, we must, and we will, maintain our military strength, as the sword and shield of freedom and the guarantor of peace. Specifically, we must and we will:
Continue the overwhelming supremacy of our strategic nuclear forces.
Strengthen further our forces for discouraging limited wars and fighting subversion.
Maintain the world's largest research and development effort ... to ensure continued American leadership in weapons systems and equipment....

Building the Peace—As citizens of the United States, we are determined that it be the most powerful nation on earth. As citizens of the world, we insist that this power be exercised with the utmost responsibility.

Control of the use of nuclear weapons must remain solely with the highest elected official in the country—the President of the United States.

Through our policy of never negotiating from fear but never fearing to negotiate, we are slowly but surely approaching the point where effective international agreements providing for inspection and control can begin to lift the crushing burden of armaments off the backs of the people of the world.... We are determined to continue all-out efforts through fully-enforceable measures to halt and reverse the arms race and bring to an end the era of nuclear terror....

National Defense—In 1960, we proposed to "recast our military capacity in order to provide forces and weapons of a diversity, balance, and mobility sufficient in quantity and quality to deter both limited and general aggression."

Since Jan. 1961, we have achieved: A 150% increase in the number of nuclear warheads and a 200% increase in total megatonnage available in the strategic alert forces; a 60% increase in the tactical nuclear strength in Western Europe; a 45% increase in the number of combat-ready Army divisions; a 15,000-man increase in the strength of the Marine Corps; a 75% increase in airlift capability; a 100% increase in ship construction to modernize our fleet; a 44% increase in the number of tactical fighter squadrons; an 800% increase in the special forces trained to deal with counter-insurgency threats.

In 1960, we proposed to create "deterrent military power such that the Soviet and Chinese leaders will have no doubt that an attack on the United States would surely be followed by their own destruction."

Since 1961, we have increased the intercontinental ballistic missiles and Polaris missiles in our arsenal from fewer than 100 to more than 1,000. Our strategic alert forces now have about 1,100 bombers, including 550 on 15-minute alert....

In 1960, we proposed "continuous modernization of our forces through intensified research and development, including essential programs slowed down, terminated, suspended or neglected for lack of budgetary support."

Since 1961, we have: Increased funds for research and development by 50% over the 1957-60 level; added 208 major new research and development projects including 77 weapons programs with costs exceeding $10 million each ...; increased, by more than 1,000%, the funds for the development of counter-insurgency weapons and equipment, from less than $10 million to over $103 million per year.

In 1960, we proposed "balanced conventional military forces which will permit a response graded to the intensity of any threats of aggressive force."

Since 1961, we have: Increased the regular strength of the Army by 100,000 men, and the numbers of combat-ready Army divisions from 11 to 16; increased the number of tactical fighter squadrons from 55 to 79...; trained over 100,000 officers in counter-insurgency skills ... and increased our special forces trained to deal with counter-insurgency by 800%....

Arms Control—In 1960, we proposed "a national peace agency for disarmament planning and research to muster the scientific ingenuity, coordination, continuity, and seriousness of purpose which are now lacking in our arms control efforts."

In 1961, the United States became the first nation in the world to establish an "agency for peace"—the Arms Control & Disarmament Agency. . . .

In 1960, we proposed "to develop responsible proposals that will help break the deadlock on arms control."

. . . After careful negotiations, experienced American negotiators reached agreement with the Russians on a nuclear test ban treaty—an event that will be marked forever in the history of mankind as a first step on the difficult road of arms control. . . .

To insure the effectiveness of our nuclear development program in accord with the momentous test ban treaty, the Joint Chiefs of Staff recommended, and the Administration has undertaken: A comprehensive program of underground testing of nuclear explosives; maintenance of modern nuclear laboratory facilities; preparations to test in the atmosphere if essential to national security, or if the treaty is violated by the Soviet Union; continuous improvement of our means for detecting violations and other nuclear activities elsewhere in the world. . . .

Goldwater Campaign

Following his nomination as Republican Presidential candidate, Goldwater charged Aug. 10 and 19 that U.S. "deliverable nuclear capacity" would be cut by 90% in the next decade under current Administration policy. Goldwater Aug. 19 released a table supporting his viewpoint by indicating that 28,570 megatons of nuclear power could be carried by current U.S. strategic weapons systems, including the manned bombers, compared with 1,656 megatons projected for the 1970s. (The Defense Department, in a statement Aug. 20, called Goldwater's table "grossly inaccurate" and said his method "seems to be that of taking newspaper guesses on warhead yields and bomber loads as facts and then subtracting all the bombers." It said: "Large numbers of strategic bombers" were to be retained at least through mid-1972; "bomber-delivered weapons do not and will not constitute 90% of our strategic force by any measure at any time in the next decade.")

Goldwater, addressing the national convention of the American Radio Relay League in New York Aug. 22, said he had opposed the 1963 nuclear test-ban treaty primarily because atmospheric nuclear explosions adversely affected communications and the USSR had more information on this subject than the U.S.

In Indianapolis Oct. 1, Goldwater charged that the Johnson Administration was guilty of "the big lie" in trying to "distort" his plea for preparedness so that "you will be frightened into thinking that we want a war." "The interim President and his curious crew . . . are plainly and simply soft on communism," Goldwater said. In Peoria, Ill. Oct. 2, Goldwater asserted that the Administration was guilty of "deceit" regarding a nuclear treaty between Great Britain, the U.S. and, "believe it or not, Red China." (The reference was to a statement that day by British Prime Min. Alec Douglas-Home that there was a draft treaty between the U.S. and Britain to limit the spread of nuclear weapons and that the treaty should include Red China to be effective. In Washington Oct. 6, Goldwater charged at a convention of United Press International editors that the Administration had "deliberately misstated the facts regarding the awesome question of nuclear responsibility just to score a political point."

Ex-Vice Pres. Richard M. Nixon campaigned in 36 states Oct. 1-Nov. 2 on a 25,000-mile tour on behalf of Goldwater. Nixon called for firmer policy in dealing with communism and defended Goldwater's views on the control of nuclear weapons. He suggested that Pres. Johnson and Goldwater face each other in a public debate on Goldwater's stand that the NATO commander should have authority to use nuclear weapons.

Goldwater's task force on defense policy issued its 2d report Oct. 11. It charged that Administration policy was responsible for a "critical slippage" of nuclear weapons development. The group, headed by ex-Defense Secy. Neil H. McElroy, contended that the slippage had occurred since the 1963 nuclear test-ban treaty had been signed because the Administration had failed to pursue the "comprehensive, aggressive and continuing" nuclear test program on which Senate approval of the pact had been predicated. There had "not been a single weapon effects test conducted since the treaty was signed," the report said. An Atomic Energy Commission spokesman retorted later Oct. 11 that "28 announced weapon-related tests" had been conducted underground by the U.S. since the treaty was signed and that not all tests were necessarily announced.

The McElroy panel, in a report issued Oct. 19, indicted Administration defense policy as having "stifled innovation, thwarted the origination of new systems and canceled promising projects." It cited failure to develop a successor to the B-52 manned bomber, cancellation of the Skybolt air-to-ground nuclear missile and Dyna-Soar manned space vehicle projects and rejection of a nuclear-power plant for the aircraft carrier *Kennedy* currently under construction. It said the A-11 plane announced by Pres. Johnson as an interceptor had been initiated in 1959 as a successor to the U-2 spy plane. An Administration rebuttal, issued later Oct. 19 by Asst. Defense Secy. Arthur Sylvester, credited the Administration with development of the SR-71 reconnaissance plane, the Minuteman-2 missile and 9 other major defense projects.

Johnson Administration's Position

Pres. Johnson, at a civic dinner in Seattle Sept. 16, spoke of the horror of nuclear war and the necessity for sole Presidential control over the use of U.S. nuclear weapons. He pledged that he would "never let slip the engines of destruction because of a reckless and rash miscalculation about our adversaries." He said his Administration had "taken every step man can devise to insure that neither a madman nor a malfunction could trigger nuclear war." The steps included (a) the "2-man rule" that "2 or more men must independently decide the order has been given" and "independently take action," (b) procedural and mechanical checks and counter-checks that "guard against unauthorized nuclear bursts," and (c) since 1961, "permissive-action links on several of our weapons" that he described as "electro-mechanical locks which must be opened by a secret combination before action is possible."

Although "the dignity and interests of our allies demand that they share nuclear responsibility," he said, and, although "the secrets of the atom are known to many," "our work against nuclear spread will go on." He also said the atomic age "creates urgent pressures" for peaceful settlements and for the U.S. "to show restraint as well as strength." In this respect, he said, "we have never rattled our rockets or come carelessly to the edge of war."

In Washington Oct. 2, Mr. Johnson addressed a group gathered to commemorate the naming of 1965 as International Cooperation Year. He said that, if reelected, he intended to call a White House conference to explore "every conceivable approach and avenue of cooperation that could lead to peace." "Cooperation with other nations and other peoples is always uppermost in our minds and is the first aim of our policies," he asserted. Alluding to Goldwater's charge that the Administration was "soft on communism," the President said: "Some" persons "may say you are 'soft' or 'hard'..., but... what greater satisfaction could come to you than the knowledge that you had entered a partnership with your government that had provided the leadership in the world that had preserved humanity instead of destroyed it?"

Defense Secy. McNamara Oct. 7 made public Administration plans to increase the number of strategic nuclear warheads in the U.S. arsenal "over the next 5 years" while "the megatonnage will remain substantially the same." McNamara did so in answer to charges by Goldwater that the Administration was planning a 90% cut in nuclear weapon delivery capability. McNamara said Goldwater's statement was "so misleading, so politically irresponsible and so damaging to our national security that it cannot be allowed to stand on the record."

In a Democratic broadcast over CBS-TV Oct. 15, Pres. Johnson hailed the 1963 nuclear test-ban treaty as "a momentous step along the road to peace" and called attention to Goldwater's vote against the pact. "Today, again those same voices oppose efforts to reach peaceful agreements," Mr. Johnson said.

Speaking in Belleville, Ill. Oct. 21, Mr. Johnson derided the Republican cry for "total victory" over communism. He said: In a nuclear war "there would not be total victory but total devastation, and the survivors would be jealous of the dead." His opponents' policies were "built on dangerous foundations, because they talk about a nuclear war as if it were inevitable and a nuclear bomb as if it were merely another weapon"; "they sound as if force or the threat of force can solve all problems, and this is dangerous." "Our military strength is vital to our security, and it is very important to our influence; but it cannot and it must not be used to compel and frighten others into following our command and our wish; that course can lead only to constant conflict."

2D PERIOD OF GENEVA TALKS

Conference Resumed

The UN 18-Nation Disarmament Committee resumed its meetings in Geneva June 9 after a 5-week recess called to permit delegates to consult with their governments. The conference remained in session until Sept. 17. The reopening of the conference was marked by statements in which the chiefs of the U.S. and Soviet delegations expressed hope for further progress on disarmament and suggested the path the negotiations might take. Neither statement materially changed the contradictory positions of the 2 powers toward specific disarmament measures.

The U.S. position was outlined in a message from Pres. Johnson, read to the conference by William C. Foster, director of the U.S. Arms Control & Disarmament Agency and head of the American delegation. Citing the progress already achieved by the conference, particularly the agreements for a limited nuclear test ban and for creation of a direct emergency communications system between Washington and Moscow, the President's message declared that "we must redouble our efforts until it [disarmament] is completed." The message said that there were 2 problems on which the U.S. was prepared to act: halting of fissionable materials production for weapons purposes and mutual destruction of the fleets of obsolete and reserve bombers held by the U.S. and Russia. Foster, commenting on past Soviet objections to the verification measures demanded by the West, added that the U.S. was prepared to restrict inspection "to inhibit . . . receipt of information which might be of military value." He said specifically that such restricted inspection could be applied to the U.S.' proposals for a "freeze" and cut-off of strategic missile production and for destruction of surplus bombers.

Speaking for the USSR, Deputy Foreign Min. Valerian A. Zorin expressed partial agreement with the suggestions in the President's message. Zorin said the USSR gave priority to proposals for the destruction of bombers; he indicated that it had decided to drop its demands for rapid extension of the Moscow nuclear test ban treaty to include underground detonations. Zorin made it clear, however, that the USSR would not join in an agreement curtailing the spread of nuclear weapons unless the U.S. abandoned its plans for formation of a joint Western fleet of nuclear missile-firing warships. Creation of such a fleet, he charged, would place nuclear weapons in the hands of West Germany and other European powers not currently possessing them.

Zorin's statement apparently contradicted the position taken by Soviet Premier Nikita S. Khrushchev in a Kremlin interview June 2 with Harold Wilson, Parliamentary leader of the British Labor Party. Wilson reported to newsmen that Khrushchev had expressed opposition to the bomber-destruction porposal and instead had called for barring the dissemination of nuclear weapons as the key to further disarmament progress. Khrushchev reportedly rejected U.S. suggestions for a freeze on nuclear-armed missiles on the ground that the U.S. had demanded inspection measures that the USSR could accept only as part of a general disarmament pact. Khrushchev was said to have attacked the plan for a Western nuclear fleet as a major obstacle to nuclear disarmament.

The apparent contradiction in the Soviet position on destruction of bombers presumably was due to a lack of clarity in the press reports from Geneva and Moscow. The Soviet delegation in Geneva had rejected the U.S. proposal for the destruction of 480 B-47 and 480 TU-16 jet bombers and instead had called for the destruction of all bombers in use by all the world's air forces. Semyon K. Tsarapkin, the chief Soviet negotiator until the April-May recess, amended the Russian plan in a statement at the conference Apr. 2. Tsarapkin said that the USSR was prepared to limit the bomber-scrapping plan to the world's major military powers in its first phase. He again rejected the U.S.' bomber-burning plan as a "cover" for disposal of its aged bombers and modernization of the U.S. Air Force.

New Stalemate

After June 9, the Geneva conference was stalemated for more than 2 months. The U.S. and Russia, the conference co-chairmen, could not agree on a plan for eliminating missiles and other means of delivering nuclear weapons.

Polish Deputy Foreign Min. Marian Naszkowski said at the conference June 11 that Poland would continue to seek an agreement on a freeze of nuclear arms in Central Europe but would do so through diplomatic channels rather than at the conference. He accused the Western powers of a "habit of constantly ceding to the views of their Bonn ally," and he said West German officials regarded the nuclear-freeze proposal as "an obstacle to their efforts to obtain nuclear weapons."

U.S. delegate Foster June 16 rejected a plan, proposed originally by Soviet Foreign Min. Andrei A. Gromyko and brought up at the conference June 9 and 16 by Soviet Deputy Foreign Min. Zorin, for the destruction within 18 months of all nuclear-warhead carriers except a few that both sides would retain as a "nuclear umbrella" until complete disarmament was achieved. Foster said the U.S. was "not prepared to make such immediate, drastic and unbalanced reductions in its nuclear forces." He stressed that there were no guarantees in the plan for its observance and that such a plan would "rapidly alter in the favor of the Soviet Union the present mix of armaments." Zorin said June 16 that a working party could be established to handle the "military and scientific details" once "an agreement in principle" had been reached on the Soviet missile plan. Foster proposed a working group that would deal with all relevant disarmament proposals, including the U.S. ones, and warned: "The conference will never get very far in solving this important problem unless it moves from generalities to details."

In a step that apparently broke a 2-year procedural deadlock, the U.S. and USSR agreed June 18 on an order of priority and scheduled definite days for the discussion of the specific disarmament proposals each had offered. Zorin also said the Soviet Union would take a "flexible position" on a U.S. plan to destroy 480 bombers if the Soviet Union would destroy an equal number of comparable aircraft. Zorin expressed a desire to seek limited arms accords. He asserted June 23 that only Soviet proposals could be referred to the proposed working group. Discussion of U.S. proposals in the negotiating group would merely repeat the "endless arguments" of the conference's plenary sessions, Zorin insisted. He emphasized that any missile-reduction negotiations would have to be based on the Soviet "nuclear umbrella" plan under which a minimum force would be retained by each side while disarmament was taking place. Foster called Zorin's conditions for establishing a working group "unacceptable."

Foster proposed June 25 that the International Atomic Energy Agency help enforce any accord on halting the production of nuclear materials for weapons use.

Zorin June 25 called for positive action on a Soviet plan to reduce military budgets. Foster criticized Moscow June 30 for being "clearly unreasonable" by trying to confine the negotiations to its "nuclear-umbrella" plan. Zorin reiterated that negotiations could be held only under such a plan.

Zorin July 2 condemned Western plans for a NATO mixed-manned nuclear fleet as aimed at "quenching the nuclear thirst of West German revenge seekers." He warned that there could be no disarmament accord unless the West scrapped plans for such a fleet. Foster retorted that Moscow was using "groundless political arguments against the multilateral force in the pursuit of its long-standing aim to disrupt NATO defensive arrangements." He reiterated the U.S. stand that "so long as hundreds of Soviet nuclear-tipped rockets are arrayed against Europe, effective European participation in strategic deterrence should be provided."

Zorin left the conference July 4 and turned over the leadership of the Soviet delegation to Semyon K. Tsarapkin. Foster left for Washington July 7 to resume his duties as head of the Arms Control & Disarmament Agency; he was replaced by Clare H. Timberlake.

(U.S. State Secy. Dean Rusk July 4 proposed an inspection system that would permit a reduction in armaments. He said in Independence Hall in Philadelphia: "We believe that the Soviet leaders recognize a common interest with us in reducing the dangers of a great war. We most earnestly hope that they will open their doors, as we are willing to open ours, to the sort of inspection which will make possible genuine progress in reducing armaments.")

Timberlake and Tsarapkin began private talks July 7 in an effort to agree on a basis for detailed bargaining on plans to destroy their missiles and other carriers of nuclear warheads. Timberlake and Tsarapkin conceded at the conference July 14 that the talks had failed but said they would continue trying. Tsarapkin stressed that "there will never be agreement" unless the West first agreed to Soviet proposals in principle.

Tsarapkin maintained July 16 that the U.S.' plan for the mutual destruction of some bombers was unacceptable and that all bombers would have to be scrapped if there were to be any accord on this point. Timberlake contended that a complete "bomber bonfire" would give the Soviet Union military superiority.

UAR delegate Abdel Fattah Hassan Aug. 13 recommended a special study of the contemplated NATO nuclear fleet with West German participation. He said plans for the fleet should be postponed until the study was completed.

Italian delegate Francesco Cavalletti and Lt. Gen. E. L. M. Burns, Canadian delegate, appealed Aug. 18 for an end to the "sterile debate" over missiles and for the exploration of a new disarmament subject.

Lij Mikael Imru of Ethiopia Aug. 20 introduced a resolution to have the UN call a conference to enact a ban on nuclear arms. Tsarapkin said the Soviet Union approved of such a ban as a measure to "reduce the possibility of nuclear war." But the conference rejected the plan. Burns said it would be illogical to pledge not to use nuclear weapons while there were vast numbers on hand. J. G. Tahourdin of Britain opposed the resolution as impractical, and the U.S. indicated firm opposition.

Timberlake Aug. 27 denied Soviet charges that Pres. Johnson's plan for a freeze on the production of nuclear weapons systems would mean the establishment of an espionage network in the Soviet Union. Timberlake said inspections would be as unobtrusive as possible.

Talks Recessed

As the Geneva conference approached a new recess, the 8 neutral conference nations (India, Sweden, Burma, Nigeria, Ethiopia, the UAR, Brazil and Mexico) Sept. 15 issued a memo expressing disappointment at the lack of progress on an underground nuclear weapons test ban and urging the nuclear powers to take "all immediate steps" to include underground explosions in the 1963 nuclear test ban treaty.

Pres. Johnson Sept. 16 sent the conference a message stressing the U.S.' desire for a disarmament agreement. He declared: "I pledge the best efforts of which my country is capable to prevent such a [devastating] war. To this end—to deter aggression—my country is maintaining the most powerful defense force in its peace-time history. But in the world of today, the quest for peace demands . . . the elimination of the causes of war and the building of a firm foundation for peace." "As you recess temporarily your deliberations in Geneva, let each nation represented here resolve to continue at home its consideration of the proposals made at this conference."

Soviet delegate Tsarapkin Sept. 17 blamed the U.S. for the "gloomy and depressing figure of zero" in the conference's achievements. He warned that "means of mass annihilation of unlimited magnitude and unlimited range" would be the alternative to disarmament. The conference recessed Sept. 17 but declared its intention to reconvene in early 1965.

(British Prime Min. Douglas-Home disclosed Oct. 2 that the U.S. and Britain had drafted a treaty to limit the spread of nuclear weapons and insisted that the treaty should include Red China to be effective. A State Department announcement said later that the draft was only a "working paper" and that Red China undoubtedly would not sign it. Pres. Johnson said at his news conference Oct. 3 that there was "no secret" about such a treaty and that Republican attacks on it were "simply some more evidence that impulsive people should probably get themselves properly briefed." He said he had announced on TV in January and in several subsequent news conferences "that we propose new agreements to stop the spread of nuclear weapons to nations not now possessing them." He said the proposal also had been made publicly in Geneva and that, "unfortunately," the Soviet Union had refused to support it and, "as all the world knows, the Chinese Communists have violently opposed any nuclear agreement of any kind.")

RED CHINESE NUCLEAR TEST

Test Predicted

U.S. State Secy. Dean Rusk warned Sept. 29 that Communist China might be on the verge of detonating its first nuclear device. Rusk's warning was reported to have been based on U.S. intelligence estimates that a Chinese nuclear test might take place within a few days, perhaps in conjunction with the celebration Oct. 1 of the 15th anniversary of the Peking (Peiping) Communist regime. Rusk's statement, issued by State Department spokesman Robert J. McCloskey, said: "For some time it has been known that the Chinese Communists were approaching the point where they might be able to detonate a first nuclear device. Such an explosion might occur in the near future. If it does occur, we shall know about it and will make the information public."

"Detonation of a first nuclear device does not mean a stockpile of nuclear weapons and the presence of modern delivery systems," the statement emphasized. The U.S., it added, "has fully anticipated the possibility of Peiping's entry into the nuclear weapons field and has taken it into full account" in U.S. military and nuclear planning.

Washington officials told newsmen that Communist China appeared to have reached an advanced stage in preparations for a nuclear test. They said information on these preparations had come from many sources, among them foreign governments, and from U.S. conventional and technical espionage. According to unattributed scientific opinion, Red China would not be able to produce sufficient plutonium to build an effective nuclear weapons stockpile for another 5 to 10 years. The *N.Y. Times* reported from Paris Oct. 8 that China had informed some friendly Afro-Asian governments that it planned to explode a nuclear device after the end of October. Among the countries reportedly advised of this were Guinea, Mali, Cambodia and Burma. China's reasons for disclosing its atomic plans beforehand were said to be 2-fold: (1) It sought to allay criticism by contending that China's possession of an A-bomb would help restore the balance of power between the West and the Afro-Asian nations; (2) Peking sought to prepare friendly nations for fresh Chinese diplomatic initiatives in Africa and Asia.

China Explodes 20-Kiloton Device

Communist China detonated its first nuclear device at 3 a.m. EST Oct. 16 at a test site reported to be in the Taklamakan Desert area of the Central Asian Province of Sinkiang. The test was announced later the same day in a statement made public by Peking's Hsinhua news agency. Confirmation was provided within a few hours in a statement issued by U.S. Pres. Johnson.

The official Chinese announcement gave no details of the test. It said only that "China exploded an atom bomb at 1500 hours on Oct. 16, 1964, and thereby conducted successfully its first nuclear test." The announcement was devoted principally to Peking's explanation of its reasons for developing a nuclear bomb and to a demand that a world summit conference be convened to outlaw atomic weapons and destroy existing nuclear stockpiles. It repeated China's past contentions that the July 1963 U.S.-British-Soviet treaty curtailing nuclear tests was "a big fraud to fool the people of the world, that it tried to consolidate the nuclear monopoly held by the 3 nuclear powers and tie up the hands and feet of all peace-loving countries" and that it increased, rather than decreased, the danger of nuclear war. *The Chinese statement said:*

"China cannot remain idle and do nothing in the face of the ever-increasing threat posed by the United States. China is forced to conduct nuclear tests and develop nuclear weapons." China proceeded from the view that "the atom bomb is a paper tiger." "China is developing nuclear weapons not because we believe in the omnipotence of nuclear weapons.... The truth is exactly to the contrary.... China's aim is to break the nuclear monopoly of the nuclear powers and to eliminate nuclear weapons."

"The development of nuclear weapons by China is for defense and for protecting the Chinese people from the danger of the United States launching a nuclear war." "The Chinese government hereby solemnly declares that China will never at any time and under any circumstances be the first to use nuclear weapons." "On the question of nuclear weapons, China will commit neither the error of adventurism nor the error of capitulationism. The Chinese people can be trusted."

"The Chinese government hereby formally proposes to the governments of the world that a summit conference of all the countries of the world be convened to discuss the question of the complete prohibition and thorough destruction of nuclear weapons, and that, as a first step, the summit conference should reach an agreement to the effect that nuclear powers and those countries, which will soon become nuclear powers undertake not to use nuclear weapons, neither... against non-nuclear countries and nuclear-free zones, nor against each other."

Communist China celebrated the nuclear test Oct. 18 with street rallies in Peking and with a special message, distributed nationally, in which its scientists and military and technical personnel were honored for having brought China to "a new stage of modernization of its national defense." The message, which referred to the detonation as a nuclear test rather than as the explosion of an atomic bomb, was signed by CP (Communist Party) Chrmn. Mao Tse-tung, by the CP Central Committee and by China's State Council (cabinet).

The Chinese government Oct. 20 released the text of a note in which Premier Chou En-lai was said to have called on world leaders to join in a summit meeting to ban nuclear weapons. The text was modelled on China's initial announcement that it had exploded a nuclear bomb and would seek such a conference. The U.S. State Department confirmed Oct. 21 that the note had been transmitted to Pres. Johnson through the U.S. embassy in Warsaw. It made clear that the Chinese proposal was unacceptable to the U.S.

Most of the information available publicly on the Chinese test was provided by the U.S. government. Pres. Johnson's initial statement Oct. 16, confirming that the Chinese test had taken place, described it as a "crude nuclear device" detonated in the atmosphere in western China. Mr. Johnson said that the detonation had been "low yield," or of a force equivalent to or less than that produced by the explosion of 20 kilotons (20,000 tons) of TNT. In his address to the nation Oct. 18, the President added that the test had been carried out at a test site near Lob Nor Lake on the eastern edge of the Taklamakan Desert in Sinkiang Province.

A statement issued Oct. 21 by the U.S. Atomic Energy Commission said that the Chinese had detonated "a fission device employing U-235 [enriched uranium]" rather than the simpler type of device that used plutonium as its explosive material. The AEC said that preliminary analysis of the radioactive debris carried by the cloud produced by the test confirmed that the Chinese test was of low yield, "roughly equivalent" to the 20-kiloton U.S. bomb used against Hiroshima in World War II. It added that "the low yield of the test coupled with other information obtained from the radioactive debris indicates that the technology of the device is that which we would associate with an early nuclear test." AEC officials conceded later Oct. 21 that the Chinese bomb had been more sophisticated in design than the Hiroshima weapon and had employed an advanced form of implosion trigger to detonate the fission materials. Most of the AEC information came from air samples taken from the bomb-produced radioactive cloud as it drifted eastward over Japan Oct. 17, the Aleutians Oct. 18, the northern Pacific Oct. 19 and Canada and the western U.S. Oct. 20.

Rep. Harris McDowell (D., Del.) reported Oct. 21 that he had been informed by State Secy. Rusk that much of the U.S.' information on the Chinese test and test site came from military reconnaissance satellites. He said, Rusk had reported, that satellite photographs had showed clearly the erection of the tower on which the Chinese nuclear device was detonated.

World Reaction

Pres. Johnson said Oct. 16 that the Chinese nuclear test came "as no surprise" to the U.S. government and that "it has been fully taken into account in planning" the U.S.' defense program and nuclear capability. In a prepared statement on the event, Mr. Johnson said that the "military significance" of the atomic blast "should not be over-estimated." Communist China was still a long way "from having a stockpile of reliable weapons with effective delivery systems," he said. Mr. Johnson stressed the U.S.' "readiness to respond to requests from Asian nations for help in dealing with Chinese Communist aggression" should Peking "eventually develop an effective nuclear capability." Mr. Johnson deplored China's "nuclear weapons program" as "a tragedy for the Chinese people, who have suffered so much under the Communist regime." "Scarce economic resources which could have been used to improve the well-being of the Chinese people have been used to produce a crude nuclear device which can only increase the sense of insecurity of the Chinese people," he declared. Although assailing the Chinese test as contrary "to the cause of peace," Mr. Johnson said that "there is no reason to fear that it will lead to immediate war." "Regretting the contamination of the atmosphere caused by the Chinese Communist test," Mr. Johnson pledged continued U.S. "efforts to keep the atmosphere clear" and to strive for "concrete, practical steps away from nuclear armaments and war."

In a nationwide TV and radio address Oct. 18 Mr. Johnson said: China's atomic test should not be treated "lightly"; "until this week only 4 powers had entered the dangerous world of nuclear explosions; whatever their differences, all are sober and serious states, with long experience as major powers in the modern world; Communist China has no such experience." Mr. Johnson cited 4 ways in which the U.S. would work to minimize "the danger of nuclear war": "First, we will continue to support the limited test ban treaty.... We call on the world— especially Red China—to join the nations which have signed it. 2d, we will continue to work for ending of all nuclear tests of every kind, by solid and verified agreement. 3d, we continue to believe that the struggle against nuclear spread is as much in the Soviet interest as in our own. We will be ready to join with them and all the world—in working to avoid it. And 4th, the nations that do not seek ... nuclear weapons can be sure that if they need our strong support against some threat of nuclear blackmail, then they will have it."

U.S. State Secy. Rusk predicted Oct. 18 that the Chinese would explode another atomic device as soon as they were capable of doing so in order to score propaganda advantage. Rusk said Peking had "upset the effort ... of every nation ... to end atmosphere testing." He said that in embarking on a nuclear program of their own the Chinese have "set back the hopes of mankind significantly."

U.S. Defense Secy. McNamara stressed at a news conference Oct. 22 that the Chinese had tested only a primitive nuclear device that posed no military threat. He said: It would be "many years" before the Chinese Communists "obtain the capability to inflict nuclear damage on this country or our allies"; the main point illustrated by the test was the "dangers of nuclear spread" as more nations obtained the capability to deveop nuclear weapons. McNamara had warned in a Chicago radio interview Oct. 3 that "tens of nations" would be able to develop nuclear weapons in 10-20 years. He explained that lower costs of production and delivery systems would permit such a situation. He called the spread of nuclear weapons "one of the most important problems we face."

Among other reactions to the Chinese atomic explosion:

●The British government said Oct. 17 that it was "deeply disappointed" that Communist China had ignored world opinion by conducting the nuclear test. The British Foreign Office statement emphasized, however, that in view of the West's strong nuclear arsenal, China could not affect the military situation in Asia or "significantly affect the balance of military power."

●The Italian Communist Party newspaper *L'Unita* said Oct. 17 that China had launched its atomic program because of "discontent" with the Soviet "atomic umbrella." The newspaper warned the "imperialist powers" to take cognizance of this new development and not put "obstacles on the road of general and controlled disarmament."

●Indian Prime Min. Lal Bahadur Shastri declared Oct. 19 that India was "confronted with a nuclear menace in Asia." He accused China of "trying to build up a mighty war machine and thus create fear in the minds of us all."

●The governments of North Vietnam and North Korea were the only Communist regimes that congratulated China on its nuclear test. A message from North Vietnamese Pres. Ho Chi Minh, published in Peking newspapers Oct. 18, called the test "a major contribution of the Chinese people and government to strengthening the forces of the Socialist camp and the struggles for national liberation and in defense of world peace."

●Peking newspapers Oct. 19 published congratulatory messages from the Japanese, Albanian and Indonesian Communist parties and the pro-Communist Pathet Lao movement in Laos.

●The Cambodian government "warmly greeted the nuclear success" in a message to Chinese Foreign Min. Chen Yi Oct. 19. The message said that "in breaking the nuclear monopoly some imperialist powers tried to keep, China has made effective preparations for complete atomic disarmament."

Touring Ohio Oct. 17, Republican Presidential candidate Barry Goldwater told a Mansfield, O. crowd that the test did not mean that Communist China "has become a nuclear threat" inasmuch as it would take, without help from other nations, "at least" 25 years to develop a weapons system capable of delivering the bomb. "If we trade with them," he told a Canton O. crowd, "then maybe in our lifetime they can build a missile."

Democratic Vice Presidential candidate Hubert H. Humphrey proposed at a press conference in Tampa, Fla. Oct. 18 that the U.S. focus the force of world opinion on Communist China in an effort to bring that country to accept the nuclear test-ban treaty. But he said this did not mean diplomatic recognition. Humphrey speculated that France might shift to acceptance of the treaty as a result of Communist China's emergence as an atomic power.

Republican Vice Presidential candidate William E. Miller told reporters in San Diego, Calif. Oct. 19 that he agreed with Pres. Johnson's desire to have Communist China sign the nuclear test-ban treaty, but he warned that "this should not open the door to recognition of Red China."

Goldwater asserted Oct. 21 that the new developments in Moscow and Peking posed a "grave" threat to U.S. "security" in that the U.S. faced "a more unified Communist movement." He asked: "Where is the Chinese-Soviet rift today?" "Can we even be sure that the Soviet Union did not take a hand in the nuclear explosion? What does the test-ban treaty mean now—if it ever meant anything?"

Abortive Diplomatic Initiatives

UN Secy. Gen. U Thant proposed at a news conference Oct. 22 that the U.S., USSR, Britain, France and Communist China meet in 1965 to discuss the banning of nuclear testing. He suggested that a "dialogue" between the 5 nuclear powers might be "very worthwhile." "Of course, there are protocol and diplomatic considerations," Thant conceded, "but I feel very strongly that they should be secondary. The primary consideration should be that of nuclear destructibility and radioactivity." He called the Chinese nuclear test "particularly regrettable" in view of (a) the 1963 agreement by the U.S., USSR and Britain to refrain from above-ground nuclear tests and (b) a 1962 UN General Assembly resolution condemning "all tests, including underground tests." Thant said he saw "some merit" in a proposal by ex-Kansas Gov. Alfred M. Landon, the 1936 U.S. Republican Presidential candidate, that the 5 nuclear powers meet. Landon had made the suggestion in a speech in Columbus, O. Oct. 20. "Since 1948 I have urged the recognition of Red China and its admission to the United Nations," Landon declared. "I have said that discussions of limitation of world armament, a World Court, even the United Nations, were useless without including China, with 1/4 of the world's population."

The Johnson Administration indicated Oct. 23 that it was not interested in either Communist China's Oct. 16 suggestion for a world summit conference to ban nuclear weapons or in U Thant's Oct. 22 proposal of a 1965 meeting of the 5 nuclear powers. State Department officials called Peking's suggestion a "sucker" proposal that was neither serious nor constructive. If Communist China really wanted to show serious interest in talks, the State Department spokesman said, it could communicate with British, French and Soviet diplomats in Peking or with the U.S. ambassador in Warsaw. The U.S. spokesman conceded that Peking would have to be a party to negotiations and agreements "at some stage . . . if such agreements are to have any real meaning. In this sense, we never have precluded the participation of any country in disarmament negotiations." But State Department officials expressed continued opposition to Communist Chinese membership in the UN or participation in the Geneva disarmament conference. They asserted that such recognition would be tantamount to rewarding Peking for a nuclear test, and they complained that some of the nations proposing such a prize were the very ones that had consistently condemned Western nuclear tests. They warned that such rewards would convince Communist China of the efficiency of aggressive deeds and thereby put the world in greater danger of Chinese belligerence.

Communist China, in an editorial Oct. 22 in the official newspaper *Jenmin Jih Pao (People's Daily),* had rejected Pres. Johnson's Oct. 18 suggestion that Peking sign the nuclear test ban treaty and help prevent the spread of nuclear weapons. The editorial asserted that Mr. Johnson's criticism of the Chinese nuclear test "boiled down to this: the United States alone can have nuclear weapons, China should not.... This is 100% tyrant's language and gangster logic." The editorial warned that Communist China had "finally gained the means of resisting the United States nuclear threat."

U.S. Amb.-to-UN Adlai E. Stevenson speculated in Louisville, Ky. Oct. 23 that the U.S. might be more willing to consider 5-power nuclear test ban talks if Communist China signed the 1963 nuclear test ban treaty.

Thant Oct. 24 appealed to the world powers to negotiate disarmament accords and settle their problems by discussion.

British Foreign Secy. Patrick Gordon Walker said at a UN news conference Oct. 27 that Britain "would consider very favorably" any suggestion advanced by Thant for halting the spread of nuclear weapons. Speaking after a talk with Thant, Gordon Walker asserted that there was "a good deal to be said" for having Communist China join the Geneva disarmament talks.

French Pres. Charles de Gaulle declared in a message to Chinese Premier Chou En-lai Oct. 30 that France was prepared to participate "at any moment" in "any serious negotiations" among the 5 nuclear powers. De Gaulle promised to "study with attention" Chou's Oct. 16 proposal for nuclear disarmament talks. De Gaulle's message also said: "On her part, France has not ceased during all of the past years to pronounce herself in favor of genuine disarmament, which naturally means that priority should be given to nuclear disarmament. On this subject, whenever the occasion has arisen, she has made detailed propositions concerning, first, the elimination of vehicles serving, or liable to serve, in the transportation of nuclear arms. Those propositions have taken into account the existing difficulty in assessing stockpiles of such devices. It is evident that disarmament cannot be conceived and cannot be put into practice if it is not accompanied by efficient control.... The French government remained ready to participate fully in any serious negotiations that could be organized among competent and responsible powers to discuss the problems of disarmament on a constructive and practical basis."

Communist Chinese Pres. Liu Shao-chi warned Oct. 30 that the U.S. faced a "serious test" in deciding whether to agree to Peking's proposal of a 5-power conference. Speaking at a Peking dinner in honor of King Mohammed Zahir and Queen Homaira of Afghanistan, Liu said the first step in Communist China's proposal would be for nuclear powers and nations about to become nuclear powers to foreswear the use of atomic weapons. He vowed that Peking would "unswervingly carry through to the end the struggle to oppose United States imperialist policies of aggression and war, smash nuclear blackmail and the nuclear threat of United States imperialism and realize the noble aim of the complete prohibition and thorough destruction of nuclear weapons."

An editorial in *Jenmin Jih Pao* declared Nov. 22 that Communist China would not participate in the 18-nation Geneva disarmament talks. "Now that China has nuclear weapons, the United States wants to drag her into the affairs of the United Nations," the editorial said. It also rejected U Thant's Oct. 22 proposal of a 5-power conference on banning nuclear testing.

British Prime Min. Harold Wilson Dec. 23 rejected Peking's Oct. 17 suggestion of a world summit conference to ban nuclear weapons. He called for detailed discussion and negotiation on disarmament first.

Tass reported Jan. 3, 1965 that Soviet Premier Kosygin had informed Communist China of the USSR's support of its summit conference proposal. Kosygin said that even though the USSR favored a "radical" agreement on nuclear weapons, it also approved of measures to "limit" and "slow down" the nuclear arms race. He suggested that the adoption of a pact denouncing the use of nuclear weapons could precede on agreement on banning and destroying atomic weapons.

THREAT OF NUCLEAR PROLIFERATION

French Testing

The French government's intentions to press ahead with its completion of an independent national nuclear striking force were reaffirmed by Pres. Charles de Gaulle in 2 major statements in 1964. The first of these was made in a radio-TV address delivered to the French people Apr. 16; the 2d was made at a formal news conference held in Paris July 23.

De Gaulle said Apr. 16: "So long as the ambition of the Soviets and the nature of their regime brings a threat of terrible conflict to bear on the free world,... France is in danger of destruction and invasion without having any certainty that her American allies, themselves directly exposed to death, would know how to prevent this for her. For France, to deny herself her own means of deterring the adversary from a possible attack on her, when she is in a position to have them, that would be drawing the lightning while depriving herself of a lightning rod. But that would also be relying entirely for her defense and, thereby, her existence and, finally, her policy, on a foreign protectorate and one that is uncertain anyway." "No! We are worth more than that!"

Speaking to an audience of newsmen, diplomats and French officials at his July press conference, de Gaulle asserted: "The fact that America and Soviet Russia possess their nuclear arsenal provides them with such security and moreover gives them, inside their respective camps, such a reason for exercising hegemony that they will not get rid of theirs, no more than any other state in their place would get rid of its arsenal.... The result is that the countries which do not have an atomic arsenal believe that they have to accept a strategic and consequently a political dependency in relation to the 2 giants." "In these conditions France...judged it necessary...to become an atomic power....[And] we are reaching results. Our first atomic air unit becomes operational this year. In 1966 we will have enough Mirage-4s and refueling planes to be able to carry at one time, over a distance of thousands of miles, bombs with a total power exceeding that of 150 Hiroshima bombs. Furthermore, we are working on moving on from series 'A' fission bombs to series 'H' fusion bombs, the latter launched from either atomic submarines, surface vessels or land.... We are in a position to think that 6 years from now our deterrent means will reach a total instantaneous power of 2,000 Hiroshima bombs. This is what certain, obviously un-thinking, opponents call France's 'little bomb.' The field of deterrence is thus henceforth open to us. For to attack France would be equivalent, for whomever it might be, to undergoing frightful destruction itself."

(It had been reported from Paris Mar. 28 that serious difficulties had been encountered with production of the Mirage-4 bomber and that no more than 6 of the planes, 3 of them prototypes, were in service. The *N.Y. Times,* quoting highly qualified Paris sources, reported that France's 3 planned missile-firing nuclear submarines, originally sched-uled for completion by 1968-70, might not be ready before 1973. The *Times* said its sources had reported that only "a few" French nuclear bombs were ready for the Mirage-4 bombers. French officials announced Oct. 10 that the U.S. had delivered 12 C-135F tanker planes intended for in-air refueling of the Mirage-4 bomber force. The planes had been sold to France despite American opposition to the construction of the French nuclear bomber command.)

French sources in Algiers had said Mar. 15 that France would end its nuclear testing program in the Algerian Sahara during the current year and shift the French nuclear test program from its 3 Sahara test sites to new sites near Tahiti in the South Pacific.

The U.S. Atomic Energy Commission acknowledged Dec. 18 that it had warned manufacturers not to sell to other countries any equip-ment that might be used in the development or testing of nuclear weapons. The warning was specifically aimed at France, which had re-fused to sign the 1963 limited nuclear test ban treaty and reportedly was preparing for 1966 atmospheric hydrogen bomb tests in the Pacific.

Multilateral Nuclear Naval Force

The USSR warned July 11 that the proposed NATO multilateral nuclear naval force (MLF) would enhance the risk of atomic war. The warnings were made in notes delivered to the Moscow embassies of the U.S., Britain, West Germany, Italy, the Netherlands, Turkey and Greece. In its protest to the West Germans, the Soviet Union declared that Bonn's efforts to seek access to nuclear weapons was "a flagrant violation of [its] international commitments." Restrictions barring West Germany from acquiring nuclear weapons, imposed on Germany under its unconditional World War II surrender, were still in force pending the conclusion of a German peace treaty, the Soviet statement said.

The Soviet protest was rejected Aug. 28 in separate but similar notes from the U.S. and Britain. Washington's message said that MLF was "entirely defensive" and that its purpose was to counter the "extensive array of Soviet nuclear weapons directed against" the West. West Germany rejected the Soviet protest Sept. 2 and upheld its right to participate in the proposed fleet under its "sovereign right of self-defense." Bonn's reply, made public Sept. 5, denied Moscow's argument that its membership in MLF would violate Germany's international commitments. Bonn declared: "The German people, through the capitulation of the *Wermacht* in 1945, by no means permanently renounced the right of self-defense."

The U.S. and West Germany were warned by the Soviet Union Nov. 14 that if they carried through their plans to establish the MLF, Moscow would "take appropriate measures" to protect its security. Characterizing MLF as "nonsense from a military viewpoint," an "authorized statement" distributed by the Tass news agency charged that the projected atomic naval force would intensify the arms race, encourage the spread of nuclear weapons, heighten international tensions and discourage disarmament. The statement said MLF would permit "revanchist and militarist circles in West Germany" to "get access to nuclear weapons" and encourage German "adventurists" to engage in "provocations."

A U.S.-West German agreement providing for "close and continuing German-American military relationships," including an expansion of joint cooperation in weapons development, was announced in a communique issued in Washington Nov. 14 at the conclusion of 3 days of talks held by Defense Secy. McNamara and West German Defense Min. Kai-Uwe von Hassel and their aides. The conferees also reaffirmed U.S.-German support for the proposed MLF "as an effective military force, as well as an instrument of unity."

India Debates Proposals

Proposals that India develop atomic weapons were debated by the national committee of India's governing Congress Party at a meeting in Guntur Nov. 7-8.

The committee Nov. 8 adopted a resolution condemning the Oct. 16 Peking nuclear test and declaring: "In the context of armed threats to our country's integrity and independence and also in the cause of world peace itself, it is the duty of the nation to be prepared to prevent and foil aggressive attempts wherever they may come from." The resolution stressed the need for worldwide disarmament. It urged that "advances in science ... be exploited only for ... peaceful development" and that "efforts be redoubled" to advance "peaceful uses of atomic energy."

The resolution was drafted by External Affairs Min. Swaran Singh, Defense Min. Y. B. Chavan and ex-Defense Min. V. K. Krishna Menon. They indicated Nov. 7 that it was intended to restate the late Prime Min. Jawaharlal Nehru's policy of renouncing nuclear weapons. But it made no such specific renunciation, and at least 12 delegates backed legislation calling for India's development of atomic weapons.

Prime Min. Lal Bahadur Shastri warned the committee Nov. 8 that "if we make the bomb, India will simply fade out as an international force for peace." He reiterated that the Indian government's policy was to use atomic energy for peaceful uses only. Shastri asserted that "talk of making bombs has no place in the deliberations of the Congress Party, with pictures of Gandhi and Nehru, apostles of peace, looking down on us."

The Canadian High Commission in New Delhi had affirmed Oct. 29 that Canada opposed any use of the plutonium generator at the Canadian-Indian research reactor at Trombay, near Bombay, for making atomic weapons. The 1956 agreement providing India with Canadian plutonium barred its use for any but "peaceful purposes."

U.S. to Study Proliferation

Pres. Johnson appointed a special panel Nov. 1 to study ways of halting the spread of nuclear weapons. White House Press Secy. George Reedy said the President had asked the new group "to explore the widest range of measures that the United States might undertake in conjunction with other governments or by itself to accomplish" the aim. The group was also directed to "examine the implications of the development of peaceful uses of atomic energy on this problem and of safeguards associated with this problem."

Among those named to the panel: Ex-Defense Undersecy. Roswell L. Gilpatric, chairman; ex-Defense Secy. Robert A. Lovett; ex-State Secy. Dean Acheson; John J. McCloy, ex-director of the U.S. Disarmament Agency; Arthur Dean, ex-delegate to the UN Disarmament Commission.

OTHER DEVELOPMENTS

Soviet 'Superweapon'

According to an apparently erroneous report Sept. 15, Soviet Premier Khrushchev told visiting members of the Japanese Diet (parliament) in Moscow that day that military officials and scientist had shown him near Moscow Sept 14 a "monstrous new terrible weapon" that could destroy humanity. He reportedly called the weapon "power without limit" but assured the visitors that he had no desire to ever use such a weapon. The report was attributed to sources close to the Japanese delegation. Khrushchev told Western and Indian newsmen in Moscow Sept. 17 that his remarks had been misinterpreted in translation. He explained: "I said that scientists had shown me the terrible weapon, which shows what mankind can do. We did not say anything about unlimited power." He denied that the weapon was a new type of nuclear bomb or that he had said it could destroy mankind.

The Soviet press agency Tass Sept. 19 published the official English version of Khruschchev's remarks to the Japanese visitors: "I had to stand all day yesterday [Sept. 14] inspecting new types of weapons. I spent the entire day among our military, scientists and engineers who work in this field. I had to spend my time doing this because as long as there are wolves in the world we must have the means to defend ourselves against the wolves. This is why we are creating the most up-to-date means of defense for our state, our people, means for the defense of peace among peoples. We are fully aware of the destructive power of this terrible weaponry and would prefer never to use it." (It was believed that the confusion had been caused by a Russian word that could be translated either as "weapon" or "weaponry." Tass first used the word "weapon" and then changed it to "weaponry." Observers pointed out that Khrushchev had made his remark about the "weapon" or "weaponry" while denouncing Communist Chinese leader Mao Tsetung, assailing China's territorial claims on Soviet territory and warning: "Our borders are sacred and inviolable and any attempt to change them by force means war.")

U.S. Satellite Detection & Defense

3 U.S. atomic-detection satellites were sent aloft by means of a single 2-stage Atlas-Agena rocket launched from Cape Kennedy at 3:22 a.m. July 17. 2 of the satellites were 292-pound Sentries whose mission was to help in establishing a system for detecting possible nuclear tests in space in violation of the nuclear test ban treaty. The 3d was a 4.5-pound satellite designed to detect any disturbances in the electrons of the Van Allen radiation belts such as might be caused by nuclear explosions.

Pres. Johnson disclosed in a Sacramento, Calif. speech Sept. 17 that the U.S. had developed 2 weapons systems capable of intercepting and destroying armed space satellites orbiting the earth. He also revealed U.S. development of an "over-the-horizon" radar that could "look around the curve of the earth" and detect a missile attack "within seconds" after its launching. Mr. Johnson said that the satellite-interceptor-systems, details of which he did not give, were already installed for use and that the new radar was being installed. He said that the U.S. had no intention to put military satellites with warheads in orbit and that "we have no reason to believe that any nation plans to put nuclear warheads into orbit."

An elaboration of the Presidential statement was made at a Pentagon news conference Sept. 18 by Defense Secy. Robert S. McNamara. He revealed that the 2 systems were (1) the Army's solid-fueled, 3-stage Nike-Zeus rocket, and (2) the Air Force's liquid-fueled Thor rocket, supplemented by 3 solid-fueled rockets. McNamara said they had been "effectively tested," had intercepted satellites in space and were "operational" under control of the Continental Air Defense Command in Colorado Springs, Colo. (3 secret satellites were launched by the U.S. Air Force from Vandenberg AF Base, Calif. Oct. 5, 6 and 23. A Thor-Agena rocket was used for the Oct. 5 shot, a Thor-Able-star for the Oct. 6 launching, and Atlas-Agena for the Oct. 23 shot.)

Other Disarmament & Peace Activites

The 12th nongovernmental Pugwash Conference, attended by 77 delegates from 25 nations, was held in Udaipur, India Jan. 27-Feb. 2. It appealed to the richer nations to divert any resources released by disarmament to the backward nations. The week-long 13th Pugwash Conference was held in Karlsbad, Czechoslovakia Sept. 13-20, with about 90 scientists from 24 Eastern and Western nations in attendance for discussions of peaceful uses of atomic energy and methods of halting the spread of nuclear weapons. At the opening session, Prof. Mikhail D. Millionshchikov, vice president of the Soviet Academy of Sciences, called for "a treaty preventing the sale of uranium which could be used for atom bombs and other military purposes."

Peace and anti-bomb groups from Sweden, Finland, Norway and Denmark held an atom-ban conference in Stockholm Mar. 14-15 and demanded the creation of a nuclear-free Nordic zone for their nations. 6 members of the Finnish Parliament attended.

The 10th World Conference against Atom & Hydrogen Bombs in Tokyo opened July 31 and was disrupted when the Soviet delegation and its supporters walked out of the meeting Aug. 1. The USSR representatives and delegations from 27 countries and 3 international organizations had boycotted the proceedings at the opening session after the Russians had been barred from conference leadership posts and were shouted down by pro-Chinese speakers. Dr. G. B. Godlette of the U.S., a member of the Soviet-controlled World Peace Council, said: "We have been forced out.... The Chinese delegation has been allowed to utilize the conference for the present vendetta against the Soviet Union." Soviet chief delegate Georgei A. Zhukov charged that the Chinese "divisionists" had made the meeting "an arena for an unbridled, slanderous campaign against the Soviet Union." Chinese delegate Tan Ming-chao charged that "the Russians came here to disrupt and confuse. The Russians have insulted the Japanese people, foreign delegations and all concerned by denouncing the conference as a puppet of Communist China and saying that the conference was trying to kick them out." The conference, sponsored by the Japanese Communist Party and left-wing peace groups, continued through Aug. 1 with only pro-Chinese representatives attending.

About 3,500 scientists and industrial observers from 71 Western and Eastern nations attended the UN's 3d International Conference on Peaceful Uses of Atomic Energy, which was held in Geneva Aug. 31-Sept. 9. UN Secretary General U Thant stressed at the opening session Aug. 31 that "only nuclear power can fill the world's immense power requirements." In a filmed message on the eve of the conference, Pres. Johnson Aug. 30 had expressed hope that atomic energy could become "a powerhouse of peace." He said the U.S. was proceeding with "an aggressive program of nuclear desalting" and would be glad to share its knowledge with other nations. "Already we have begun cooperative exchanges with Mexico, with Israel and with the Soviet Union," he added. Soviet Premier Khrushchev warned in a message to the conference Aug. 31 that the military use of atomic energy presented an obstacle to its peaceful use. He called for a "most rapid" solution to the disarmament question and a pledge by nuclear powers not to share nuclear weapons information with other nations.

The U.S., Britain and the Soviet Union Aug. 5 observed the first anniversary of the signing of the nuclear test ban treaty by issuing a joint declaration pledging all possible efforts to solve international problems by negotiations. The statement said in part: "We declare our intention to do everything possible for the solution through negotiations of unresolved international problems in order to strengthen general peace." (Khrushchev was quoted in the London *Sunday Times* Aug. 15 as saying in an interview Aug. 13 that he would be willing to attend a high-level nuclear disarmament conference in 1965. "A new initiative would be welcome," and the Soviet government would allow inspection if it "came after a disarmament agreement," he said. Interviewed in the Kremlin June 2 by British Labor Party leader Harold Wilson, Khrushchev had called for a ban on further dissemination of nuclear weapons as the key to disarmament progress. Khrushchev was said to have expressed opposition to Western proposals for mutual destruction of strategic bombers and for a freeze on nuclear-armed missiles. He was reported to have told Wilson that the U.S., in advancing these plans, had demanded inspection measures that the USSR could accept only as part of a general arms agreement.)

Pres. Johnson Dec. 30 urged Soviet Pres. Anastas I. Mikoyan and the new Soviet premier, Aleksei N. Kosygin, to join him in promoting agreements on disarmament and arms-control programs. The Johnson appeal, in a New Year's letter, stressed the President's hope of finding a means to stop the spread of nuclear weapons as well as of achieving a complete worldwide ban on nuclear tests. Mr. Johnson recommended a "cutoff" of production of fissionable materials intended for weapons use and suggested steps to encourage the peaceful use of nuclear power. He proposed a "verified freeze in existing offensive and defensive strategic nuclear delivery systems."

Pope Paul VI, in his broadcast Christmas message Dec. 22, expressed alarm over a "militarism no longer focused on the legitimate defense of the countries concerned or on the maintenance of world peace, but tending rather to build up stockpiles of weapons ever more powerful and destructive." He urged world disarmament and possible diversion of military spending for humanitarian ends.

1964's NUCLEAR TESTS

U.S. Explosions

All U.S. nuclear tests conducted during 1964 were underground. The dates, force and sites of the tests:

Date	Force	Site
Jan. 16	Low yield	Nevada test site
Jan. 23	Low yield	Nevada test site
Feb. 20*	Low-intermediate	Nevada test site
Mar. 13**	Low yield	Nevada test site
Apr. 14	Low yield	Nevada test site
Apr. 15	Low yield	Nevada test site
Apr. 24	Low-intermediate	Nevada test site
Apr. 29	Low yield	Nevada test site
May 14	Low yield	Nevada test site
May 15	Low yield	Nevada test site
June 11*	Low yield	Nevada test site

Date	Force	Site
June 25	Low yield	Nevada test site
June 30*	Low yield	Nevada test site
July 16	Low yield	Nevada test site
Aug. 19	Low yield	Nevada test site
Aug. 24	Low-intermediate	Nevada test site
Aug. 28	Low yield	Nevada test site
Sept. 4	Low yield	Nevada test site
Oct. 2	Low-intermediate	Nevada test site
Oct. 9§	30 kiloton	Nevada test site
Oct. 16	Low yield	Nevada test site
Oct. 22†	5 kiloton	Baxterville, Miss.
Oct. 31	Low yield	Nevada test site
Nov. 5 ‡	10 kiloton	Nevada test site
Dec. 5	2 low yield	Nevada test site
Dec. 16	Low yield	Nevada test site
Dec. 18¶	Low yield	Nevada test site

Soviet Explosions

Sept. 18***	Less than 5 kiloton	
Oct. 25***	5 kiloton	Novaya Zemlya
Nov. 16***		Semipalatinsk

Other Explosions

July 17 (U. S.-British)***	Low yield	Nevada test site
Oct. 16 (Red China)★	Low yield	Lob Nor test site
Nov. 19 (French)***		Sahara

---

* Tests described as detonations in "a series to develop devices for use in possible later excavation experiments."

** A small amount of radioactivity escaped accidentally from this underground nuclear explosion, and some of it fell on Las Vegas. The AEC described the fallout as of "very low level."

§ According to Dr. John S. Foster Jr., director of the AEC's Lawrence Radiation Center, this test demonstrated the feasibility of producing heavy elements from nuclear explosion.

† Explosion designed to see if U.S. detection devices could spot nuclear explosions by foreign powers. The first U.S. nuclear device exploded east of the Mississippi River.

‡ Test designed to determine possible industrial uses of nuclear explosions in breaking up underground rock for ore, gas and oil recovery.

¶ The object of this test was to develop excavation techniques for sea-level canal building.

*** Underground test.

★ Atmospheric test.

1965

Continued testing by both Communist China and France during 1965 accentuated the need for preventing further proliferation of nuclear arms. Besides the rapid advance of the Chinese nuclear program, NATO plans for nuclear sharing among the alliance's members—including West Germany—aroused Soviet apprehensions. The danger of proliferation, along with the efforts to extend to underground tests the 1963 Moscow partial test ban treaty, was the most important item on the disarmament agenda. Inconclusive talks were held within 3 UN bodies: the UN Disarmament Commission in New York Apr. 21-June 16, the 18-Nation Disarmament Committee in Geneva June 27-Sept. 16 and the 20th session of the UN General Assembly in New York Sept. 23-Dec. 3.

INCREASED GREAT-POWER ARMAMENTS

U.S. Defense Budget & Military Programs

Pres. Johnson told the U.S. Congress in a special defense message Jan. 18 that he planned (a) to reduce defense expenditures for the 2d consecutive year and (b) to develop the Poseidon missile to replace the Polaris A-3 submarine missile in 3-4 years. But except for continuing current development options, no major programs for a new manned bomber, anti-missile missile or fallout shelter construction were planned. "Today we can walk the road of peace," the President said, "because we have the strength we need.... We covet no territory, we seek no dominion, we fear no nation, we despise no people. With our arms we seek to shelter the peace of mankind.... We seek to avoid a nuclear holocaust."

Defense expenditures for fiscal 1965 were estimated at about $49.3 billion ($2 billion less than in fiscal 1964), and the President said he expected that fiscal 1966 expenditures would approximate $49 billion. He cited 2 main reasons for this "leveling-off": (1) the U.S. had "achieved many of the needed changes and increases" in its military force structure; (2) the benefits of the "rigorous cost-reduction program" started 4 years previously were being realized. Barring international complications, Mr. Johnson predicted, defense spending would "constitute a declining portion of our expanding annual gross national product."

The President further reported that: U.S. strategic nuclear power on alert had increased 3-fold in 4 years; tactical nuclear power had been "greatly" expanded; U.S. forces had been made "as versatile as the threats to peace are various"; U.S. special forces, "trained for the undeclared, twilight wars of today," had been expanded 8-fold; combat-ready Army divisions had been increased by 45%; the Marine Corps had been increased by 15,000 men; airlift capacity to move troops had been doubled; tactical Air Force firepower to support divisions in the field had been increased 100%. The U.S.' strategic retaliatory forces included more than 850 land-based intercontinental ballistic missiles, more than 300 nuclear-armed missiles in Polaris submarines and more than 900 strategic bombers, half of them ready at all times to be airborne within 15 minutes. Work on the new Poseidon strategic weapon system was scheduled to begin in 1965. (The cost of development and production was estimated at $2 billion.) The Poseidon was to have double the payload (and 8 times the "kill capability") of the Polaris A-3 plus increased accuracy and flexibility. 2 other strategic weapons system starts were also scheduled: (1) "A series of remarkable new payloads," including penetration aids" to get missiles "through any defense"; "guidance and re-entry vehicle designs to increase... effectiveness... against various kinds of targets"; methods of reporting arrival of missiles on target. (2) A new short-range attack missile (SRAM) to be carried by the B-52 or smaller bombers.

Procurement and deployment of the Minuteman II and Polaris A-3 missiles were to be continued, as was the replacing of outdated Atlas and Titan I missiles, Mr. Johnson reported. Military aircraft plans called for: (a) a request for $300 million to improve and maintain B-52 bombers; (b) the elimination of 2 squadrons of the earliest B-52s (the B-52Bs); (c) the phasing out of the remainder of the B-47 forces during fiscal 1966; (d) continued development of "engines and other systems for advanced aircraft to retain our option for a new manned bomber"; (e) continued deployment of the SR-71, "which will enter the active forces this year"; (f) the beginning of large-scale procurement of the F-111 and A-7 Navy attack aircraft; (g) continued installation of over-the-horizon radars. Other plans included: (1) a start on construction of 4 nuclear-powered attack submarines and 10 destroyer escorts; (2) continued development of a smaller atomic-power plant for aircraft carriers; (3) continuation of the existing fall-out shelter program and a start on a program to increase shelter inventory through surveys of private homes and other small structures; (4) continuation of research and development on alternative weapons systems so that the U.S. would have the options of meeting attack with anti-ballistic missiles or with manned interceptors or surface-to-air missiles against bombers (development of the Nike-X anti-missile system would be continued).

(The dollar value of the entire U.S. military establishment rose by $2.1 billion in the 12 months ended July 1, 1964 to a $173.5 billion total, according to Defense Department figures. Expensive new combat weapons such as intercontinental missiles and improved facilities for supporting them were the chief factors in the rise. The Navy's value was put at $67 billion, the Air Force's at $66 billion and the Army's at $37 billion.)

Pres. Johnson Jan. 25 sent Congress his budget for fiscal 1966. For the first time since 1950, payments in 1966 for defense, international and space programs, estimated at $61.8 billion, were expected to account for less than half of federal total payments. The defense budget as projected according to military missions (for fiscal years, in billions):

	1965	1966
Strategic retaliatory forces	$ 5.3	$ 4.5
Continental air-missile defense	1.8	1.8
General purpose forces (all services)	18.1	19.0
Airlift and sealift forces	1.5	1.5
Reserve forces	2.1	2.0
Research and development (not included elsewhere)	5.1	5.4
General support	14.3	14.6
Retired pay	1.4	1.5
Total obligational authority	$49.6	$50.5
New obligational authority	$48.7	$47.4
Prior year funds	$ 1.0	$ 3.1

The budget provided for military manpower as of June 30, 1966 (current manpower in parentheses) of: Army 953,000 men (963,000); Navy 685,000 (674,000); Marines 193,000 (190,000); Air Force 809,000 (829,000).

Fiscal 1966 Atomic Energy Commission (AEC) expenditures were budgeted at $2.5 billion, down $170 million from 1965. Expenditures for development and production of nuclear weapons in 1966 were to decrease by $19 million from 1965 levels. A decline of $29 million in test program expenditures in 1966 was possible, Mr. Johnson said, if the U.S. proved able in 1965 "to resume atmospheric testing" because of "violation by others of the limited nuclear test ban treaty."

The AEC presented its annual report to Congress Jan. 29. It asserted that an underground nuclear effects test at the Mercury, Nev. test site Aug. 19, 1964 had helped uphold the Administration's pledge that the test ban treaty would not substantially hinder U.S. military preparedness. The report said: The test was "one of the most important events conducted to date as well as the most costly [$5.5 million].... If the test ban were not in being, the event would normally have been conducted in the atmosphere. However,... methods were found to derive the desired data from the underground event." (The test, designated Alva, apparently demonstrated that even without atmospheric testing the U.S. could measure the precise effects that an unfriendly nuclear detonation would have on American nuclear weapons.) The report disclosed a program to "increase the hardness and penetration capability of missile warheads so that their vulnerability to enemy anti-ballistic missile countermeasures is decreased." It also noted the addition to the U.S. nuclear stockpile of "new warheads for the Polaris, Subroc and Minuteman missile systems and new nuclear artillery projectiles and atomic demolition devices."

Defense Secy. Robert S. McNamara presented his annual "military posture" accounting to the House Armed Services Committee in closed session Feb. 18. According to excerpts released prior to the session, McNamara urged a fall-out shelter system, opposed new manned bomber production and reaffirmed the U.S.' defensive commitment to its allies. "In order to preclude any possibility of miscalculation by others, I want to reiterate," he said, that, although the U.S. "would itself suffer severely in the event of a general nuclear war, we are fully committed to the defense of our allies. 2d, we do not view damage limitation as a question of concern only to the U.S. Our offensive forces cover strategic enemy capabilities to inflict damage on our allies in Europe just as they cover enemy threats to the continental U.S."

McNamara's report contended that offensive weapons could be acquired much more cheaply than defensive facilities. "At the level of spending required [$25 billion] to limit fatalities to about 40 million in a large first strike against our cities," it said, "we would have to spend on damage limiting programs about 4 times what the potential aggressor would have to spend on damage creating forces." Included in the report was a table, based on projected population in the 1970s of 210 million for the U.S., indicating that 122 million Americans would die in the event of a Soviet nuclear attack limited to military targets. (McNamara noted that such a limitation was "unlikely.") If urban centers were included in the attack, the death toll was estimated at 149 million. If $5 billion were invested for a full fall-out shelter program, the respective death tolls were estimated at 90 million and 120 million. If $8.5 billion were added to the fall-out shelter investment to provide limited deployment of a low-cost missile defense system, and if $1.5 billion were spent for new manned bomber defenses, the death tolls were estimated at 59 million and 96 million; if a total of about $17 billion were spent for anti-missile defenses and $3 billion for bombers, plus the fall-out shelters, the death tolls were estimated at 41 million and 78 million.

McNamara told the committee that parts of the distant early warning line (DEW line) were "either obsolete or of marginal value." The items of questionable value included 22 off-shore radar ships and some aircraft, which, he said, would be eliminated at an eventual saving of $266 million.

A bill authorizing $15,402,800,000 in fiscal 1966 for procurement of aircraft, missiles and ships for the armed services and for defense research and development was passed by the House May 26 and the Senate May 27 and was signed by Pres. Johnson June 11. $8,958,300,000 of the authorization, $219.9 million more than the Administration had requested, was for procurement. The unrequested funds included $150.5 million for a nuclear-powered guided missile frigate and $133.6 million for the construction of 2 more nuclear-powered attack submarines. The bill's authorizations: Procurement—Army $598,200,000 (aircraft $344,500,000, missiles $253,700,000). Navy and Marine Corps $4,013,800,000 (aircraft $1,915,800,000, missiles $377 million ships $1.721 billion). Air Force $4,346,300,000 (aircraft $3,550,200,000, missiles $796,100,000).

Despite the importance of the military spending recommended in the federal budget, the possibility of disarmament was reported not to represent an economic danger to the U.S. The White House Sept. 5 released a 92-page report in which the 13-member Committee on the Economic Impact of Defense & Disarmament concluded that "even general and complete disarmament would pose no insuperable problems" to the U.S. economy. "Indeed, it would mainly afford opportunities for a better life for our citizens," the report said. The report, however, warned that major policy decisions would have to be made because of non-defense factors if economic growth and prosperity were to be maintained. It estimated that the gross national product probably would increase by $210 billion to an $870 billion total by 1970 and that federal revenues, at current tax rates, would rise therefore by about $50 billion to a $165 billion annual total. Such an increase in taxation would have to be offset by new tax cuts or by greater federal spending if economically depressing reductions in demand for goods and services were not to result, the committee held.

Soviet A-Tests & Armaments

The U.S. Atomic Energy Commission (AEC) announced Jan. 16 that the Soviet Union apparently had conducted the biggest underground nuclear test in its history Jan. 15. "The United States yesterday recorded seismic signals from an event in the Soviet nuclear testing area in the Semipalatinsk region [of Soviet central Asia]," the AEC reported. It tentatively estimated the explosive force at about 100 kilotons (in the low intermediate range). But a new AEC estimate Jan. 19 upgraded the blast to the "intermediate range"—200 kilotons to a megaton. The Seismological Institution at Uppsala University in Sweden Jan. 15 had recorded "an apparent nuclear underground explosion" that took place near Semipalatinsk. It estimated the explosive force at perhaps as high as a megaton. The Swedish news agency's scientific expert said the signals received "almost surely came from the first known underground explosion of an H-bomb."

The AEC announced Jan. 19 that the U.S. "detection system has now detected a certain amount of venting connected with the test." It said: "The amounts of radioactivity measured to date will not produce measurable exposures to persons. In view of the treaty banning nuclear weapons tests in the atmosphere, in outer space and under water, the Department of State has asked the government of the Soviet Union for information on this event." (High-flying U.S. planes were reported to have picked up air samples containing very small amounts of radioactive debris, apparently from the explosion, over the northern Pacific outside Soviet territory Jan. 18-19.)

The USSR denied Jan. 25 that it had violated the test-ban treaty. The denial was made by Soviet Amb. Anatoly F. Dobrynin at a meeting with U.S. State Secy. Dean Rusk after the U.S. had requested information about the Jan. 15 test. The U.S. State Department said in a statement issued on the meetings: "... the Soviet government has stated that the nuclear explosion was carried out deep underground on Jan. 15 and that some radioactive debris leaked into the atmosphere. However, the [Soviet] oral reply states that the amount is so insignificant that the Soviet government excludes the possibility of a violation of the limited test ban treaty."

William C. Foster, head of the U.S. Arms Control & Disarmament Agency, told the House Foreign Affairs Committee Jan. 26 that U.S. security officials were convinced that radioactive leakage from the Jan. 15 test apparently was accidental. He said that, in any case, the fallout apparently did not violate the test ban treaty's intent.

The U.S. State Department declared Feb. 18 that it was not satisfied with the USSR's Jan. 25 explanation that the amount of radioactivity in the Jan. 15 explosion was "insignificant" and therefore not a violation of the test-ban treaty. But the department Mar. 9 issued a statement saying: It had reached "the preliminary conclusion" that, although the test "may have constituted a technical violation," "on the basis of what we now know the event does not represent a threat to our national security or to the test ban treaty. Nor, standing alone, does it represent a resumption of tests prohibited by the treaty."

The U.S. AEC announced Mar. 3 that seismic signals had been recorded from "an event" in the Soviet underground nuclear test area near Semipalatinsk. If the "event" was a nuclear test, the AEC said, its force yield would be in the low-intermediate range (20-200 kilotons). Sweden's Seismological Institute at Uppsala had reported earlier Mar. 3 that it had detected a strong explosion in the test area.

U.S. speculation that the Soviet Union planned to orbit nuclear weapons in violation of a 1963 UN General Assembly resolution increased as a result of a Nov. 7 military parade in Moscow's Red Square at which the USSR displayed an "orbital missile."

Soviet Finance Min. Vasily F. Garbuzov Dec. 7 presented a record state budget for 1966 to the Supreme Soviet. Military expenditure under the budget would be 13.4 billion rubles—or $14.7 billion at the official Soviet rate of one ruble to $1.11. The 13.4 billion-ruble figure exceeded by 600 million rubles Soviet defense spending in 1965, but the increase in the total budget to a record 105.4 billion rubles would keep defense spending at about 12.8% of total expenditures. In 1963, when Soviet defense cutbacks were first announced the military share of the budget was 16.1%.

Red China's Nuclear & Military Growth

Communist China announced May 14 that it had "exploded another atom bomb over its western areas" at 10 a.m. that day and thus had "successfully concluded its 2d nuclear test." The Chinese communique continued: "Following on the explosion of China's first atom bomb on Oct. 16, 1964, this nuclear test is another important achievement scored by the Chinese people in strengthening their national defense and safeguarding the security of their motherland and world peace.... It is a great victory for the party's general line of Socialist construction. It is a great victory for Mao Tse-tung's thinking.... China is conducting necessary nuclear tests within defined limits and is developing the nuclear weapon for the purpose of coping with the nuclear blackmail and threats of the United States and for the purpose of abolishing all nuclear weapons.... China will never be the first to use nuclear weapons.... Together with all the peace-loving countries and people of the world, the Chinese government and people will, as always, continue to strive for the noble aim of the complete prohibition and thorough destruction of nuclear weapons."

The Chinese announcement indicated that the nuclear device had been dropped from a plane. U.S. sources estimated the force of the detonation as equivalent to that produced by the explosion of perhaps a little more than 20 kilotons (20,000 tons) of TNT—a yield generally described as in the low-intermediate range.

The U.S. State Department had warned Feb. 16 that Communist China was preparing for its 2d nuclear test. The department declared in a statement: "The United States has reason to believe that Communist China is preparing for another nuclear test. The United States government deplores this indication that the leaders of Communist China are, in the face of worldwide condemnation of atmospheric nuclear testing, continuing such tests." A U.S. State Department spokesman May 14 called it "deeply regrettable" that China had tested a 2d nuclear device "in total disregard of the test-ban treaty."

Soviet Premier Aleksei N. Kosygin told Indian correspondents visiting Moscow May 14 that he did "not see a direct threat of nuclear war in present circumstances." He insisted there was "no nuclear blackmail from China" and asserted: "I do not think any sane person can think of using nuclear weapons. Nuclear war is impossible in our time."

Indian and Japanese spokesmen, in remarks before the 114-nation UN Disarmament Commission in New York May 14, criticized Peking for conducting a 2d A-test. Vishnu C. Trivedi of India called the test "a genetic and health danger" to present and future generations. He warned: "The explosion conducted...is an attack not only on all that we stand for and all the efforts that we are making but it is also an attack on all of humanity." Akira Matsui of Japan declared: "To us the most regrettable development of all during the past year was the explosion of a nuclear device last October by a neighbor of ours, the People's Republic of China, with the manifest intention of becoming a nuclear power." He termed the 2d explosion a defiance of all UN disarmament efforts. Halim Budo of Albania had told the UN Disarmament Commission May 11 that "freedom loving people" had welcomed the first Chinese explosion as a defense against U.S. blackmail.

Gen. Lo Jui-ching, Chinese Army chief of staff, had called previously for "realistic" preparations for nuclear war. Writing in *Hung Chi (Red Flag),* the ideological journal of the Chinese Communist Party, Lo warned that China would attack non-Communist countries if war began and that ground armies, rather than weapons, would be the decisive factor. (The Peking Communist Party newspaper *Jenmin Jih Pao* had reported, however, that Communist China did not have enough small arms or ammunition for all its military training requirements. It said: "The army recently had conducted an exhibition of substitute equipment made by the soldiers to save money for the state." "Mass inventions, creations and technical innovations helped solve some problems in military training that previously had not been answered.")

Communist China, in a major policy declaration released Sept. 2 in Peking and published in newspapers throughout the country Sept. 3, urged revolutionaries in underdeveloped countries to wage a "people's war" aimed at "encirclement" of the U.S. and other capitalist countries. The statement, issued on the 20th anniversary of the World War II victory over Japan, was written by Defense Min. Marshal Lin Piao, Communist Party deputy chairman and a deputy premier. The article discussed Mao Tse-tung's military-revolutionary strategy; it said that following this strategy, the Chinese Communists, relying on a peasant base, had gradually encircled the cities and had won the Chinese civil war. Such a strategy, said Lin, pursued on a worldwide scale by revolutionaries in underdeveloped nations, could be used to defeat the capitalist countries, which he viewed as the "cities of the world."

Emphasizing the superiority of conventional over nuclear warfare, Lin wrote: "U.S. imperialism relies solely on its nuclear weapons to intimidate people, but these weapons cannot save U.S. imperialism from its doom. Nuclear weapons cannot be used lightly. U.S. imperialism has been condemned by the people of the whole world, for its towering crime of dropping 2 atomic bombs on Japan. If it uses nuclear weapons again, it will become isolated in the extreme. Moreover, the U.S. monopoly of nuclear weapons has long been broken; U.S. imperialism has these weapons, but others have them too. If it threatens other countries with nuclear weapons, U.S. imperialism will expose its own country to the same threat.... However highly developed modern weapons and technical equipment may be and however complicated the methods of modern warfare, in the final analysis the outcome of a war will be decided by the sustained fighting of the ground forces, by the fighting at close quarters on battlefields, by the political consciousness of the men, by their courage and spirit of sacrifice. Here the weak points of the U.S. imperialism will be completely laid bare, while the superiority of the revolutionary people will be brought into full play. The reactionary troops of U.S. imperialism cannot possibly be endowed with the courage and the spirit of sacrifice possessed by the revolutionary people. The spiritual atom bomb that the revolutionary people possess is a far more powerful and useful weapon than the physical atom bomb."

The Red Chinese nuclear buildup continued, however. The *Wall Street Journal* reported from Washington July 13 that Communist China was building a fleet of long-range submarines capable of launching missiles armed with atomic warheads. The report said that Red China might be able to mount a submarine-launched nuclear attack within 2 to 3 years. China, according to the report, was building Russian-designed G-class diesel-electric submarines equipped with 3 vertical tubes in the conning tower for missile launching. The Russian G-class submarine had a range of 44,000 miles.

At the NATO Council meeting in Paris, Dec. 15, U.S. Defense Secy. McNamara stressed the growing nuclear capability of China. He made these estimates: By 1967, Peking would have enough fissionable material to begin a small stockpile of atomic weapons. By 1967, it would also have developed a medium-range ballistic missile with an atomic warhead. It would have several launchers for medium-range missiles deployed by 1968 or 1969 and possibly "several dozen" by 1975. And by 1975, China would have deployed intercontinental ballistic missiles armed with atomic warheads and capable of hitting targets in the U.S. and Western Europe. China currently had an army of 2,300,000 plus a large trained militia. China spent about 10% of its gross national product (GNP) on defense as compared with about 2% of GNP spent on defense in India, Pakistan and Brazil. Judging by China's current declarations, Peking planned to use military force to support "revolutionary wars." China's next target would be Thailand.

New French A-Bomb & Missiles

The annual report of the French Atomic Energy Commission, made public July 12, said that France had developed a "new nuclear explosive device." No details were released, but the N.Y. Times reported July 13 that the device was a "smaller, more powerful" weapon that could be more easily carried by France's Mirage-4 jet bombers than its 12-foot predecessor, which had to be mounted outside the bomber. (The French air force had received its first nuclear bombs in mid-1963.) The commission's report added that (1) research continued on an atomic warhead for strategic ballistic missiles; (2) construction of new test sites in the South Pacific (in the Tuamotu Islands) was proceeding as scheduled; (3) the transfer from Sahara bomb testing sites to the Pacific in mid-1967 would cause no delays in trials of atomic and hydrogen bombs; (4) the commission's manpower had reached 26,231, its budget about $1 billion by the end of 1964.

France's accent on atomic power was emphasized at the July 14 Bastille Day parade in Paris, where 12 deltawinged Mirage-4s were displayed publicly for the first time in a low-level fly-past. Defense Min. Pierre Messmer told the French National Assembly Oct. 21 that France's independent "atomic armament is an accomplished fact." 2 squadrons (12 planes each) of Mirage-4s were almost combat ready, Messmer said, and in 1966 50 of the 62 bombers would be "largely" operational. In 1966, he said, the strategic nuclear force would absorb 26% of the $4.4 billion defense budget. (The French Army Oct. 15 had released a photo of a device described as an operational French nuclear bomb with an explosive force of 60 kilotons [equivalent to the energy released by the detonation of 60,000 tons of TNT]. The U.S. Army July 22 had apologized to France for a July 16 incident in which a U.S. Air Force jet made 4 photo-reconnaisance passes over the French nuclear production plant at Pierrelatte, near Lyon.)

French Defense Ministry sources confirmed Oct. 12 that France planned to build 30 underground silos for strategic missiles in Haute Provence (southeastern France). The silos would be dispersed over a 220-square-mile area of the Albion Plateau. Construction would begin in 1966 and take 3 years.

East-West Strength Compared

The Institute for Strategic Studies, a private London-based research organization, reported Nov. 18 a decline in the U.S.' numerical superiority in strategic missiles. The institute, releasing its annual survey of world military strength (entitled The Military Balance, 1965-1966), said that the number of U.S. inter-continental ballistic missiles had dropped from 925 in 1964 to 854 in 1965 as a result of the retiring of obsolescent Atlas missiles. The number of Soviet strategic missiles, however, had risen from 200 to 270 in the same period. Other institute estimates of East-West strength:

Fleet ballistic missiles	U. S.—	541	USSR—	120
Medium-range missiles	U. S.—None		USSR—	750
Long-range heavy bombers	U. S.—	625	USSR—	200
Medium bombers	U. S.—	430	USSR—	1,250
Aircraft carriers	West—	38	Communist bloc—	0
Cruisers	West—	31	Communist bloc—	20
Escorts	West—	591	Communist bloc—	268
Nuclear-powered submarines	West—	62	Communist bloc—	40
Conventional submarines	West—	186	Communist bloc—	416

The institute survey included a section on the nuclear-weapons potential of nations without atomic arms but with atomic reactors for power generation and research. 26 research reactors were currently operating in such nations. By 1970, it said, 20 power reactors—having a greater bomb-producing potential than research reactors—would be in operation in such nations. At the current rate of plutonium production, according to the survey, Canada could produce enough plutonium for 16 Nagasaki-type bombs, West Germany could produce 10, India 4, Sweden 3 and Israel one. By 1970 Canada's power reactors could produce plutonium for 224 bombs, by 1972 India could produce enough for 230, West Germany for 170, Japan for 92, Italy for 120, Sweden for 32 and Czechoslovakia for 30. (5 kilograms of plutonium were required for a bomb.)

An examination of defense expenditures by nations as percentages of gross national product for 1963-4 revealed that Israel was spending the highest figure—10.7%. The U.S. spent 8.9%, the United Arab Republic 8.6%, Britain 6.7%, Portugal 6.2% and Yugoslavia 6%. Estimates for other Communist-bloc countries were lower but based on different data.

Army strength of the NATO nations was 4,961,000, of which 2,896,000 men was assigned to NATO. Communist-bloc strength was estimated at 5,830,000, of which 2,925,000 men were assigned to the Warsaw Pact.

UN DISARMAMENT COMMISSION ACTIVITY

Soviet Initiative

Soviet Amb.-to-UN Nikolai T. Fedorenko proposed to UN Secy. Gen. U Thant Mar. 31 that a full disarmament debate be held by all 114 UN members as soon as possible. Fedorenko urged that the debate be conducted at UN headquarters in New York within the framework of the UN Disarmament Commission, which had met briefly in Aug. 1960 and had turned the issue over to the Geneva disarmament conference. U.S. Amb.-to-UN Adlai E. Stevenson responded to Fedorenko's request by saying that, although the U.S. favored "a negotiating committee [the Geneva conference] to a debating committee [the Disarmament Commission]," the U.S. would agree to "participate constructively" in any disarmament debates. (The Geneva conference had recessed in Sept. 1964 without noticeable progress.) Stevenson reiterated in a note to Thant Apr. 9 that the U.S. still felt the Geneva conference was "the most suitable forum in which to negotiate concrete disarmament measures" but that "we are, however, also agreeable to a meeting of the Disarmament Commission in the meantime if a majority of the members accept it." 36 nations had agreed to such a meeting.

The UN Disarmament Commission, consisting of all 114 UN member nations, began discussions at UN headquarters in New York Apr. 21. The commission unanimously elected Mohamed Awad el-Kony of the United Arab Republic, as chairman. U Thant warned the commission that "there is evidence that we may be approaching yet another crucial point in the nuclear arms race" and stressed the need to halt the spread of nuclear weapons. (The UN General Assembly had established the commission in 1952 to work under the jurisdiction of the Security Council on matters previously assigned to the UN Atomic Energy Commission and the Commission for Conventional Armaments.

It had been enlarged since 1958 to include all UN members and was to report to both the Council and Assembly.)

At the commission's next meeting, held Apr. 26, Fedorenko charged that the Pentagon had ordered the 1945 Hiroshima and Nagasaki atomic bombings merely "as an experiment" and currently regarded Vietnam as a "proving ground for other kinds of weapons." He accused the U.S. of maintaining a million troops abroad to fight "imperialist" wars and to serve as a bridgehead for "nuclear" or "colonial" wars. Stevenson replied that Fedorenko's accusations confirmed his fears that the USSR had requested the reconvening of the commission only to provide a propaganda forum. Stevenson declared: "If this day's work is what the Soviet Union had in mind..., we shall have little constructive accomplishment in disarmament to look forward to, I fear."

Warnings against Proliferation

British Disarmament Min. Lord Chalfont warned the UN Disarmament Commission Apr. 28 that atomic civil wars within nations could become a worldwide menace if the spread of nuclear weapons were not halted. He declared: "It is even possible, in the context of a nuclear free-for-all, that weapons might get into the hands of people wanting to upset the established government of their own country. The idea of nuclear revolution may be too terrible for sane men to contemplate, but we should not deceive ourselves. It is one of the logical ends of the unrestrained spread of nuclear weapons."

Indian delegate B. N. Chakravarty told the commission May 4 that if the UN really expected to halt the spread of nuclear weapons, it would have to give guarantees that countries lacking such weapons would not be subject to nuclear attack. He condemned Peking's Oct. 1964 nuclear test explosion as a "cynical disregard for human welfare" and open defiance of the 1963 nuclear test ban treaty. He called for a ban on underground A-tests.

Gen. E. L. M. Burns, Canadian representative, told the commission May 7 that a "reasonable period of time" ought to be given for the nuclear powers to scrap "this most dangerous [atomic] weapon" but that nonnuclear nations could not refrain permanently from trying to obtain nuclear weapons if superpowers retained atomic arsenals. He urged a quick resumption of the Geneva disarmament negotiations. (Canadian External Affairs Secy. Paul Martin had proposed in Geneva May 3 that countries agreeing not to acquire atomic weapons be guaranteed against nuclear attack. He said at the 11th general assembly of the World Veterans Federation that "the principal problem in the field of disarmament before us today" was to prevent more countries from obtaining independent nuclear attack capabilities.)

Algerian representative Tewfik Bouattoura told the commission May 10 that worldwide disarmament talks, with Communist China present, would be especially desirable.

But Mrs. Alva Myrdal of Sweden May 10 expressed doubt about the usefulness of any world conference in the current politically tense atmosphere. Instead, she urged that the Geneva disarmament talks be reopened. Mrs. Myrdal suggested that the commission agree on a 3-point program: (a) a treaty to ban underground tests as well as those coming under the 1963 treaty (which prohibited tests in space, in the atmosphere or under water); (b) a halt in the production of fissionable materials for military purposes; (c) a pact to halt the spread of nuclear weapons to states that did not have them. Sweden May 10 became the 4th member of the Geneva disarmament conference to suggest to the commission that any agreement to halt the spread of nuclear weapons would have to be linked with an agreement by the nuclear powers to stop weapons production. Canada, India and the UAR had made the same suggestion.

Irish Foreign Min. Frank Aiken suggested to the Disarmament Commission May 12 that emphasis be placed on an immediate pact to halt the spread of nuclear weapons. "There is every indication that the number of states with an embryonic nuclear arsenal will be doubled within a few years," he declared, and there was "very little time left" to initiate a treaty.

Hans R. Tabor of Denmark recommended May 13 that the Geneva disarmament conference be resumed soon and that Communist China be allowed to speak there. He also urged France to end its boycott of the Geneva conference and agree to become the 18th conference nation, as had been stipulated in 1962.

Frank H. Corner of New Zealand warned May 18 that French plans to test a hydrogen bomb in the South Pacific might "lead others to do likewise."

Representatives of Pakistan, Nepal, Kenya, Tunisia and Rwanda urged May 21 that Communist China be invited to future disarmament negotiations. But Nationalist Chinese delegate Yu-chi Hsueh warned May 25 that including Communist China in such negotiations would cause them to fail.

Call for Further Talks

The UN Disarmament Commission June 11 proposed a world disarmament conference that would include Communist China. The commission June 15 approved a U.S. proposal for an early resumption of negotiations by the 18-member UN Disarmament Committee in Geneva. These were the last major actions taken by the commission before its recess June 16. The vote on the resolution to call a world disarmament conference was 89-0, with the U.S., France and 14 other nations abstaining. (U.S. delegate William C. Foster, director of the U.S. Arms Control & Disarmament Agency, had told the commission June 9 that a world disarmament conference "would only delay negotiations...in the 18-nation Disarmament Committee.") The proposal, presented by Yugoslavia and 35 Asian and African states, was supported by all Communist countries. The resolution left the final decision on calling the conference to the UN General Assembly and recommended that the Assembly give the matter "urgent consideration" at its 20th session scheduled to begin Sept 21. (All 114 members of the Disarmament Commission were members of the General Assembly.) A key paragraph of the text welcomed "the proposal adopted at the 2d Cairo conference of nonaligned countries in Oct. 1964 for the convening of a world disarmament conference to which all countries would be invited."

The U.S. proposal June 1 for a resumption of the Geneva meetings was approved by 83-1 vote, with 18 abstentions (including the Soviet bloc and France). The proposal asked the committee to concentrate on: (1) the writing of a new treaty to prevent the spread of nuclear weapons to states that did not have them and (2) the broadening of the 1963 limited test ban treaty to include underground tests. The only opposing vote was cast by Albania and was a reaction to the resolution's language criticizing the continuation of testing. France's abstention was linked to its refusal to participate in the committee's negotiations during the past 4 years; its boycott had reduced the committee to an effective membership of 17 nations.

The 7-week Disarmament Commission conference ended June 16. The close of the conference was marked by an apparent U.S.-Soviet agreement not to press for action on rival disarmament proposals. The Soviet Union abandoned proposals, submitted to the commission May 27 by Soviet delegate Federenko, calling for (a) a world conference on banning nuclear weapons and (b) the liquidation of all overseas military bases. The U.S. agreed not to ask for a vote on its June 1 proposals for the negotiation of agreements to stop producing fissionable material for weapons, to transfer "sizable" quantities of such material to peaceful uses and to discuss a freeze on the number of strategic delivery vehicles capable of carrying nuclear weapons.

NATO & NUCLEAR POLICY

A-Mine Belt Opposed by USSR

The USSR objected Jan. 18 to a plan, discussed at a Dec. 1964 NATO meeting in Paris by Gen. Heinz Trettner, West German armed forces inspector general, for the creation of an atomic mine field in Central Europe along the borders of the Iron Curtain.

Soviet Deputy Foreign Min. V. S. Semenov gave U. S. Amb.-to-USSR Foy D. Kohler a note predicting that "an 'atomic mine belt' would... increase international tensions and the danger of an outbreak of a nuclear conflict in which many countries could be involved."

The note to West Germany asserted that the stockpiling by the U.S. of nuclear demolition charges in Germany "immeasurably increases the danger of nuclear conflict" and that the Soviet bloc would be forced to take countermeasures if an atomic mine belt were erected.

A spokesman for the West German government maintained Jan. 19 that there was no atomic mine belt along the West German side of the Iron Curtain and that none was planned. (U.S. officials had explained that U.S. troops in West Germany had nuclear devices that could be used in the event of an invasion.)

In separate notes to the Soviet Foreign Ministry, West Germany and the U.S. denied Apr. 23 that West German military leaders planned an atomic mine field across Germany and along the Czechoslovak border.

(Belgian Foreign Min. Paul-Henri Spaak had suggested Mar. 17, in a report to the NATO Council, that NATO discuss with the Communist bloc a proposal to establish a nuclear-free zone in Central Europe. The plan had been suggested originally by Polish Foreign Min. Adam Rapacki in 1957. As presented in its final form in a 1959 Soviet memo, the Rapacki plan called for "a zone free of atom, hydrogen and rocket weapons" in Poland, Czechoslovakia, East Germany and West Germany. The U.S. and Britain rejected the plan as giving the Warsaw Treaty powers military supremacy in Central Europe because of their numerical superiority in conventional strength. Spaak's suggestion that the plan be reexamined was based on his talks with Rapacki in February.)

A-Use Consultation Proposed

The NATO defense ministers conferred in Paris May 31-June 1 on future defense commitments of the alliance's members. At the May 31 meeting, U.S. Defense Secy. Robert S. McNamara proposed the establishment of a "select committee" of 4 or 5 NATO powers to study ways to improve consultation on the use of nuclear weapons. The projected committee's dual purpose, according to McNamara, would be to study ways: (1) to improve and extend allied participation in any decision to use nuclear forces, strategic or tactical; (2) to "improve communications to insure that agreed consultations concerning a decision to use nuclear forces can take place as expeditiously as possible." The committee would be composed of the defense ministers of the 4 or 5 governments represented. (Semyon K. Tsarapkin, Soviet delegate to the UN Disarmament Commission meeting in New York, criticized McNamara's proposal June 2. He said it would give West Germany more power in NATO nuclear planning.) McNamara emphasized that the projected committed was not related to the U.S. proposed multilateral nuclear force (MLF) or Britain's proposed Atlantic force.

McNamara suggested that Europe should be more concerned about small dangerous crises than about the threat of an all-out Soviet nuclear attack. He called for "small, fast-breaking mobile forces" to deal with such situations. (By comparison, French strategy demanded massive retaliation in response to all aggression, large or small.)

McNamara disclosed at the meeting June 1 that the U.S. had increased the number of its nuclear warheads in Europe by 10% since Jan. 1. By the end of 1965, he said, NATO forces in Europe would be supplied with "100%" more nuclear warheads than in 1961. He told newsmen June 1 that reports that the U.S. was planning a "denuclearization" of Europe were "completely untrue."

In their final communique June 1, the ministers agreed to study McNamara's proposal for a nuclear policy committee.

The proposal of a NATO committee to improve Western consultation on the use of nuclear weapons was rejected by France at a meeting in Paris July 7 of the NATO Permanent Council. Jacques Schricke, a member of the French delegation, told the Council that the proposal concerned a "technical" matter that did not merit the attention of the defense ministers. He said, that if other NATO powers wanted to proceed with the proposal without French participation, Paris would raise no objection. (France's refusal to participate in the proposed committee was in line with Pres. Charles de Gaulle's 1958 proposal for a tripartite nuclear directorate—France, Britain and the U.S.—and his opposition to the integration of France's independent nuclear force within NATO.)

Regardless of French opposition, defense ministers of 10 NATO nations—Belgium, Britain, Canada, Denmark, Greece, the Netherlands, Italy, Turkey, West Germany and the U.S.—met in Paris Nov. 27 and set up a "Special Committee on Nuclear Consultation." NATO members that did not attend the meeting were France, Iceland, Luxembourg, Norway and Portugal. A communique published Nov. 27 announced that the 10-nation committee would have 3 subcommittees: The first would study ways to improve joint planning for the use of nuclear weapons in the event of war; the 2d would study ways to improve communications, and the 3d would seek means to improve intelligence and information exchanges. The U.S. and Britain would be represented on all 3 subcommittees. West Germany, Italy and Turkey were on the first committee; Canada, Denmark and the Netherlands on the 2d; Canada, Belgium and Greece on the 3d. NATO Secy. Gen. Manlio Brosio of Italy, presided at the Nov. 27 meeting and was appointed permanent chairman of a 10-nation steering group composed of the ambassadors to NATO from the 10 nations of the "Special Committee on Nuclear Consultation." The communique said the steering committee would make an interim report at the December plenary session of the North Atlantic Council.

U.S. spokesmen in Paris Nov. 27 emphasized that the newly created committee was not to be understood as a substitute for a multilateral nuclear force or Atlantic nuclear force (MLF and ANF), both of which were still under consideration. A West German spokesman expressed "satisfaction" with the new committee and said West Germany wanted to be a "partner" and have "adequate influence on nuclear planning and choice of targets." But West German Defense Min. Kai-Uwe von Hassel said in Bonn Nov. 29 that "consultation does not imply co-ownership [of nuclear weapons], but co-ownership insures consultations."

McNamara told the 10 NATO defense ministers Nov. 27 that 5,000 U.S.-supplied nuclear warheads were currently located on European soil. In the next 6 months, he said, the force would be increased by 20%. This would represent a "doubling of nuclear weapons strength in Europe over the past 5 years." In addition to the atomic weapons at the disposal of NATO, McNamara said, the U.S. strategic forces had more than 5,000 warheads—including Polaris-submarine missiles, U.S.-based Minuteman missiles and B-52 bomber warheads.

A communique issued Dec. 16 at the end of the semi-annual NATO Council meeting of foreign ministers noted that the ministers had "discussed" a procedural report by Secy. Gen. Brosio on the new 10-nation "Special Committee on Nuclear Consultation." French Foreign Min. Maurice Couve de Murville had warned during the discussion Dec. 14 against permitting the committee to assume a permanent status. He suggested that the committee last no longer than May 1966, when it would present its recommendations at the next NATO Council meeting. Couve de Murville's suggestion was opposed by Brosio, West German Foreign Min. Gerhard Schroeder, British Permanent Foreign Office Undersecy. Sir Paul Gore-Booth and U.S. State Secy. Dean Rusk. Rusk and Schroeder said the committee should be allowed to decide on its own future and warned that the Soviet Union should not be permitted to exercise a veto over NATO defense and nuclear sharing. Couve de Murville was reported Dec. 14 to have dropped his proposal to limit the life of the committee to May 1966.

Erhard-Johnson Meetings

West German Chancellor Ludwig Erhard met June 4 in Washington with Pres. Johnson. A communique released after their meeting said the U.S. "will maintain its forces in Europe, backed by nuclear power, so long as they are wanted and needed for the peace and security of Europe."

The 2 leaders conferred again in Washington Dec. 20-21. Their conversations were concentrated mainly on the problem of nuclear sharing within the NATO alliance. State Secy. Rusk, Defense Secy. McNamara, Treasury Secy. Henry H. Fowler, West German Foreign Min. Schroeder and Defense Min. von Hassel also participated in the discussions.

A West German-U.S. communique dated Dec. 21 said: Mr. Johnson and Erhard had affirmed that "Germany and the other interested partners in the alliance [NATO] should have an appropriate part in nuclear defense." Erhard "emphasized that . . . Germany neither intended nor desired to acquire national control over nuclear weapons." Mr. Johnson stated that "arrangements could be worked out to assure members of the alliance not having nuclear weapons an appropriate share in nuclear defense." The 2 men "agreed that discussion of such arrangements be continued between the 2 countries and other . . . allies." They agreed to uphold "the principle of non-proliferation of nuclear weapons. . . . They were of the view that [NATO] alliance nuclear arrangements would not constitute proliferation of nuclear weapons and, in fact, should contribute to the goal of preventing the spread of nuclear weapons."

West German press chief Karl-Gunther von Hase said at a White House press conference Dec. 21 that an "appropriate" participation in NATO nuclear defense meant: "Upward development. More. In the direction of more [than] what is now." In order "to defend oneself in the nuclear field one has to have weapons," he said. White House Press Secy. Bill D. Moyers said the U.S. interpreted the communique to mean that the U.S. was ready for further discussions of nuclear sharing.

It was reported Dec. 20 that Erhard had proposed to Johnson a plan to create a NATO force of 10 Polaris-armed nuclear submarines. The submarines would be supplied by the U.S. and Britain, and the project would be financed jointly by NATO members. Sen. Clinton P. Anderson (D., N.M.), a member of the Joint Congressional Committee on Atomic Energy, told newsmen Dec. 20 that a majority of the committee opposed joint financing or joint manning by NATO allies of Polaris-armed submarines made available by the U.S. and Britain for an Atlantic nuclear force.

Other NATO Developments

Britain Feb. 23 issued a defense White Paper that advocated a major redeployment of NATO forces, with less stress on nuclear defenses and more on conventional warfare. (U.S. Defense Secy. McNamara was said to agree with the idea.) The White Paper indicated that the Labor government was considering abandoning its 1964 campaign call for renunciation of Britain's independent nuclear deterrent.

Gen. Lyman L. Lemnitzer, supreme NATO commander, urged at a news conference in Paris Mar. 16 that plans to increase the alliance's Mobile Force from one brigade of 5,000 men be encouraged. The plans were being considered by the NATO Council. He said the force had nuclear weapons and could be deployed as far away from NATO headquarters as northern Norway.

The British Defense Ministry Aug. 27 announced a decision to equip some units of the British Army of the Rhine (BAOR) with light artillery pieces to replace Corporal missiles. The British statement followed sharp criticism in West Germany of Britain's decision to discontinue its use of the Corporal, a U.S. Army-developed missile capable of delivering a nuclear warhead. The British statement said: "NATO has long known that Corporal would reach the end of its useful operational life about the end of 1966 and has been informed in the usual way.... We continue to believe that NATO forces must maintain an effective tactical nuclear capability. In addition to Corporal, BAOR is currently equipped with [U.S. Army-developed] Honest John rockets and 8-inch howitzers, both of which have a nuclear capability and which we plan to retain after Corporal has been phased out. In preparation for the phasing out next year, we are concentrating the missile launchers into one larger unit to make the best use of available manpower. Since the same number of launchers will remain, this amalgam will not significantly affect the operational capability of our Corporal force."

West German press chief von Hase had announced in Bonn Aug. 25, after a meeting of the West German cabinet, that the Bonn government intended to seek early discussion within NATO of the British decision to withdraw Corporal. Von Hase also announced that Swidbert Schnippenkoetter, Bonn's commissioner for disarmament and armaments control and observer at the Geneva disarmament conference, had been instructed to confer with Gen. E. L. M. Burns, the Canadian delegate to the conference, and the 2 met in Geneva Aug. 26.

Ex-Chancellor Konrad Adenauer told a West German election campaign audience Aug. 27 that the British decision was "a devastating blow for us...." "Do they not realize," he asked, "how they destroy the trust of the German people in our allies?"

The *N.Y. Herald Tribune* had reported from Ottawa Aug. 22 that the Canadian Defense Department had decided not to replace nuclear strike aircraft based in West Germany as they became unserviceable.

British Foreign Secy. Michael Stewart Oct. 11 conferred in Washington with State Secy. Dean Rusk. It was reported that Stewart gave priority to an East-West anti-nuclear proliferation treaty rather than to Britain's earlier proposal for an Atlantic nuclear force (ANF) within NATO.

The *N.Y. Times* Oct. 16 quoted a U.S. Defense Department official as saying plans for a multilateral nuclear force had been dropped. The "matter is academic," he said.

But the State Department Oct. 18 issued a statement saying: The U.S. "has not foreclosed either the MLF or the ANF or any other proposals that may be developed . . . [to] meet the nuclear problem of the alliance without proliferation."

West German Chancellor Ludwig Erhard Nov. 10 told the Bundestag in a major policy statement: NATO must "adjust . . . to new political and military conditions. It is in particular necessary to solve such problems as result from the fact that some members of the alliance now have nuclear weapons while others have not. All allies should . . . be given a share in . . . nuclear defense, which should be in keeping with the extent of the danger threatening them and with the extent of the burdens they bear. We are thinking in terms of a joint nuclear organization, and we participate in relevant deliberations with the allied powers. We have repeatedly made known that we do not desire national control of nuclear weapons. We should, however, not be kept out of any nuclear participation simply because we are a divided country. . . . We enjoy special relations with the United States, Great Britain and France. . . . The United States bears the main defense burden of NATO; it possesses an arsenal of nuclear weapons . . . superior to that of the Soviets; it maintains . . . 240,000 troops in Germany. . . . Our vital interests command us to cooperate closely with the U.S.A. politically and militarily."

A U.S. Defense Department spokesman confirmed Nov. 22 that tactical fighter-bombers of 9 NATO nations (Belgium, Britain, Canada, France, Greece, Italy, the Netherlands, West Germany and Turkey) were currently "armed" with U.S. atomic warheads. The spokesman insisted that the weapons remained under U.S. control and could not be used without U.S. authorization. White House Press Secy. Bill D. Moyers said Nov. 22: "As has often been stated, we have made nuclear warheads available to our NATO allies, but custody of all such warheads remains with the United States." The Defense Department and White House statements followed a Nov. 21 *N.Y. Times* article that had asserted: "For more than 6 years, United States nuclear warheads have been mounted secretly on planes and missiles of West Germany and other . . . [NATO] allies, according to sources close to the atomic weapons program." The *Times* article, by John W. Finney, said: During 1958 hearings on the amendment to permit the sharing of nuclear information under the Atomic Energy Act, "the impression was left by

Administration officials that the warheads [to be allocated to NATO allies] would be kept under a separate American lock and key and only turned over to the allies in the event of attack"; "under current controls, at least 2 United States sentries stand guard over the nuclear-armed plane, and allied pilots cannot enter the cockpit without the approval of the American servicemen." Nuclear warheads were also "mounted on some of the German-manned Pershing ballistic missiles with a 400-mile range."

The U.S.' control of these NATO warheads "has existed more in principle than in fact. Only in recent years, it is reliably reported, have the controls been strengthened to the point where unauthorized use of the warheads by an ally can be regarded as a highly unlikely possibility." The added controls, the *Times* suggested, came as a result of a 1960 inspection tour of European NATO installations by Rep. Chet Holifield (D., Calif.), chairman of a Joint Congressional subcommittee on atomic energy.

The Defense Department's Nov. 22 acknowledgement of the arming of NATO planes with U.S. nuclear warheads, said the *Times* Nov. 23, came after it was noted that Deputy Defense Secy. Cyrus R. Vance had said in an Aug. 28, 1964 speech at the Veterans of Foreign Wars convention that "Allied fighter-bomber squadrons are equipped with our [tactical nuclear] weapons." The Defense Department's initial response Nov. 20 to a question by the *Times* reporter had been: "It is department ... policy not to discuss location, numbers or operations involving nuclear weapons." The department issued an identical statement Nov. 21 but added: "No matter where they are located, United States warheads are always under U.S. custody."

Holifield Nov. 15 and U.S. Atomic Energy Commissioner John G. Palfrey Nov. 16 (in speeches at the joint annual meeting of the Atomic Industrial Forum and the American Nuclear Society in Washington) had indicated prior to the *Times'* Nov. 21 story that NATO allies had U.S. nuclear warheads. Holifield, criticizing the proposed multi-lateral nuclear force, said West German military units already had nuclear weapons "whose firepower far exceeds all the explosives of World War II." Palfrey said a "permissive actions links" system, a combination of electronic and mechanical devices, prevented unauthorized use of nuclear weapons currently mounted on West German planes. Palfrey suggested an "imaginative extention of the present arrangements so that West Germany could be equipped with nuclear weapons capable of reaching the Soviet missile sites." The U.S. would maintain custody of and control over the new weapons, he said.

A West German Defense Ministry spokesman, Col. Hasso Viebig, said in Bonn Nov. 22 that no West German pilot could board a plane carrying a nuclear weapon without the permission of the President of the U.S. He said no West German weapons system commanded by West Germans had been equipped with atomic weapons.

Italian Defense Min. Giulio Andreotti told the Italian Parliament Nov. 23, in response to a question citing the *Times* disclosure, that Italian aircraft could be equipped with "nuclear armaments [only] in the event of an emergency and then only with the permission of a nuclear power." Andreotti declined to answer a question as to whether nuclear weapons were currently on Italian soil.

Soviet Premier Aleksei N. Kosygin accused the U.S. Dec. 6 of "trying to build up tensions, to create an atmosphere conducive to war." In a Kremlin interview with *N.Y. Times* associate editor James Reston, Kosygin said: "You have the multilateral force, the allied nuclear force, the McNamara council or committee [NATO's Special Committee on Nuclear Consultation].... These only result in uniting the forces of one camp.... It compels us to muster our own forces and react to what you do." "The West Germans have built an army of 500,000 men with your help. They have ... your nuclear weapons on their territory, and they are clamoring for their own nuclear weapons. This causes us concern." "They have trained personnel, delivery vehicles, all that is necessary to start a nuclear war. They have achieved all this with your assistance."

Soviet Foreign Min. Andrei A. Gromyko said Dec. 9 that the U.S. would have to discard any plans it might have for nuclear sharing within NATO if it wanted to make progress towards an East-West disarmament treaty against nuclear proliferation. Gromyko told the Supreme Soviet: "People cannot be deluded by [U.S.] references to effective controls, guarantees, systems of locks and keys.... Since the goal of non-proliferation of nuclear weapons and nuclear access for West Germany's Bundeswehr are incompatible, the Soviet government hopes that the ... United States will take a more realistic stand and will agree to an international treaty to ban the spread of nuclear weapons."

An 18-month cruise by the mixed-manned *Claude V. Ricketts* had ended in Norfolk Va. Dec. 1. The ship, with a crew of 355 from NATO countries, had made a 50,000-mile trip to demonstrate the feasibility of a mixed-manned allied nuclear navy. U.S. Adm. Thomas H. Moorer, commander of NATO's Atlantic forces, said Dec. 1: "If the decision is made to continue mixed manning, the experience we have received certainly proves its feasibility."

GENEVA TALKS RESUMED

Preparations for Negotiations

Pres. Johnson asked Congress Jan. 15 to extend the authorization of the Arms Control & Disarmament Agency for 4 years and to increase its funds. Mr. Johnson lauded the agency's record, saying its achievement "has refuted the doubts of those who questioned whether there was effective work for such an agency to perform." He said he "fully" shared in the conclusions expressed by the agency's director, William C. Foster, that the agency's work "has become an integral part of our over-all national security policy" and that "the need for arms-control measures is becoming even more acute as more nations develop a nuclear capability."

A bill authorizing appropriations of $30 million over fiscal 1966-8 for the Arms Control & Disarmament Agency was passed by the House Apr. 13 and Senate May 14 and was signed by Pres. Johnson May 27.

The Soviet Union's acceptance of renewed disarmament negotiations was disclosed by Pres. Johnson July 13 at his White House news conference. The President said that the USSR had notified the U.S. the previous day that it "was agreeable to the resumption of negotiations of the 18-nation Disarmament Committee at Geneva." Mr. Johnson said that Foster had "met with the Soviet spokesman in New York on June 15 . . . on instructions to urge reconvening of the Disarmament Committee as soon as possible. Yesterday's Soviet response is an encouraging development." (The USSR had abstained June 15, when the UN Disarmament Commission had adopted a U.S. proposal calling for reconvening of the Geneva committee.)

British Disarmament Min. Lord Chalfont said in London July 13 that Britain, in concert with her allies, had prepared a draft treaty designed to halt the proliferation of atomic weapons and intended to present the draft to the Geneva committee. "If nuclear weapons become so widespread," he said, "the chances are that sooner or later they will get into the hands not only of irresponsible governments but even possibly of irresponsible individuals."

West German Foreign Min. Gerhard Schroeder had conditioned Bonn's acceptance of such a treaty on the prior establishment of joint nuclear defense security within NATO. In a newspaper interview in Bonn July 3, he had said that "a form of organization must be worked out which will meet the security requirements of the non-nuclear members of NATO. If this happens through the creation of a multilateral nuclear force or an equally valid solution, Germany would be able to renounce *vis-a-vis* her allies the acquisition of her own nuclear weapons."

The danger of nuclear weapons proliferation was emphasized by Chairman Glenn Seaborg of the U.S. Atomic Energy Commission in an interview published July 12 in *U.S. News & World Report.* An agreement must be reached, he said, "to stop the spread of nuclear weapons to additional countries beyond the 5 [the U.S., Britain, France, USSR and Red China] that have them."

In response to a question from newsmen about the USSR's decision to resume negotiations in Geneva, U.S. Amb.-at-Large W. Averell Harriman said July 22 during a private visit to Moscow: "I don't think they would go [to Geneva] unless they were serious in carrying out negotiations." (The *N.Y. Times* reported July 25 that Kosygin, during his talks with Harriman, had stressed the need for a treaty against proliferation of atomic weapons and had argued that such an agreement would be impossible if a Western nuclear force gave West Germany a share in the control of nuclear weapons.)

Opening Statements

The 18-nation UN Disarmament Committee reconvened July 27 in Geneva after a 10-month recess. The committee's 17 participating members included 4 NATO powers—the U.S., Britain, Canada and Italy; 5 Warsaw Treaty nations—the USSR, Czechoslovakia, Bulgaria, Poland and Rumania; and 8 non-aligned states—Brazil, Burma, Ethiopia, India, Mexico, Nigeria, Sweden and the UAR. France, the committee's 18th member, continued to boycott the negotiations. Communist China, not a UN member, had been excluded from the negotiations.

No action was taken by the committee at its first 3 plenary sessions, held July 27, 29 and Aug. 3. At the meetings, devoted largely to general statements of position by the participating delegations, both the USSR and the NATO powers expressed their acceptance in principle of proposals for an agreement to prevent the spread of nuclear weapons to non-nuclear states. They clashed over the Soviet insistence that Western plans for nuclear sharing within NATO were not compatible with the principle of non-proliferation and that the U.S. involvement in the war in Vietnam was not consistent with serious disarmament negotiations.

At the opening session July 27, William C. Foster, head of the U.S. delegation, read a statement to the committee from Pres. Johnson. The President's message declared that "the effort to diminish danger—to halt the spread of nuclear power—and bring weapons of war under increasing control" was in the interest of all nations. The U.S., Mr. Johnson said, would pursue 4 major aims at the talks: (1) prevention of proliferation of nuclear weapons, (2) effective limitation of existing nuclear weapons and their delivery systems, (3) a fully comprehensive nuclear test ban treaty and (4) the participation of many nations in the disarmament discussions. Foster, in his own remarks, alluded to the Vietnam situation by saying that "the dangers posed by the arms race . . . and the threatened proliferation of nuclear weapons will not wait until the guns are stilled." He acknowledged that the Western delegations had arrived without an agreed joint disarmament proposal and said that further discussions of the matter would have to be held by the 4 powers.

Semyon K. Tsarapkin, chief Soviet delegate, told newsmen after the July 27 session that unless the U.S. and Britain dropped their plans for sharing nuclear weapons within NATO, the USSR could not subscribe to any agreement to prevent the spread of such weapons. In his address to the conference, delivered at the Aug. 3 session, Tsarapkin called for an end to the Vietnamese war. "The Geneva conference," he declared, "cannot bypass the actions of the United States in Vietnam, where it is using its troops and bases for an aggressive imperialist and punitive war." It is "imperative," he said, "that the guns be silenced, that the aggression of the United States... cease, in order that the... Western powers show... their readiness to solve the urgent problems" of disarmament. Tsarapkin again demanded that the West abandon its proposals for nuclear sharing on the ground that West Germany attempts to acquire nuclear weapons must be blocked. West German "revanchist" circles, he said, hoped to use nuclear blackmail to recover former German territory incorporated in Eastern Europe.

Lord Chalfont, British state minister with responsibility for disarmament, read a message from Prime Min. Harold Wilson to the committee at its July 29 session. Wilson's message stressed the danger that nuclear proliferation could bring "nuclear war by mistake, miscalculation, accident or madness." In his own address, Chalfont emphasized the necessity for an immediate treaty against proliferation. Other questions, such as inspection, verification and a test ban including underground tests, were more difficult to negotiate and could be deferred, he said. Chalfont added that an agreed Western draft treaty would not be presented to the committee unless it were acceptable to non-nuclear powers. He mentioned the case of India, where, he said, there were pressures to produce nuclear weapons as a result of Red China's atomic tests.

Italian Foreign Min. Amintore Fanfani told the committee July 29 that the scope of the disarmament talks should be widened to prepare the way for an East-West detente. The conference, he said, "might even create the indispensable conditions for a negotiated solution of the Vietnam problem, just as Pres. Johnson hoped for through the intermediary of the United Nations."

Meetings of experts of the 4 NATO powers' disarmament delegations took place in Geneva several times in late July to iron out a joint Western draft treaty for submission to the committee. The 4 powers primarily discussed current British and Canadian disarmament proposals. The British proposal aimed at a simple undertaking by the nuclear powers not to give nuclear weapons to non-nuclear states and a parallel pledge by non-nuclear powers not to acquire or manufacture such weapons. In addition, the plan contained an escape clause that would permit the USSR to withdraw from its commitment if West Germany acquired direct access to nuclear weapons. (Tsarapkin, on arrival in Geneva July 25, told newsmen: "What is the use of...an escape clause in an agreement which would be without value from the very beginning.") The Canadian proposal called for a collective guarantee in which all nuclear powers would pledge their aid to non-nuclear nations in the event of a nuclear attack on them. The proposal also included a system of verification and inspection by the UN's International Atomic Energy Agency. (The British proposal was presented at a meeting of the NATO Council July 26 in Paris. The *N.Y. Times* reported that Chalfont argued that a simple treaty was needed to avoid negotiating complications with the USSR. He reiterated the British view that nuclear sharing within NATO was compatible with a non-proliferation agreement. Werner Krueger, acting West German press chief, said at a Bonn news conference July 26 that West Germany "insists on no conditions or preconditions to participate in an agreement limiting the dissemination of nuclear weapons.")

U.S. Presents Draft Non-Proliferation Pact

A U.S. draft treaty to prohibit the proliferation of nuclear weapons was submitted at a plenary session of the Geneva conference Aug. 17 by William C. Foster, head of the American delegation. The U.S. proposal was immediately repudiated by Soviet delegate Tsarapkin. It also was criticized by the NATO allies of the U.S. present at the conference, in particular by the British delegate, Lord Chalfont. The committee took no action on the plan at its plenary sessions Aug. 17 and 19; it adjourned Aug. 19 with the plan on the agenda for further discussion.

In a statement released Aug. 17 in Geneva and Washington, Pres. Johnson described the U.S. proposal as an "important step forward in the search for disarmament." The proliferation of nuclear weapons, he said, was the "gravest of all unresolved human issues." He added that "the time to halt nuclear spread is before its contagion takes root."

Under the U.S. draft, nuclear-armed states would pledge (1) "not to transfer any nuclear weapons into the national control of any non-nuclear state either directly, or indirectly through a military alliance" and (2) "not to assist any non-nuclear state in the manufacture of nuclear weapons." In turn, each non-nuclear state would undertake (a) "not to manufacture nuclear weapons...or to receive the transfer of such weapons into its national control, either directly, or indirectly through a military alliance" and (b) "not to seek or to receive assistance in the manufacture of nuclear weapons, or itself grant such assistance." The most controversial passage of the U.S. proposal provided that both nuclear and non-nuclear states would pledge "not to take any...action which would cause an increase in the total number of states and other organizations having independent power to use nuclear weapons." The passage was interpreted to permit the formation of multi-national nuclear weapons-sharing groups so long as one of the existing atomic powers participated and possessed a veto over the group's use of nuclear weapons.

Tsarapkin, who had received details of the proposal in advance, told reporters Aug. 16 that the U.S. draft was a "joke." At the plenary session Aug. 17, he said the USSR would not consider any plan unless it explicitly prevented West Germany from obtaining direct or indirect access to nuclear weapons through any of the nuclear sharing plans under consideration within NATO. In reply to a question posed by Lord Chalfont at the Aug. 19 meeting as to what the USSR meant by "access" to nuclear weapons and why Tsarapkin had in the past attacked U.S. Defense Secy. Robert S. McNamara's proposal for a NATO nuclear committee, Tsarapkin told reporters Aug. 19 that by "access" he meant to include "the whole complex of nuclear sharing." "Not the right to fire nuclear weapons alone, but sharing in nuclear strategy, nuclear training, contact in any form with nuclear weapons, and so on." "The draft treaty," he declared, "does not prevent this, therefore it is not a basis for negotiations." (*Pravda* had said July 20 that "the McNamara proposal is perhaps even more dangerous than the multilateral project because its implementation would allow Bonn 'to have its say' in the use of all nuclear forces of the NATO countries, not only some Polaris missiles.")

Chalfont said at an Aug. 17 press conference that the U.S. draft had left open a "theoretical" loophole that Britain would prefer to see closed. "The language used," he said, "... does not rule out the possibility that an association of states might be set up with the capacity to make use of nuclear weapons by the decision of a majority of its members—in other words, without the veto of an existing nuclear power. It is true that such an association could not, under this draft, come into existence unless one of the existing nuclear powers had ... abandoned its independent control of nuclear weapons, so that in any event the total number of nuclear entities would not be increased. Nevertheless, we would ... like to see these articles amended in order to make it absolutely clear that we are opposed to the creation of any association capable of using nuclear weapons without the consent of an existing nuclear power."

Foster said at a Geneva press luncheon Aug. 18 that differences between the U.S. and British views were more theoretical than real. The U.S. position, he said, "is that the charter for any Atlantic force must provide for our [U.S.] consent to the firing of nuclear weapons. If, however, the nations of Europe were to achieve the kind of political authority capable of deciding on behalf of all members on the use of nuclear weapons, we feel that reconsideration of the provisions of the charter for the Atlantic force would be appropriate. But even then, any revision of the charter would be possible only with the approval of all of its parties." There was only one possibility, Foster said, that such a force could change to some form of majority control. "That would arise," he said, "if one of the [existing] nuclear participants were to turn over to the force all of its weapons and also give up its veto over them. That would be in conformity with the draft treaty . . . since it would not involve any increase in the number of nuclear decision-making entities."

(The London *Times* reported Aug. 18 that Canada and Italy also questioned the U.S. plan. Canada demanded additional safeguards for non-nuclear states, and Italy called for a moratorium on the acquisition of nuclear weapons by non-nuclear states in the event the major powers failed to agree on an anti-proliferation treaty.)

Positions of Minor Powers on Proliferation

West Germany's observer at the Geneva talks, Swidbert Schnippenkoetter, conferred Aug. 13 with Tsarapkin. After the meeting Tsarapkin told reporters he had urged Bonn to give up its claim to nuclear weapons. The best way to insure German security was through effective disarmament, Tsarapkin said. Schnippenkoetter, according to Tsarapkin, had said that West Germany favored disarmament, but had to have access to nuclear weapons as a security measure only. (Ex-West German Chancellor Konrad Adenauer said at a Christian Democratic Union election meeting in Munster Aug. 19 that the U.S. draft ultimately would mean "the surrender of Europe to the Russians." The *N.Y. Times* and London *Times* reported Aug. 20 that the Bonn government dissociated itself from Adenauer's statement.)

Among other developments at the Geneva conference:

V. C. Trivedi, Indian delegate to the conference, told the committee Aug. 12 that India would not agree to the "unrealistic and irrational proposition that a non-proliferation treaty should impose obligations on non-nuclear powers while the nuclear powers continue to hold on to their . . . status . . . by retaining and even increasing their deadly stockpiles." He proposed that the nuclear powers pledge not to give nuclear weapons to non-nuclear states and also to cease the production of atomic weapons and begin to reduce their existing stocks. Only with such a pledge, he said, would the non-nuclear states sign an anti-proliferation treaty. Trivedi criticized the U.S. for not accepting "some theoretical risks" to achieve a comprehensive test ban treaty covering underground tests. (The U.S. opposed such a test ban unless it was accompanied by an on-site inspection system.)

Mrs. Alva Myrdal, the Swedish delegate, said Aug. 10 that "the test-ban issue is politically probably the most tractable—both as between the different nuclear powers and between them and the non-nuclear ones." A total ban on tests, she said, "would *de facto* achieve the same result, as far as the non-nuclear powers are concerned, as a non-dissemination treaty."

Canadian delegate E. L. M. Burns had accused the USSR Aug. 5 of blocking a comprehensive test ban by its refusal to demonstrate that it could scientifically detect all underground tests by agencies operating from its own national territory, thus obviating the necessity for the on-site inspection system called for by Canada and the U.S.

The *N.Y. Herald Tribune* reported Aug. 12 that Tsarapkin, at a press luncheon Aug. 11, had withdrawn the USSR assertion that no progress in disarmament negotiations could be made while the war in Vietnam continued. In response to a question as to whether the USSR maintained that a settlement in Vietnam was a pre-condition for a disarmament agreement, Tsarapkin was reported to have said: "We are not eager to bind the 2 together. Then we would have a permanent stalemate."

A 3-man delegation from East Germany, headed by Deputy Foreign Min. Georg Stibi, arrived Aug. 8 in Geneva to observe the conference.

Indonesian Pres. Sukarno declared July 24 in Jakarta that Indonesia would produce an atom bomb for defensive purposes in the near future. Brig. Gen Hatono, director-general of the Indonesian Logistical Command, said July 28 in a Jakarta newspaper interview that Indonesia's first atom bomb test would occur in November after the 2d Afro-Asian conference. He added that ground-to-ground missiles were being tested in West Java "capable of destroying Singapore and Kuala Lumpur by pressing a button."

(Mohammed Hassanein Heikal, editor of Cairo's *Al Ahram* and a close associate of UAR Pres. Gamel Abdel Nasser, wrote Aug. 20 that Israel was preparing to explode a nuclear device. Israel, he said, planned to propose an accord with the UAR to ban production of A-weapons. "Naturally, Egypt will refuse to become a party in any agreement with Israel," he said, and "Israel can then use this as a pretext to produce atomic weapons.")

(Indian Prime Min. Lal Bahadur Shastri said Oct. 19 that India would maintain its current policy of not manufacturing nuclear weapons. 86 members of the Indian Parliament [representing all parties] had presented Shastri Sept. 23 with a letter calling on India to begin to make atomic weapons. The letter said: "India's survival . . . , in the face of collusion between China and Pakistan, casts a clear and imperative duty on the government to make an immediate decision to develop our nuclear weapons.")

Conference Concludes Discussions

The 18-nation UN Disarmament Committee recessed Sept. 16. Before the recess, Soviet delegate Tsarapkin Aug. 31 had formally rejected the U.S.' Aug. 17 proposal of an anti-proliferation treaty. The U.S. draft treaty, he said, was designed to bring West Germany into the nuclear club. There was no basis for negotiation "as yet," he declared. Lord Chalfont, chief British delegate, said Tsarapkin's "as yet" statement constituted the first Soviet step "toward genuine negotiations."

Jozef Goldblat, chief Polish delegate, told the committee Sept. 2 that Western proposals left open the possibility of the creation of various forms of nuclear partnerships under which non-nuclear powers could get access to nuclear weapons. He said West Germany could obtain nuclear weapons through the creation of a NATO nuclear force.

Chalfont told the committee Sept. 9 that the Soviet-bloc countries would have to realize that the security of NATO would not be bargained away.

Francesco Cavaletti, chief Italian delegate, presented Sept. 14 a draft declaration under which non-nuclear nations would unilaterally renounce acquisition of nuclear weapons for a limited period during which the existing nuclear powers would attempt to agree on disarmament. Tsarapkin told reporters the Italian draft would not prevent indirect access to nuclear weapons under NATO. U.S. chief delegate Foster and Chalfont were reported to have backed the Italian proposal.

The discussions also envisaged the possibility of extending the test ban to underground explosions. Foster told the committee Sept. 2 that a U.S. underground nuclear test to be conducted later in 1965 in the Aleutian Islands would add to techniques for detecting underground nuclear tests. He said the U.S. was constructing a prototype array of 525 detectors covering an area in Montana 120 miles in diameter. According to Foster, the detectors would achieve a signal-to-background-noise ratio at least 10 times better than previous methods. A worldwide system of such detectors, he said, would permit detection of about 80% of all earth tremors with force of more than a few kilotons. But, he emphasized, the remaining 20% could not be identified by instruments alone. He called on the USSR to disclose its research data and participate in East-West technical discussions to justify its claim that instruments located on its own territory could identify all tremors of possible military significance and that, as a consequence, on-site inspection as demanded by the Western powers, was unnecessary.

Mrs. Alva Myrdal, Sweden's delegate, proposed the establishment of a worldwide system of seismic arrays to advance research on remaining test-ban verification problems.

Tsarapkin said Sept. 7 that the USSR would sign "without delay" a UAR proposal under which the 1963 test ban would be extended by a formal agreement to bar underground tests registering above 4.75 on the seismic magnitude scale, and nations would voluntarily agree to a moratorium on smaller tests. The proposal had been presented Aug. 17 by UAR delegate Abdel Moneim El-Kaissouny. Foster rejected the UAR proposal because of its failure to include on-site inspection. There was no way to distinguish between small underground tests and natural earth tremors, he said, and "half-way measures may create suspicions."

Tsarapkin replied that detection systems located on any nation's territory were "absolutely sufficient" to identify tests conducted elsewhere. Chalfont said Sept. 9 that Britain would consider the UAR proposal but added that the seismic magnitude of an underground test varied with the geological structure of the site and the technical means used to reduce shock waves (e.g., detonating the nuclear device in a large cavity, a process known as "decoupling"). He proposed that scientists from East and West meet to discuss ways to extend the test ban to include tests large enough to be identified by existing instruments. Burns, the Canadian delegate, backed Chalfont's proposal. Tsarapkin rejected it as leading to a "quagmire of technical discussion."

Foster told reporters Sept. 14 that the conference had "come a long way" toward a non-proliferation agreement and that discussions were ending "on a note of hope." He left Geneva Sept. 16 for Paris to report to the NATO ministers.

The 8 non-aligned members of the committee (Burma, Brazil, Ethiopia, India, Mexico, Nigeria, Sweden and the UAR) Sept. 15 submitted 2 memoranda to the conference: The first called for an agreement to bar the proliferation of nuclear weapons and halt all nuclear testing; it emphasized that an anti-proliferation accord should be linked to or followed by definite steps to stop the nuclear arms race and to limit, reduce and ultimately eliminate existing stocks of nuclear weapons. The 2d memo supported a U.S. and British request to the USSR for the exchange of scientific information on the identification of underground tests; the memo lauded the request as a step toward a comprehensive test ban. The non-aligned 8 also recommended that the committee reconvene in Jan. 1966.

At its Sept. 16 meeting, the 240th since the committee's creation in 1962, the participating members unanimously adopted a report to the UN General Assembly. The report said the committee was prepared to resume its work after the disarmament issue was examined by the General Assembly at its 20th session, which convened Sept. 21 at UN headquarters in New York. The report summarized the differing proposals presented to the committee but made no recommendation for action on the 2 major issues discussed during the conference: (1) how to prevent proliferation—the spread of nuclear weapons to non-nuclear powers—and (2) how to extend to underground testing the existing 1963 test ban, which barred nuclear tests in the atmosphere, under water and in space. The report discussed the U.S.' Aug. 17 proposal of a non-proliferation treaty and Italy's Sept. 14 proposal of a unilateral renunciation of nuclear weapons by non-nuclear powers. The report noted the USSR's expressed approval of the Aug. 17 UAR proposal to ban underground testing.

The State Department disclosed Dec. 4 that the U.S. and the USSR had agreed to renew disarmament negotiations within the Geneva committee in late Jan. 1966.

UN GENERAL ASSEMBLY

Goldberg Proposes Destruction of A-Arms

At the opening of the UN General Assembly's regular debate on world affairs, U.S. Amb.-to-UN Arthur J. Goldberg proposed to the USSR Sept. 23 that the U.S. and Soviet Union agreed to destroy part of their nuclear arsenals. In a major policy address, Goldberg announced that the U.S. was prepared to destroy enough American nuclear weapons to make, 60,000 kilograms of uranium-235 available for peaceful uses. The U.S. would do so, he said, if the USSR provided 40,000 kilograms in a similar manner. The proposal differed from previous U.S. offers to cut back the production of fissionable material or to transfer to peaceful use fissionable material produced for use in weapons. The earlier offers included no offer (as demanded by the Soviets) to destoy existing nuclear weapons.

Goldberg said the "goal of general and complete disarmament . . . is a necessary and indispensable goal." "The first priority," he declared, ". . . must be given to halting the spread of nuclear weapons. . . . That is why the United States has tabled in the 18-Nation Disarmament Committee the full draft of a treaty binding its signers from taking any action to increase the number of states and other organizations having power to unleash nuclear weapons." "We believe," he continued, "assurances of support against threats of nuclear blackmail should be available to nations which have foresworn a nuclear capability of their own."

In regard to underground nuclear testing, Goldberg said the U.S.' "vigorous research program indicates the possibility of substantial improvement in seismic detection capabilities." The U.S., he added, "insist[s] on the minimum amount of inspection necessary in the present state of science to give confidence to all that a comprehensive test ban [one including a ban on underground tests] is actually being observed." He said the U.S. would invite a large number of UN members to visit the Montana test detection site Oct. 12-13 to inspect its detection capabilities. Goldberg then announced the new U.S. offer to destroy existing nuclear weapons. He said:

"We must . . . take steps to reduce the dangers stemming from the high level of nuclear capabilities. There is no reason to wait. We are prepared to take practical steps here and now.

"First, we should take steps to halt the accumulation of strategic nuclear delivery vehicles.

"2d, the United States proposes a verfied halt in production of fissionable material for weapons use and the transfer of fissionable materials to peaceful purposes.

"The United States is ready to transfer 60,000 kilograms of weapons-grade U-235 to nonweapon uses if the Soviet Union would be willing to transfer 40,000 kilograms.* If the USSR accepts this proposal, each of us would destroy nuclear weapons of our own choice so as to make available for peaceful purposes such amounts of fissionable material.

"Moreover, the United States government stands ready, if the Soviet Union will do likewise, to add to this transfer associated plutonium obtained from the destroyed weapons in an agreed quantity or ratio and to place the material thus transferred under the International Atomic Energy Agency or equivalent safeguards."

USSR Offers Non-Proliferation Draft

Soviet Foreign Min. Andrei A. Gromyko, addressing the Assembly Sept. 24, submitted a draft treaty to prevent the proliferation of nuclear weapons. The draft was designed to prevent the formation of nuclear-weapons sharing groups such as the U.S.-backed NATO nuclear force (MLF) plan.

Under the USSR's proposal, nuclear powers would undertake not to transfer nuclear weapons "in any form" to "states or groupings of states not possessing nuclear weapons, or to grant the aforesaid states or groups of states the right to participate in the ownership, disposition or use of nuclear weapons." In a passage designed to prevent the creation of a NATO nuclear force, Article I of the Soviet draft would prohibit transfer of nuclear weapons "to units of armed forces of states which do not [currently] possess nuclear arms even if these armed forces are under the command of a military alliance." Article II of the Soviet draft would require non-nuclear powers not to produce or acquire nuclear weapons from other states and would prohibit acquiring control of nuclear weapons within "military alliances." In his address, Gromyko reiterated Soviet opposition to a NATO nuclear sharing arrangement that would include West Germany.

Gromyko also called for a world disarmament conference to be convened in 1966. All states, including non-members of the UN, should be eligible to attend.

Debate on Arms & Disarmament

Czechoslovak Foreign Min. Vaclav David Sept. 27 supported the Soviet Union's proposal for an anti-proliferation treaty covering nuclear weapons.

French Foreign Min. Maurice Couve de Murville, addressing the UN General Assembly Sept. 29, said: The Vietnamese war and the absence of Communist China from "the framework that is available to all the other powers" were major obstacles to progress toward disarmament. It was not "possible to separate disarmament problems from the

---

*60,000 kilograms of U-235 would release about 1,000 megatons of nuclear energy (one megaton equals the energy released by the detonation of one million tons of TNT), equivalent to about 1/3 of a ton of TNT for each human being on earth.

framework in which they . . . fall, that is to say, the problems of war and peace." "France desires dissemination [of nuclear weapons] no more than any other country . . . [and] knows . . . that the powers that find themselves with . . . atomic weapons will never agree to share them with others. . . . In reality, behind the discussions that are being pursued in Geneva or elsewhere . . . lie the major international problems, and first of all—why not say so?—that of the future of Germany. . . . Dissemination . . . is a by-product of and not the root of the evil." "Everything depends . . . on the behavior of the biggest [world powers]. Special responsibilities are incumbent upon those that possess nuclear weapons. On their agreement . . . the peace of mankind ultimately depends."

Albanian Foreign Min. Behar Shtylla said Sept. 30: "What one has called a 'nuclear umbrella' amounts to a plan to disarm the other countries while the 2 super nuclear powers conserve . . . atomic weapons to intimidate . . . other countries."

Danish Foreign Min. Per Haekkerup said Oct. 1 that the UN could make no progress in disarmament without the participation of Communist China.

Ethiopian Foreign Min. Ato Ketema Yifru said that his government backed an anti-proliferation Oct. 5 treaty covering nuclear weapons but that such a treaty must be linked to plans calling for the elimination of existing stocks of atomic weapons.

New Zealand Finance Min. Harry R. Lake expressed "the . . . concern of his government regarding the continuing French plans to carry out . . . thermonuclear explosions in the South Pacific." Rumanian Foreign Min. Corneliu Manescu Oct. 8 backed the admission of Red China to the UN and supported Peking's 1964 demand for a summit meeting of chiefs-of-state to prohibit and destroy nuclear weapons.

Pope's Plea for Disarmament

Addressing the UN General Assembly Oct. 4, Pope Paul VI voiced support for the "fruitful formula of co-existence" and delivered a strong plea for "disarmament." He said:

"Not the ones against the others, never again, never more! It was principally for this purpose that the organization of the United Nations arose: against war, in favor of peace! Listen to the lucid words of the great departed John Kennedy, who proclaimed, 4 years ago: 'Mankind must put an end to war, or war will put an end to mankind.' . . . It is peace that must guide the destinies of peoples and of all mankind. . . .

"Peace, as you know, is not built up only by means of politics, by the balance of forces and of interests. It is constructed with the mind, with ideas, with works of peace. You labor in this great construction. But you are still at the beginnings. . . . It is toward that new history, a peaceful, truly human, history, as promised by God to men of good will, that we must resolutely march. The roads thereto are already well marked out for you and the first is that of disarmament.

"If you wish to be brothers, let the arms fall from your hands. One cannot love while holding offensive arms. Those armaments, especially those terrible arms, which modern science has given you, long before they produce victims and ruins, nourish bad feelings, create nightmares, distrust and sombre resolutions; they demand enormous expenditures; they obstruct projects of union and useful collaboration; they falsify the psychology of peoples. As long as man remains that weak, changeable and even wicked being that he often shows himself to be, defensive arms will, unfortunately, be necessary.

"You, however, in your courage and valiance, are studying the ways of guaranteeing the security of international life, without having recourse to arms.... Let unanimous trust in this institution grow, let its authority increase; and this aim, we believe, will be secured....

"We rejoice in the knowledge that many of you have considered favorably our invitation, addressed to all states in the cause of peace from Bombay last December, to divert to the benefit of the developing countries at least a part of the savings that could be realized by reducing armaments. We here renew that invitation...."

Non-Proliferation & Disarmament Resolutions

The UN General Assembly Nov. 19 approved by 93-0 vote a resolution calling on "all states to take all necessary measures to conclude ... a treaty preventing the proliferation of nuclear weapons." The U.S., Britain and the USSR voted for the resolution; France, Cuba, Guinea, Pakistan and Rumania abstained. Albania did not vote; its delegate, Halim Budo, said Nov. 19 that the resolution was "aimed at reinforcing the monopoly of the atomic super-powers." The resolution, sponsored by the 8 non-aligned members of the 18-nation Geneva Disarmament Committee (Brazil, Burma, Ethiopia, India, Mexico, Nigeria, Sweden, and the UAR), had been adopted Nov. 8 by the Assembly's First (Political & Security) Committee by 83-0 vote with 6 abstentions—Mali plus the 5 nations abstaining in the Nov. 19 vote.

The resolution called on the 18-nation committee to "reconvene as early as possible with a view to negotiating an international treaty to prevent proliferation of nuclear weapons." The resolution stated that the proposed treaty must be "void of any loop-holes" that would permit nuclear or non-nuclear powers to cause or allow "direct or indirect" proliferation of nuclear weapons. The text represented a compromise of U.S. and USSR proposals before the committee by avoiding mention of nuclear-sharing agreements within military alliances. USSR delegate Nikolai Fedorenko had told the committee Oct. 18 that the U.S.-proposed NATO MLF constituted a violation of the principle of non-proliferation. William C. Foster, director of the U.S. Arms Control & Disarmament Agency, said Oct. 18 that the Sept. 24 Soviet draft of a non-proliferation treaty could not be accepted by the U.S. because it was directed against NATO.

Gen. E. L. M. Burns, Canadian delegate, told the committee Oct. 19 that the USSR proposal was inadequate because it provided for no system of verification and inspection.

Lord Chalfont, the British disarmament minister, said Oct. 21 that non-proliferation was for the UK "an article of faith with which all other arrangements, including those within NATO, must be consistent."

After the Assembly's vote Nov. 19, UN Secy. Gen. U Thant told the Assembly that "all members" of the 18-nation Geneva committee should renew their efforts to draft a non-proliferation treaty. Because France had boycotted the 18-nation committee since 1962, Thant's use of the word "all" was considered an indirect appeal to Paris to participate in disarmament negotiations. France's UN delegation had taken no part in the 3-week deliberation by the Assembly's First Committee on proliferation.

Foster had said in First Committee discussions Oct. 18 that the fact that the USSR had presented a draft treaty indicated that there was a "basis for hope" in negotiations. Fedorenko said Oct. 26 that "the question of non-dissemination of nuclear weapons should be singled out from the mass of other questions and that every effort should be concentrated on the speediest possible solution of the problem." (Foster said Oct. 27 that implementation of the U.S.' Sept. 23 proposal to transfer fissionable material to peaceful uses in return for a USSR agreement to do the same would mean the destruction of "several thousand weapons" by each side. He asserted that the destruction could be carried out in "a way that secret design features ... are not revealed.")

(A preparatory committee representing 19 Latin American governments met in Mexico City Aug. 20-Sept. 7 and approved a warning against the spread of nuclear weapons to Latin American nations. The declaration was proposed as a preamble to a projected anti-proliferation treaty that the preparatory committee was expected to draft in Apr. 1966. Much of the discussion at the meeting was over whether an anti-proliferation treaty could be effective without Cuba's participation; Cuba boycotted the meeting. Of the 3 Latin American nations currently capable of making nuclear weapons—Argentina, Brazil and Mexico— only Mexico pressed for an anti-proliferation treaty. Mexican Foreign Undersecy. Alfonso Garcia Robles was the chairman of the meeting.)

The General Assembly's First Committee Nov. 23 approved by 91-0 vote a resolution sponsored by 43 Afro-Asian states, calling for a world disarmament conference that would include Communist China. Voting for the resolution were the USSR, Britain and the U.S.; France abstained. The U.S. had abstained in June when a similar resolution had been approved by the UN Disarmament Commission. The 2-paragraph resolution (a) called for the adoption of a proposal of the Oct. 1964 Cairo conference of non-aligned states to convene a world disarmament conference to which all countries would be invited and (b) "urge[d] that the necessary consultations be conducted with all countries for the purpose of establishing a widely representative preparatory committee which will take appropriate steps for the convening of a world disarmament conference not later than 1967."

U.S. Amb.-to-UN Goldberg told the committee Nov. 23: The U.S.' vote for the Afro-Asian resolution meant the U.S. agreed "only in principle to convene a conference"; the U.S. had "reservations concerning the utility of a world disarmament conference"; a final U.S. decision to participate in such a meeting "remains to be taken in the light of the results of consultations and preparations"; a "small initial group" should first discuss "areas of agreement on disarmament questions"; this "group" should include nuclear powers and states with "major peaceful nuclear programs...[and] several which have played leading roles in developing the idea for a world disarmament conference."

Halim Budo of Albania and Sori Coulibaly of Mali, both of whom voted for the resolution, had told the committee Nov. 22 that Communist China would be unlikely to participate in a world disarmament conference if it were held under UN auspices. The resolution, as approved Nov. 23, did not specify any link between the UN and the proposed conference.

By 112-0 vote, with France abstaining and Nationalist China not participating, the General Assembly Nov. 20 adopted a resolution calling for a world disarmament conference that would include Communist China. U Thant told the Assembly after the vote that if a preparatory meeting for the proposed conference or the conference itself requested "the assistance of the facilities of the Secretariat," he would answer that request. Thant said the conference would have to be "open to all countries." He added that it was the UN that bore "the direct responsibility for the maintenance of international peace" and that under the UN Charter the UN had disarmament responsibilities. (The Communist Chinese Foreign Ministry in Peking Dec. 1 released a statement saying China "will certainly not take part" in the UN-proposed disarmament conference. It asserted that "China will never enter into relations with the United Nations and any conference connected with it before the restoration of her legitimate rights in the United Nations and expulsion of the Chiang Kai-shek clique from the organization." Communist Chinese Foreign Min.-Vice Premier Chen Yi had said Sept. 29 that "China is ready to render assistance" to countries that have requested aid in "building atomic reactors" for "peaceful use." "Any country with a fair basis in...science and technology will be able to manufacture atom bombs, with or without China's assistance. China hopes that Afro-Asian countries will be able to make atom bombs themselves, and it would be better for a greater number of countries to come into possession of atom bombs." A-bombs, however, were not very important. "If you are cold, you cannot wear an atom bomb; if you are hungry, you cannot eat an atom bomb." China's own "nuclear weapons will only be used for defense," he said.)

The General Assembly Dec. 3 concluded its discussion of disarmament for the current (20th) session by adopting 3 resolutions that had been approved by its First Committee:

●The first resolution, adopted by 92-1 (Albania) vote, with France and the USSR among 14 nations abstaining, contained 3 provisions: (1) It urged all nations to suspend all nuclear weapons tests. (2) It called on all nations to observe the 1963 treaty banning nuclear tests in the atmosphere, under water and in outer space. (3) It requested the 18-nation Committee on

Disarmament to continue with a sense of urgency its work on a comprehensive test ban treaty and arrangements banning effectively all nuclear weapons tests in all environments, taking into account the improved possibilities for international cooperation in the field of seismic detection. The resolution had been presented in the First Committee Nov. 24 by 26 sponsor nations, mainly Afro-Asian states; it was approved in the committee Nov. 26 by 86-0 vote (13 abstentions).

In committee debate on the resolution, U.S. delegate Foster, director of the U.S. Arms Control & Disarmament Agency, said Nov. 26 that U.S. support for the resolution did not mean Washington had dropped its view that an inspection system was required for an effective test ban. He said: "We share the regret that it has not yet been possible to reach agreement on a verified test ban that would halt all testing, but in the absence of such agreement, the United States finds its necessary . . . to continue underground testing as permitted by the limited [1963] test-ban treaty. The USSR also is conducting such tests." "It is in the spirit of . . . [the 3d] paragraph [of the resolution] that we shall . . . seek to achieve agreement" on a test-ban treaty providing for detection and verification. Foster Nov. 25 had opposed a 32-nation proposal for an unverified test ban. He said the proposal, which was backed by the USSR, was "unacceptable" because it would prevent the establishing of "a stable and permanent comprehensive test ban." Soviet delegate Tsarapkin said Nov. 26 that the U.S. had raised the inspection issue to prevent agreement by asking for what amounted to espionage rights. The British representative, Sir Harold Deeley, had called on the USSR Nov. 24 to enter scientific and technical discussions for the purpose of setting up an effective test ban.

●The 2d disarmament resolution adopted by the Assembly Dec. 3 called on the 18-nation Disarmament Committee to resume its work with a view to making progress towards general and complete disarmament. The resolution was adopted 102-0 with 6 abstentions (France, Albania, Algeria, Guinea, Mali, Tanzania). It had been approved earlier Dec. 3 by 78-0 First Committee vote (4 abstentions).

●The final resolution adopted Dec. 3 called on all states not to use nuclear weapons on the African continent. It was adopted by 105-0 vote (France and Portugal abstaining). It had been approved by the First Committee Dec. 1 by 105-0 vote (South Africa, France and Portugal abstaining). The resolution had been presented by 28 African states and was based on a July 1964 heads-of-states' declaration made in Cairo.

Prime Min. Harold Wilson of Great Britain addressed the General Assembly Dec. 16 while in the U.S. for meetings with Pres. Johnson. He insisted on the need in 1966 for "an effective and water-tight treaty to stop the spread of nuclear weapons." He said there must be an "unequivocal agreement" among nuclear states not to grant nuclear capability to non-nuclear nations and a similiar declaration by non-nuclear nations not to build or attempt to acquire atomic weapons. He also held that a "dialogue" would have to be established with Communist China on disarmament.

OTHER DEVELOPMENTS

Kennedy Calls for Nuclear Treaty

Sen. Robert F. Kennedy (D., N.Y.), in his first major address to the U.S. Senate, declared June 23 that the U.S. "should initiate at once negotiations with the Soviet Union and other nations with nuclear capability or potential, looking toward a non-proliferation treaty." Kennedy asserted that "we have not ourselves done all we can to secure a non-proliferation treaty. The most prominent example," he said, "is the question of the [Western] multilateral force [MLF] and the variant Atlantic nuclear force [ANF]." The USSR, he said, "has absolutely refused to conclude a non-proliferation agreement as long as we go forward with the MLF or the ANF. We have not abandoned the MLF plans, because West Germany feels it must have a greater role in nuclear deterrence. But if a non-proliferation treaty can be concluded," he declared, "it will be in the national interest of every nation." He called for "a form of nuclear guarantee to West Germany and other countries of Europe" which would not be rejected by the USSR.

Kennedy urged "that the work of the Gilpatric Committee...appointed by the President to study the problem of nuclear proliferation be carried forward by all concerned government agencies at once." (The *N.Y. Times* reported July 1 that the committee, established in Nov. 1964 by Pres. Johnson, had recommended, in a top-secret January report to the President, that a non-proliferation treaty be given priority over nuclear sharing within NATO.) Kennedy said that Communist China would have to be included in negotiation to establish an anti-proliferation treaty, but he added that "if we must ultimately have the cooperation of China, and the Soviet Union, and France, and all other nations with any nuclear capability..., it does not follow that we should wait for that cooperation before beginning our efforts."

Kennedy said in a Senate speech Oct. 13 that Red China should be asked to participate in the deliberations of the 18-nation Geneva Disarmament Committee. Senate majority leader Mike Mansfield (D., Mont.) and Sen Joseph S. Clark (D., Pa.) supported Kennedy's proposal.

Kennedy, in a Los Angeles speech Nov. 5, again called on the world's major powers to "make compromises" on issues of nuclear defense, including the MLF issue, for the sake of an eventual abolition of nuclear weapons.

Couve de Murville & Stewart in Moscow

French Foreign Min. Maurice Couve de Murville visited the Soviet Union Oct. 28-Nov. 2 and conferred with Soviet Foreign Min. Andrei A. Gromyko, Premier Aleksei N. Kosygin and other Soviet leaders. Tass said Kosygin had suggested that French Pres. de Gaulle might "find a visit here attractive in solidifying France's position as a completely independent European nuclear power." A French-Soviet communique Nov. 2 "emphasized the risks of dissemination of nuclear arms in the world." Gromyko stressed the importance of an "international conference on disarmament"; Couve de Murville said "it remained to the [5] nuclear powers primarily to begin the realization [of disarmament]."

British Foreign Secy. Michael Stewart, accompanied by Lord Chalfont, disarmament minister, visited Moscow Nov. 29-Dec. 3. They conferred Nov. 30 with Gromyko. British sources said that the discussion centered on disarmament and that Stewart had stressed Britain's intention to prevent joint nuclear planning within NATO from resulting in the acquisition of nuclear weapons by non-nuclear states. Stewart insisted that Britain would not accept the Soviet view that plans for a NATO nuclear force would have to be abandoned before there could be any agreement on an East-West pact to prevent the spread of nuclear weapons. He argued that discussions with non-nuclear states (such as West Germany) on the use of nuclear weapons in emergency did not constitute nuclear proliferation, and he said that the control of atomic weapons would remain with current nuclear powers even if NATO set up a new multinational force. British sources described Gromyko as unimpressed with Stewart's argument.

At a press conference Dec. 3, before flying back to London, Stewart said that the 2 sides "will continue to search for ... agreement" in disarmament. He indicated that the discussion had centered on the word "access"; the Soviet leaders sometimes used the word broadly to mean any closer consultation between nuclear and non-nuclear powers; at other times they used it to mean actual control of the use of nuclear weapons. (British sources had said Nov. 30, after the Stewart-Gromyko meeting, that if all the USSR was opposed to was West Germany's obtaining the capability to "press the button" through a NATO nuclear-sharing plan, then agreement on an East-West non-proliferation pact could be reached because Britain also opposed proliferation of such a capability.)

Other Discussions

A White House Conference on International Cooperation was held in Washington Nov. 28-Dec. 1. It was convened by Pres. Johnson in connection with the UN International Cooperation Year. The meeting was attended by about 5,000 private citizens and government officials. They discussed advisory reports submitted by 30 committees on various subjects, including disarmament. Disagreement between government officials and private citizens became evident Nov. 30 during a session on the report of the committee on arms control and disarmament, headed by Dr. Jerome B. Weisner, dean of MIT's School of Science. The report recommended (a) a 3-year moratorium on the development of an anti-missile missile, (b) a non-aggression pact between NATO and the Warsaw Pact countries, (c) bi-lateral disarmament talks with Communist China, (d) priority to nuclear non-proliferation treaty over creation of a NATO multi-lateral nuclear force and (e) a joint withdrawal of some troops from East and West Germany. These proposals were criticized by Administration officials, including Asst. State Secy. John M. Leddy and Deputy Disarmament Agency Director Adrian S. Fisher. Sen. Joseph S. Clark (D., Pa.), commenting on this official reaction, asserted that "the intermediate levels in the Department of State are almost allergic to any change in the *status quo.*" Clark criticized the panel for unwillingness "to face up to the crucial challenge" of total disarmament, and he offered a resolution reaffirming U.S. interest in a comprehensive disarmament treaty. The resolution was ruled out of order by John J. McCloy, a member of the U.S. Disarmament Agency's advisory committee and moderator of the session.

Following a meeting Dec. 8 between Soviet Amb.-to-U.S. Anatoly F. Dobrynin and U.S. Ambassador-at-Large Llewellyn Thompson, the U.S. State Department announced Dec. 10 that it had received assurances from the USSR that it did not intend to place nuclear weapons in orbit around the earth.

The 15th Pugwash Conference was held in Addis Ababa, Ethiopia Dec. 29, 1965-Jan. 3, 1966. According to an interview published in the Soviet government newspaper *Izvestia*, 87 scientists from 31 nations (including 50 scientists from 20 countries of Africa, Latin America and Asia) attended the conference. Prof. Mikhail D. Millionshchikov, vice president of the USSR Academy of Sciences and chairman of the Soviet delegation to the conference, said the conference "once again expressed the opinion that the full security of all nations could be insured only with an agreement . . . on general and complete disarmament."

1965's NUCLEAR TESTS

U.S. Explosions

All U.S. nuclear tests conducted during 1964 were underground. The dates, force and sites of the tests:

Date	Force	Site
Jan. 13	Low yield	Nevada test site
Jan. 14	Low yield	Nevada test site
Jan. 18	Low-intermediate	Nevada test site
Jan. 21	Low yield	Nevada test site
Feb. 3	Low yield	Nevada test site
Feb. 4		Nevada test site
Feb. 16	Low yield	Nevada test site
Feb. 18	Low yield	Nevada test site

Date	Force	Site
Mar. 3	Intermediate	Nevada test site
Mar. 26		Nevada test site
Apr. 5		Nevada test site
Apr. 14*	Low yield	Nevada test site
Apr. 21	Low yield	Nevada test site
May 7	Low yield	Nevada test site
May 12	Low-intermediate	Nevada test site
May 14	Low-intermediate	Nevada test site
May 21	Low yield	Nevada test site
June 11	Low yield	Nevada test site
June 17**	Low yield	Nevada test site
July 23	Low-intermediate	Nevada test site
Aug. 6	Low yield	Nevada test site
Aug. 27	Low yield	Nevada test site
Sept. 1	Low yield	Nevada test site
Sept. 17	Low yield	Nevada test site
Sept. 22		Nevada test site
Oct. 10		Nevada test site
Oct. 29†	80 kiloton	Amchitka Island
Nov. 12	Low yield	Nevada test site
Dec. 3	Intermediate	Nevada test site
Dec. 16	Low yield	Nevada test site
Dec. 16	Low-intermediate	Nevada test site

Soviet Explosions

Jan. 15***§	Intermediate	Semipalatinsk
Mar. 3***		
Sept. 18***		
Oct. 8***	Low-intermediate	Central Asia
Nov. 21***		
Nov. 22***	Low-intermediate	Semipalatinsk

Chinese Explosion

May 14★	Low-intermediate	

---

* Part of Plowshare Program to develop peaceful uses of atomic energy (other tests were presumably weapons related). Test released a "very small amount of radioactivity" into the atomosphere but not enough to endanger health or violate the 1963 nuclear test-ban treaty, according to the AEC.

** Part of Defense Department's Vela Program for improving methods of identifying underground tests.

† Purpose of the test was to produce data useful for administering a possible future ban on underground nuclear tests. The explosion was detected 3,200 miles away by the Advanced Research Projects Agency's detection center near Billings, Montana.

§ The USSR admitted Jan. 25 that some radioactive material had leaked into the atmosphere. It asserted that the amount was "so insignificant" as not to violate 1963 test ban treaty.

*** Underground test

★ Atmospheric test.

1966

While the armaments of the great powers, including France and Communist China, continued to expand during 1966, the 18-Nation Disarmament Committee met in Geneva Jan. 27-May 10 and June 14-Aug. 25 and made some progress toward a non-proliferation agreement. Perhaps the most significant step toward arms control during 1966 was a U.S.-Soviet agreement, announced at the UN Dec. 8, on a draft treaty banning the placing of mass-destruction weapons in outer space. The treaty was unanimously indorsed by the UN General Assembly Dec. 19 and was to come into force on ratification by 5 countries, among them the U.S., Britain and USSR.

ARMS RACE ACCELERATES

U.S. Nuclear Weapons & Ships

In its annual report to Congress, the U.S. Atomic Energy Commission (AEC) Jan. 31 announced that progress had been made during 1965 towards better protection of U.S. nuclear-armed intercontinental missiles against enemy attack. According to the report, laboratory and field tests had identified certain designs that would improve protection for missiles. The report said: "The designs are under further study, with the purpose of producing...a system with hardness [*i.e.*, safety against enemy attack] balanced against all possible threats." According to the report the U.S. Navy had 59 nuclear-powered ships and submarines in operation and 45 other under construction or authorized. Vice Adm. Hyman G. Rickover had told the Joint Congressional Atomic Energy Committee Jan. 26 that the proposed 2d nuclear-powered aircraft carrier would need refueling only once during its projected 25-year life span. Original cores in the proposed ship would last 13 years; the cores in the only existing nuclear-powered carrier, the *Enterprise,* had to be replaced after 4 years.

With the launching at Groton, Conn. July 21 of the *Will Rogers,* the U.S. completed the construction of its 41-ship Polaris nuclear submarine fleet. The *Will Rogers,* armed with 16 nuclear-tipped Polaris missiles with a range of 2,500 nautical miles, was one of 31 *Lafayette-*class subs.

A bill authorizing $2,259,958,000 in fiscal 1967 for the AEC was passed by the House May 9 and Senate May 10 and was signed by Pres. Johnson May 21. The authorization total was $14,862,000 less than the AEC request. Among the bill's authorizations: Raw materials $163,015,000; special nuclear materials $354,228,000; weapons $649 million (33% of total authorizations for operating expenses); reactor development $430,822,000 (including $81,980,000 for operating expenses of the civilian reactor program); development of space propulsion systems $79,100,000; development of small nuclear power sources for space and terrestrial applications $45,350,000; general reactor technology research program $59.1 million; advanced reactor research $24.7 million; physical research $258.9 million.

Chinese Testing

3 nuclear explosions—its 3d, 4th and 5th—were achieved by Communist China during 1966.

The first of the year's 3 Chinese nuclear blasts took place May 9 at the Sinkiang Province test site near Lob Nor. Hsinhua, the Communist Chinese news agency, reported that at "4 p.m. [Peking time]...China successfully conducted... an explosion which contained thermonuclear material." This was the first Chinese claim of the use of "thermonuclear material" in a test. The May 9 test, like China's 2 earlier tests, was conducted in the atmosphere. The Hsinhua announcement, similar to the statements issued after earlier tests, hailed the "explosion" as a "new important achievement scored by the Chinese people in their efforts to further strengthen their national defense and safeguard the security of their country and the peace of the world." The success of the test was called a tribute to China's "People's Liberation Army," to its "scientists, technicians... workers, functionaries, who, under the correct leadership of the Communist Party of China and holding still higher the great red banner of Mao Tse-tung's thought, gave prominence to politics... and adhered to the '4 firsts.'" Hsinhua explained the "4 firsts": "First place must be given to a man in handling the relationship between man and weapons; to political work in handling the relationship between political and other work; to ideological work in relation to other aspects of political work; and, in ideological work, to the ideas currently in a person's mind as distinguished from ideas in books."

Hsinhua said: "China's purpose in conducting necessary and limited nuclear tests and in developing nuclear weapons is to oppose the nuclear blackmail and threats of U.S. imperialism... and to oppose the U.S.-Soviet collusion for maintaining nuclear monopoly and sabotaging the revolutionary struggles of all oppressed peoples and nations." China's "possession of nuclear weapons is a great encouragement to the peoples who are fighting... for their own liberation as well as a new contribution to the defense of world peace." China repeated its proposal, made following its first and 2d tests, for a summit conference of all countries of the world to discuss the complete prohibition and thorough destruction of nuclear weapons." The U.S., "in disregard of the statements of... [China,] continued to develop and mass produce nuclear weapons..., further expanded its nuclear bases all over the world and stepped up its nuclear blackmail and threats against China and the whole world." China's "sole purpose in developing nuclear weapons is defense, and her ultimate aim is to eliminate nuclear weapons.... [At] no time and in no circumstances will China be the first to use nuclear weapons." China was "convinced that a nuclear war can be prevented" if "all peace-loving... countries work together and persevere in the struggle."

Technical estimates of the nature of the Chinese test, aside from the Chinese announcement that the test "contained thermonuclear material," came principally from U.S. agencies. A State Department spokesman May 9 said the yield from the test was "in the same general range" as China's earlier 2 tests. (The first 2 had been in the low-yield range, *i.e.,* producing a blast force equivalent to less than 20,000 tons of TNT, or 20 kilotons.) But the State Department May 11 increased its estimate of the yield to about 130 kilotons, thereby placing it in the low-intermediate range (20-200 kilotons). The Atomic Energy Commission May 13 released a statement that did not estimate the size of the Chinese test but did say that Communist China had not produced a hydrogen bomb explosion: "Preliminary debris analysis indicated the 3d Chinese nuclear test on May 9 was not a thermonuclear weapon. The test was probably an experimental device, either attempting to increase the yield of the previous low-yield fission device [*i.e.,* an atomic bomb with a blast force of less than 20 kilotons] or looking toward an eventual thermonuclear capability. Specifically, the device employed enriched uranium, the same fissionable material that was used in the previous Chinese tests. It did not contain plutonium. The thermonuclear material, lithium-6, was present, although its specific function in the device is not yet clear."

An AEC statement May 20 declared: "Information now available . . . indicates that the yield [of the May 9 test] was in the lower end of the intermediate range." (The intermediate range was 200,000 to a million tons of TNT, or 200 kilotons to one megaton.) The AEC's May 20 statement, by re-estimating the force produced by the Chinese test to about 10 times the force originally estimated by the State Department, led to renewed speculation that the Chinese had achieved some form of thermonuclear reaction.

The *N.Y. Times* reported May 21 that the presence of the thermonuclear material lithium-6 in the test, in addition to the yield of the explosion, indicated that a thermonuclear reaction had occurred because a yield of more than 200 kilotons was greater than that usually obtained from just a fission bomb. According to the *Times,* the largest fission bomb ever tested by the U.S. at its Nevada test site had a yield of 74 kilotons. It was conceivable that the Chinese had achieved the 200-kiloton explosion using a fission device alone. But such an explosion would require the use of large amounts of fissionable material, which was thought to be in short supply in China. U.S. "experts" had therefore concluded that China's large yield had been accomplished by the combination of a fission and a fusion (thermonuclear) reaction. (A fusion reaction provided the main explosive force of the hydrogen bomb.)

The U.S. Public Health Service reported May 20 that radioactive air samples from the Chinese test had been collected May 14-17 over Colorado, Idaho, California, North Carolina, Florida, Illinois and Utah. The report said the radioactive levels were lower than those following the earlier Chinese tests and presented no health hazard.

The State Department, which had announced Apr. 28 that a Chinese nuclear test would be conducted in the near future, described the Chinese test May 9 as "part of . . . [a] deliberate and costly . . . program to acquire nuclear weapons" that disregarded the "desires . . . of people throughout the world who may suffer from the ill effects of atmospheric nuclear testing, which most of the world has banned by adherence to the limited test ban treaty." The statement reiterated Pres. Johnson's 1964 pledge, issued 2 days after the first Chinese test Oct. 16, 1964, that the

U.S. would defend non-nuclear nations against nuclear blackmail. State Secy. Dean Rusk said in testimony before the Senate Foreign Relations Committee May 9 that he did not believe the Chinese test would "have any serious effect on the situation in Southeast Asia."

Among other reaction to the Chinese test: *May 9*—The Soviet news agency Tass reported the test in a one-line statement without comment.... *May 10*—Indian Foreign Min. Swaran Singh told the Indian Parliament that the test was in "arrogant defiance" of world wishes. The North Vietnamese News Agency reported that Pres. Ho Chi Minh had sent a message of congratulations to the Chinese leaders. Ho said that Chinese possession of nuclear weapons was "a great stimulus to the peoples now endeavoring to fight against U.S. imperialist aggression." ... *May 11*—New Zealand Prime Min. Keith Holyoake said in Wellington that the test was "evidence" of China's "determination to fly in the face of international opinion." ... *May 12*—Premier Eisaku Sato of Japan called a cabinet meeting to discuss the test. Japan's leading newspapers said the Chinese test heightened the urgency of a national debate on Japan's defenses. Takao Kosaka, a scientist at Niigata University in Tokyo, said the fallout from the May 9 test was 33 times more radioactive than that from China's earlier tests.

Announcing its 2d nuclear test of 1966, Communist China said Oct. 27 that it had successfully exploded on target a nuclear weapon carried by a guided missile. Hsinhua reported: "On Oct. 27, 1966 China successfully conducted over its own territory a guided missile-nuclear weapon test. The guided missile flew normally, and the nuclear warhead accurately hit the target at the appointed distance, effecting a nuclear explosion." The test was China's 4th nuclear explosion but the first involving a missile delivery. The Chinese communique continued:

"This successful test marks the fact that China's science, technology and defense capabilities are advancing at even greater speed under the brilliant illumination of Mao Tse-tung's thought.... [Its] complete success ... was ensured by the Chinese People's Liberation Army and China's scientists, technicians ... workers and functionaries, who, enthusiastically responding to the call of ... [Defense Min.] Lin Piao and holding high the great red banner of Mao Tse-tung's thought, put politics in the forefront ... and, propelled by the great proletarian cultural revolution, ... displayed the spirit of self-reliance, hard work, collective wisdom and efforts and wholehearted cooperation.... China's purpose in developing nuclear weapons is precisely to oppose the nuclear monopoly and nuclear blackmail by the United States and the Soviet Union acting in collusion.... The conducting of necessary and limited nuclear tests and the development of nuclear weapons by China are entirely for the purpose of defense, with the ultimate aim of destroying nuclear weapons. We solemnly declare once again that at no time and in no circumstances will China be the first to use nuclear weapons...."

The U.S. AEC said Oct. 27 that preliminary estimates indicated that the yield from the test had been in the "low to low-intermediate range, similar to the first Chinese test." (Low-yield tests produced less energy than would result from the explosion of 20 kilotons [20,000 tons] of TNT; low-intermediate-yield tests produced force in the 20-200-kiloton range.) It was reported Nov. 1 that preliminary analysis of the radioactive debris from the test indicated that China had used enriched uranium as the material for the warhead. (Natural uranium consisted mainly of non-fissionable U-238; enriched uranium, from which most of the U-238 had been removed by expensive, highly sophisticated technological processes, consisted more than 90% of fissionable U-235.)

Although there was no immediate confirmation of the Chinese claim that the warhead had been carried by a guided missile, it was reported Oct. 28 that preliminary data seemed to indicate that the missile had been fired 400 miles to its target—China's Sinkiang Province test site near Lob Nor. The U.S. State Department said in a statement Oct. 28: "We have been aware of the Chinese efforts to develop missiles as well as nuclear weapons. A test of the type reported by Peking falls within the time period we have foreseen. We see no reason to alter our estimate of when they might have an operational capability. It can be expected that there will be further tests of this kind." (Defense Secy. Robert S. McNamara had estimated in Dec. 1965 that Red China might have an operational medium-range ballistic missile by 1967.)

Among other reactions to the test reported Oct. 28: The State Department accused China of "polluting the atmosphere in defiance of world opinion." UN Secy. Gen. U Thant said the test "is to be regretted," as is "any atomic explosion anywhere at any time." A Japanese government statement said the test "went counter to the hope of mankind." Japanese General Defense Agency director Eikichi Kambayashiyama said that although Asian nations must be shocked, Japan must not react by developing its own nuclear capability. North Vietnamese Pres. Ho Chi Minh said the test had provided a great stimulus to the cause of preserving world peace.

Pres. Johnson commented on China's latest nuclear tests in a speech delivered Oct. 30 at Kuala Lumpur during a state visit to Malaysia. He pledged that the U.S. would protect any nonnuclear nation from "the threat of nuclear blackmail." He warned that Chinese Communist efforts to create an atomic stockpile impeded the drive for international arms controls and "also invites danger to China itself." "For the leaders of China must realize," Mr. Johnson asserted, "that any nuclear capability they can develop can—and will—be deterred." The President deplored "the pursuit of national nuclear power by too large a part of the underdeveloped world as a tragic fact, for bread is the need of millions who face starvation every day and bombs are too often purchased at the price of bread."

It was reported that Communist China might have used a triple-stage (or fission-fusion-fission) nuclear device in the year's 3d Chinese nuclear test—conducted at the Lob Nor test site in Sinkiang Province Dec. 28. The test was confirmed by the U.S. AEC Dec. 28 and announced officially by Communist China Dec. 29. (The U.S. State Department had reported Nov. 29 that Communist China was preparing to conduct a test "in the near future.") The Chinese announcement said that the test had been "successfully conducted" and that it had raised "China's science and technology in the field of nuclear weapons to a new level."

The AEC's Dec. 28 announcement said the test had produced a yield of "a few hundred kilotons." (Unofficial sources estimated that the yield was 300 kilotons.) A further AEC announcement Dec. 30 revealed that preliminary analysis of the radioactive debris from the explosion indicated that the device tested "involved thermonuclear material" and utilized some normally nonfissionable uranium-238 as "fissionable material." The reference to the U-238 suggested that China might have tested a triple-stage bomb, the "dirtiest" and most powerful type known. (In such a device, normally stable U-238 is placed around the thermonuclear material used in a hydrogen bomb; the emission of high-energy neutrons from the hydrogen explosion causes fission in the U-238 and thereby greatly increases the power and radioactive "dirtiness" of the weapon.) Some U.S. experts suggested, however, that the presence of U-238 might indicate that China had been unable to separate completely from the stable U-238 the fissionable U-235 that was used as the atomic triggering device in a thermonuclear weapon.

Chinese Nuclear Strength & Disarmament

Testifying before the Joint Congressional Committee on Atomic Energy Mar. 7, U.S. Defense Secy. McNamara predicted that China would have within 2 or 3 years a "warhead delivery capability" for a nuclear attack on countries within a 700-mile radius. He said he was particularly "disturbed" about such power in view of "aggressive statements of her leaders" and of the implication from the sacrifice China was enduring to attain its nuclear position. The implication was, he said, that China was getting in position "to support such words with instruments of war of the most terrible kind." McNamara appeared before the committee to support a treaty to prevent the spread of atomic weapons. He said a pact should be part of a "comprehensive program" that should include some form of protection to the nonnuclear states against nuclear attack or large-scale conventional attack.

Chrmn. J. W. Fulbright of the Senate Foreign Relations Committee, apprised of McNamara's view of China's aggressive pose, said the aggressiveness "could just as well be because they fear attack by countries on their border who have nuclear power." Asked to specify what countries, Fulbright asked: "What do you consider 55,000 men in Korea?"

A report on its Communist China hearings was released May 20 by the Far East & Pacific Subcommittee of the House Foreign Affairs Committee. It asserted that China could become a "major military threat" to the U.S. and USSR—particularly after probably achieving intercontinental missile capability in about 1975.

State Department press officer Robert J. McCloskey confirmed May 11 that the U.S. had turned down a Red Chinese suggestion—made about a year previously—that the 2 nations formally pledge not to use nuclear weapons against each other. Chinese Premier Chou En-lai had announced May 9 that the U.S. had rejected the Chinese proposal. McCloskey said the offer had been rejected because the Chinese "profess to believe that such a public declaration without controls would constitute a sufficient guarantee" whereas "we do not [believe so], and we have given our views to the Chinese." McCloskey said the Chinese had not demonstrated a "constructive interest" in U.S. disarmament proposals; he cited China's refusal to sign the 1963 test ban treaty. He said that the U.S. had proposed a mutual ending of the production of fissionable materials and a freeze in the number of strategic (i.e., long-range) delivery systems but that the Chinese had not responded. (It was assumed that the U.S. proposals had been made at the regular meetings of the U.S. and Communist Chinese ambassadors to Warsaw. U.S. Amb.-to-Poland John A. Gronouski, in Washington for consulations, told newsmen May 11 that disarmament was among the subjects he had discussed with the Chinese ambassador.)

State Secy. Dean Rusk said at a May 17 news conference that the U.S. had rejected the Chinese proposal because "mere declarations on such matters would not be adequate." He said: The U.S. had "put forward . . . far-reaching proposals about limiting nuclear weapons and freezing and possibly reducing nuclear weapons delivery vehicles." In addition, the U.S. had "suggested they [China] ought to be associated with the preparatory arrangements for a world disarmament conference, but we've had no indication from the Chinese that they are willing to do that." (The UN General Assembly's 1965 resolution calling for a world disarmament conference that would include Communist China had proposed that a "preparatory committee" be set up to plan for the conference.)

Sen. Robert F. Kennedy (D., N.Y.) May 12 had criticized the U.S.' rejection of the Chinese proposal. Speaking in the Senate, Kennedy acknowledged that Peking's proposal might not have been sincere, but he asked "whether this will be well understood in the rest of the world unless we now take . . . affirmative steps to make clear our desire to reach effective control over nuclear weapons with the Communist Chinese." Kennedy proposed that the U.S. invite Communist China to participate in the Geneva disarmament committee meetings and offer to negotiate with them "anywhere in the world." Senate Democratic leader Mike Mansfield (Mont.) and Sen. George S. McGovern (D., S.D.) supported Kennedy's remarks.

Chou En-lai's May 9 statement had been made at a Peking reception for visiting Albanian Premier Mehmet Shehu. He asserted that his government had proposed that the U.S. and China "undertake the obligation of not being the first to use nuclear weapons against each other, but U.S. imperialism rejected the idea...."This rejection had forced China to continue developing nuclear weapons, Chou declared. Shehu described the 3d Chinese test as a "very great victory." Nuclear weapons "in the hands of revolutionaries educated in Marxism-Leninism and Mao Tse-tung's thought are in the service of peace and socialism and throw our enemy into panic," he declared. A joint communique on Chou's talks with Shehu, signed May 11, announced Albania's "full support of the Chinese government for a summit conference of all the countries of the world to discuss the question of complete prohibition and thorough destruction of nuclear weapons."

Communist China June 20 rejected a U.S. proposal of a "no first use" pledge on atomic weapons if China agreed to sign the 1963 Moscow test ban treaty. *Jenmin Jih Pao,* the Chinese Communist Party daily, said that the proposal had been made May 25 during a meeting of the 2 nations' ambassadors in Warsaw. It asserted that China would "determinedly continue to develop nuclear weapons" and would attend no world disarmament conference. It rejected the U.S. proposal as another "big fraud."

5 French Atmospheric A-Tests

France exploded 5 nuclear bombs in the atmosphere July 2-Oct. 4. This was France's first nuclear testing since Mar. 1963. The experiments, which included one "safety test" not involving an explosion, were held at the newly-developed Centre d'Experimentation du Pacifique (Experimental Center of the Pacific). They were France's first tests in the Pacific, and they raised to 9 the number of atmospheric tests conducted by France. About 13,000 French personnel had been brought to the test area for construction and other work involved in the tests. Preparations at the site had taken 2 years. Pres. de Gaulle, on a world tour, witnessed the 3d test Sept. 11.

The first 3 bombs in France's 1966 series were described in French communiques as "plutonium fission devices" (or A-bombs). They were exploded July 2, July 19 and Sept. 11 at the Mururoa Atoll, 750 miles southeast of Tahiti. The first bomb was said to have produced energy within the "tactical range," or equivalent to the explosion of less than 100,000 tons (100 kilotons) of TNT. It was exploded aboard a barge in Mururoa's lagoon. *Le Monde* reported July 5 that observers said the resulting mushroom cloud indicated that the blast had been in the lower tactical range. The 2d bomb, dropped by parachute from a Mirage-4 jet bomber, produced a force of about 60 kilotons. The 3d, suspended from a ballon above the lagoon, produced energy believed to have been equivalent to 100 kilotons. De Gaulle saw the 3d test from a position 25 miles away aboard the command cruiser *De Grasse.* He was believed to have been the first head of state to witness a nuclear explosion.

The last 2 bombs of the 1966 series were exploded Sept. 24 at Fangataufa Atoll, 800 miles south of Tahiti, and Oct. 4 at Mururoa Atoll. According to an official communique, the Oct. 4 test, "like its predecessor, contained plutonium and thermonuclear material but in a different configuration." Authorities said the force of the Oct. 4 explosion was equivalent to 400 kilotons. (Defense Min. Pierre Messmer had announced July 2 that "after the first test [in the current series], we will increase in strength and will have, at the end of the series, explosions at least as powerful as the Chinese ones." Communist China's May 9 test was of a device equivalent in power to France's Oct. 4 bomb.)

The "safety test," conducted July 21, was designed to check the effectiveness of a nuclear bomb's safety mechanism in the event of an accident occurring during stocking or transport. The bomb was dropped on Mururoa Atoll; it burst on contact with the ground but did not explode.

France had announced the tests May 17 and had warned shipping companies and airlines to stay clear of the danger area, which was defined as a circle around Mururoa with a radius of 400 nautical miles. Japan, Australia and New Zealand protested the proposed tests, as did Brazil, Chile, Peru, Colombia and Ecuador. De Gaulle had said May 4 that tests were necessary for France to be able to carry out its policies of "world equilibrium" and peace. He said the tests posed no danger to countries in or around the Pacific.

Following the July 2 test, the U.S. State Department issued a statement expressing regret "that France has resumed nuclear testing in the atmosphere." The statement urged France, which was not a signatory to the 1963 Moscow treaty banning nuclear tests in all environments except underground, "to adhere to the treaty and join in the effort to extend the ban on testing to include underground nuclear tests." Britain expressed "regret that France continues to ignore the principle of the partial test ban treaty and to test nuclear weapons in the atmosphere, thus causing an increase in the level of radioactivity." The Soviet news agency Tass reported the test briefly, without comment.

France July 3 dismissed the criticism as "irritating moralizing" and said the precautions for the test had been "particularly severe" in comparison to those taken by other nuclear powers in their testing.

France Aims at Nuclear Independence

French Pres. de Gaulle had asserted Feb. 21 that France must develop a nuclear force of its own in order to end its dependence on U.S. nuclear protection and in order to avoid being drawn into America's wars. "The Western world is no longer threatened...as it was at the time when the American protectorate was set up in Europe under the cover of NATO," de Gaulle declared. The fact that the USSR had developed a "nuclear power capable of striking the United States directly" meant that the U.S.' decision "as the eventual use of their [nuclear] bombs [had become] indeterminate," he said. Finally, with the dissipation of "prospects of world war breaking out on account of Europe . . . , conflicts in which America engages in other parts of the world . . . risk . . . being extended so that the result could be a general conflagration."

In what was regarded as the most comprehensive explanation of France's position, Premier Georges Pompidou told the National Assembly Apr. 20 that NATO's nuclear strategy was dictated by the U.S. He said:

The North Atlantic Council had at one time "unanimously . . . approved what is generally called the 'strategic concept' of NATO." Under this concept, supported by France, NATO was committed to all-out nuclear retaliation should any NATO nation suffer a conventional or nuclear attack. This strategy "was that of massive and immediate atomic retaliation. Officially it remains the NATO doctrine. . . . But, in actual fact, this strategic concept approved by the NATO Council, unanimously, still theoretically in effect, has been abandoned by the Supreme Command in favor of the concept of the flexible response [under which NATO would measure its military response to that used by the attacker in an attempt to avoid all-out nuclear war].

The NATO alert system was of no value to France. It would give the U.S. a "useful alert time on the order of 15 minutes. This is not negligible. . . . But for Europe, and for France in particular, in the event of a missile attack, the 15 minutes becomes one or 2. In other words, there is no alert or warning at all. . . . For France, the alert will be given by the bombs if they happen to explode on our soil." Nevertheless, the U.S.' strategic situation, with its additional 15 minutes, was "not basically different" from France's. Hence, both countries had based their nuclear defense policy on "'counterstrike,' that is, the fact of disposing of a large enough and sufficiently dispersed nuclear force . . . to be sure of being able to launch such retaliation [after an enemy attack] that the adversary is destroyed. This is the . . . line of reasoning, on our scale, that makes us choose the atomic submarine as the principal weapon of our future strategic force." "What we criticize" about the flexible response doctrine "is its being specifically conceived on the basis of America's geographical location . . . ,limiting the atomic battlefield by sparing the territory of the Soviet Union and therefore the territory of the United States, and thereby creating a psychological risk, that of making it believed that the war could remain localized between the Atlantic and the Polish frontier in the East, that is to say, in Europe, but a Europe doomed to destruction."

The Cuban missile crisis of 1962 was an example of the nuclear risks that NATO presented to France: "Faced with the threat, . . . Pres. Kennedy took immediate steps. He did not consult us, but informed us, quickly, although after the fact. . . . We agreed with Pres. Kennedy. But, even before we announced our position—while the NATO forces were supposed to be outside the conflict, and while, even if they had been advised to take precautionary measures, no coded alert system had been set up—the American forces in Europe, including those in France, had been placed in a state of alert and , I might add, alert of the highest degree." France could, therefore, even if it did not "declare war," become a "target for atomic bombs."

As for criticism that France's current nuclear strike force, dependent on Mirage-4 jet bombers, was vulnerable and obsolete: Nuclear war "would be preceded by a period of perceptible political tension, of military movements large enough for us to be put on the alert. And naturally we have foreseen these circumstances and have set up a dispersal and alert system for our strategic force that would shelter at least part of it from the initial destruction."

N.Y. Times Washington correspondent John Finney reported Apr. 17 that for more than a year the U.S. had been refusing to supply France with enriched uranium fuel that it had promised under a 1959 agreement. According to Finney, French diplomatic officials in

Washington had revealed the U.S. refusal to fulfill the agreement, and U.S. officials confirmed their refusal without discussing reasons. The *Times* reported from Paris Apr. 20 that French officials had said that the U.S. had refused to deliver nuclear fuel under the 1959 agreement since Nov. 1964. Previously, the U.S. had delivered 374 of the 968 pounds of fuel called for in the agreement. The Times cited U.S. "circles" as charging that France had exceeded the agreement in attempting to build an atomic striking force composed of submarines firing Polaris-type missiles. According to the U.S. officials, as explained in the *Times,* France was supposed to use the "hunter-killer" type submarines, capable of destroying other submarines, but not for an atomic striking force. The semi-official Agence France Presse (AFP) Apr. 19 had distributed a statement in which "authorized [French] circles" said that "during the signing of the [1959 nuclear fuel] accord and afterward, [no question had been raised] of a difference between a pursuit submarine and a Polaris submarine." Premier Pompidou said in his Apr. 20 speech to the National Assembly that France had chosen "the atomic submarine as the principal weapon of our future strategic force."

AFP said that while the U.S. had agreed to give France uranium for testing a "land-based prototype submarine propulsion plant," it had given "other countries... technical information on the building of the submarine itself." (In 1958 the U.S. had agreed to give Britain one nuclear submarine propulsion unit plus information on manufacturing nuclear weapons.)

In an interview published Apr. 13 in the weekly French magazine *Paris-Match,* State Secy. Dean Rusk acknowledged that the U.S. had been preventing French military planes en route to the Tuamotu Islands, the South Pacific side of France's projected nuclear tests, from flying over the U.S. on the grounds that the French tests violated the 1963 test-ban treaty. A State Department spokesman said May 20 that the U.S. had refused to issue an export license for "high-performance" computers required by France for its nuclear weapons program. The U.S., he said, had licensed the export of computers to France "which are not to be involved in the French atomic weapons program."

In its annual report July 12, the French Atomic Energy Commission announced that France would produce enough high-quality enriched uranium in less than a year to begin the construction of its first H-bomb. Defense Min. Messmer had announced July 2 that France would have nuclear-tipped missiles in operation by 1969.

De Gaulle said during his semi-annual press conference Oct. 28: France's nuclear capability "will, by next year, exceed several thousand kilotons, and will exceed 100,000 kilotons within 4 years, when it becomes thermonuclear." "France's accession to the rank of atomic power" was both "an essential and unprecedented guarantee of her own security" and "a new and liberating factor" for the world that would reduce tension and break the "stifling rigidity" existing between the 2 power blocks. "We are going to see...the permanently and gravely dangerous game that was called the cold war growing blurred."

NATO Strategy

Defense ministers of 5 North Atlantic Treaty Organization nations—Robert S. McNamara of the U.S., Denis Healey of the UK, Kai-Uwe von Hassel of West Germany, Roberto Tremelloni of Italy and Ahmet Topaloglu of Trukey—met Apr. 28-29 in London to discuss nuclear strategy and planning in the event of war. The 5 nations comprised the first and most important of 3 subcommittees set up in Nov. 1965 as part of a projected permanent 10-nation NATO "Special Committee on Nuclear Consultation." Also participating in the talks were NATO Secy. Gen. Manlio Brosio, chairman of the 10-nation committee, and Gen. Lyman Lemnitzer, Supreme Commander, Allied Powers in Europe. A communique on the talks, published Apr. 29, stated that at their next meeting, scheduled for July, the 5 nations would "consider possible modifications in organization and procedure to permit a greater degree of participation in nuclear planning by non-nuclear nations across the whole spectrum of planning, and to make possible appropriate consultation in the event their use is considered." The communique said the ministers had agreed that the total number of "tactical nuclear weapons" at the alliance's disposal in Europe (reported at 6,000) was "adequate."

The U.S. Defense Department Apr. 30 denied press reports from London that McNamara had proposed changes in NATO's nuclear defense strategy at the Apr. 28-29 meeting. "At no time, in no way," said the Defense Department statement, "did the United States propose a change in the use of nuclear weapons in defense of NATO territory. Secy. McNamara emphasized again, as he had before, the belief of the United States government that NATO must possess both non-nuclear and nuclear forces adequate to deal with a wide range of threats, with the power appropriate to each."

The Pentagon statement was an apparent response to an article published Apr. 30 in the *Washington Post.* The article, written by Don Cook in London, said that McNamara had proposed a new policy of automatic but limited and controlled nuclear responses to attacks on NATO territory. Cook said: This strategy would replace the "pause theory," instituted in 1961 by Pres. Kennedy, under which the U.S. President retained the decision to commit NATO to nuclear war. McNamara was currently "proposing that plans be drawn up for use of nuclear weapons in 3 carefully controlled categories." In the first, pre-positioned "nuclear demolition charges or land mines" would be used to "block strategic invasion points if NATO territory were to be invaded." The 2d included the "use of nuclear anti-aircraft weapons in the event of an air attack against" NATO territory. The 3d involved anti-submarine nuclear weapons "in the event of an attack against naval forces or ports." Although the U.S. President would retain the decision to escalate NATO's nuclear response, the current McNamara proposals "would end the present uncertainty in NATO as to whether, and when, nuclear weapons would [initially] be used in European defense."

Cook noted that French Premier Pompidou, in his address to the French National Assembly Apr. 20, had criticized the U.S.' decision in 1961 to introduce the "pause theory" without consulting the other allies. "McNamara's new proposals," said Cook, "put forward in 2 days of meetings ... [in London], will go a long way toward restoring a balance and putting nuclear weapons back into NATO war plans."

The 5-nation nuclear planning subcommittee had met for the first time in Washington Feb. 17-18. It was reported that at the 2-day meeting, West Germany and Italy had expressed dissatisfaction with a plan to bar the eventual development of a NATO nuclear force in which they would participate. West Germany and Italy were described as unwilling to accept a joint NATO nuclear planning committee as a substitute for a NATO nuclear force. A State Department official said Feb. 23 that the nuclear planning committee "was never designed ... as a substitute for whatever nuclear arrangements would become possible for the alliance."

State Secy. Dean Rusk told the Joint Congressional Committee on Atomic Energy Feb. 23 that "no one in NATO has been talking about any arrangement which would involve the proliferation of nuclear weapons," and "no NATO nuclear sharing proposal would increase the number of independent nuclear entities."

Rusk Apr. 27 denied that the U.S. had "foreclose[d] a possible Atlantic nuclear force or any other collective approach" giving West Germany or other NATO nations participation in "the management of nuclear power." Rusk described as a "misstatement of facts" a report in *N.Y. Times* Apr. 27 that the "Johnson Administration has decided to ask West Germany to forgo indefinitely even nominal ownership of part of an allied nuclear weapons system and to be content with improved consultation on nuclear strategy." Rusk said the nuclear sharing problem remained "major unfinished business." The *N.Y. Times* story, by diplomatic correspondent Max Frankel, said: Ex-State Secy. Dean Acheson, who was currently serving as adviser on NATO affairs, had "opposed the idea [of nuclear sharing] and is reported to have persuaded" Rusk and State Undersecy. George W. Ball "to squelch it." "The West Germans ... will have to be satisfied with membership in a new consultative committee on nuclear questions, which they have thus far maintained is no substitute for participation in nuclear defense."

The 5-nation sub-committee met in Rome Sept. 23 to continue discussions on a proposal to put the committee on a permanent basis. A communique at the conclusion of the talks recommended "a framework of permanent arrangements for nuclear planning in NATO" in order "to bring about more effective allied participation." McNamara announced at the meeting that the U.S. had about 7,000 tactical nuclear warheads—or double the 1961 figure—available for NATO forces in Europe. McNamara said he had made the announcement to counter "absolutely false rumors" that the U.S. intended to reduce the number of nuclear weapons assigned to NATO forces.

West German Chancellor Ludwig Erhard conferred with Pres. Johnson in Washington Sept. 26-27. The 2 statesmen "emphasized their great interest in an early termination of the armaments race" and "agreed that the proliferation of nuclear weapons into the national control of non-nuclear states must be checked." They "noted with satisfaction" the Sept. 23 recommendation of the NATO Nuclear Planning Working Group to establish a permanent nuclear planning committee within the alliance.

Thant's Warning

In his annual report on UN activities, issued Sept. 18, Secy. Gen. U Thant warned against the accelerating armaments race: "The past year has regrettably seen a reversal of the trend of recent years toward some progress in the stabilization and reduction of armed forces and military budgets." France and Red China had contined to test nuclear weapons in the atmosphere. Underground nuclear testing by the U.S., USSR and Britain had continued. Nuclear proliferation was becoming increasingly dangerous as a result of the growing numbers of nuclear reactors capable of producing "plutonium, which, when processed in a separation plant, can be used to make nuclear weapons, by techniques that are no longer secret. According to some estimates, by 1980 nuclear power reactors will produce more than 100 kilograms of plutonium every day." (100 kilograms of plutonium were sufficient to produce about 10 atomic bombs.)

East-West Strength Compared

The Institute for Strategic Studies in London reported Sept. 22 that, in contrast to the situation a year previously, there were more men under arms in NATO than in the Warsaw Pact force. The institute, releasing its annual survey of world military strength (entitled *The Military Balance, 1966-1967*), reported that total active armed strength of the NATO nations was 4,700,000 men, of whom 3,200,000 were assigned to NATO, while Communist-bloc strength was estimated at 5,800,000 men, of whom 2,800,000 were assigned to the Warsaw Pact. The report said the NATO superiority had resulted from the increase in the size of the U.S. armed forces to meet the demands of the Vietnamese war.

The USSR was reported to be maintaining at least 12 army divisions "at combat strength" in the Far East and another 5 divisions "in the 2d category of readiness," a condition described as "below combat strength but not requiring major reinforcements in the event of war."

The report stated that the USSR had deployed anti-ballistic missile defenses around Moscow and Leningrad.

Little change in the relative strategic power of the 2 blocs was noted in the report. The U.S. had slightly increased its numerical superiority of strategic missile forces over those of the USSR, while both sides increased the total number of missiles in operation. Comparative strength in strategic weapons:

	U.S.	USSR
Intercontinental ballistic missiles	934	300
Fleet ballistic missiles	624	150
Intermediate range missiles	None	750
Long-range heavy bombers	595	200
Medium bombers	222	1,200

Communist China was reported to be developing a ballistic missile delivery system for nuclear weapons. Institute estimates of East-West naval strength:

	West	Communist Bloc
Carriers	37	0
Cruisers	22	20
Escorts	623	239
Nuclear-powered submarines	70	50
Conventional submarines	195	395

An examination of 1964-5 defense expenditures by nations as percentages of gross national product indicated that South Vietnam had spent the highest figure—15.2%. Israel, 2d, spent 11.7% and was followed by Communist China 10% (according to the institute's own calculations), Formosa 9%, the UAR 8.6%, the U.S. 8%, Britain 6.8% and Portugal 6.5%. The institute noted that figures for Communist-bloc countries could not be compared with those of the West since they were based on different data.

GENEVA TALKS

Opening Messages

The UN 18-Nation Disarmament Committee reconvened in Geneva Jan. 27. It had been in recess for 4 months while disarmament was discussed at the 20th session of the UN General Assembly. Highlighting the opening meeting of the committee were messages from Pope Paul VI and Pres. Johnson. The pope's message, the first by a pontiff to the UN Disarmament Committee, contained an "urgent appeal" to the delegates to make progress toward disarmament. It was "becoming more and more obvious," Paul said, "that no lasting peace can be established among men until there has been an effective, general and controlled reduction in armaments."

Pres. Johnson's message, read to the committee by William C. Foster, director of the U.S.Arms Control & Disarmament Agency, urged the Soviet Union to participate with the U.S. in the joint "destruction of thousands of nuclear weapons." Mr. Johnson suggested that regional pacts to control "non-nuclear arms races" be set up.

He proposed this 7-point disarmament program:

Non-proliferation—"Let us seek a non-proliferation treaty which, in the words of the United Nations General Assembly, is 'void of any loopholes which might permit nuclear or non-nuclear powers to proliferate, directly or indirectly, nuclear weapons in any form.' We are prepared to sign such a treaty, making it applicable to nuclear and non-nuclear countries alike. We are prepared to work with other countries to assure that no non-nuclear country acquires its own nuclear weapons, gains national control over nuclear weapons, achieves the power itself to fire nuclear weapons or receives assitance in manufacturing, or testing nuclear weapons. We are prepared to agree that these things should not be done directly or indirectly through 3d countries or groups of countries, or through units of the armed forces or military personnel under any military alliance."

Controls on peaceful uses of nuclear energy—"We must continue to secure application of the International Atomic Energy Agency [IAEA] or equivalent international safeguards over peaceful nuclear activities. . . . I urge agreement that all transfers of nuclear materials or equipment for peaceful purposes to countries which do not have nuclear weapons be under IAEA, or equivalent international safeguards. . . .The major nuclear power should accept in increasing measure the same international safeguards they recommend for other states."

Guarantees to non-nuclear nations—"So that those who forswear nuclear weapons may forever refrain without fear from entering the nuclear arms race, let us strive to strengthen United Nations and other international security arrangements. Meanwhile, the nations that do not seek the nuclear path can be sure that they will have our strong support against threats of nuclear backmail."

Underground test ban—"The perils of proliferation would be materially reduced by an extension of the limited test ban treaty to cover underground nuclear tests. For such an extension, the United States will require only that number and kind of inspections which modern science shows to be necessary to assure that the treaty is being faithfully observed."

Nuclear stockpile reduction—"Let us seek agreement not to increase, and indeed to reduce, nuclear materials in weapons stockpiles. The United States continues to urge a verified halt in the production of fissionable materials for use in weapons. We continue to urge that such a halt be accompanied by the transfer of large quantities of fissionable material to peaceful purposes, under international safeguards. We continue to urge the demonstrated destruction of thousands of nuclear weapons by the United States and the USSR to produce this fissionable material."

Delivery systems reduction—"I urge continued exploration of the terms and conditions which could make acceptable to all the proposal I put before you in 1964 for a freeze on offensive and defensive strategic bombers and missiles designed to carry nuclear weapons. If progress can be made here, the United States will be prepared to explore the possibility of significant reductions in the number of these delivery vehicles."

Non-nuclear arms reduction—"Let us not forget that resources are being devoted to non-nuclear arms races all around the world. These resources might better be spent on feeding the hungry, healing the sick and teaching the uneducated....We suggest, therefore, that countries, on a regional basis, explore ways to limit competition among themselves for costly weapons often sought for reasons of illusory prestige."

In a message to the UN Disarmament Committee Feb. 2, Soviet Premier Aleksei N. Kosygin called for a ban on "the use of nuclear weapons against non-nuclear states . . . which have no nuclear weapons on their territory." Kosygin's message, distributed in Moscow by the offical news agency Tass, declared the USSR's support for a treaty against the proliferation of nuclear weapons to non-nuclear nations. It said: "The Soviet government fully supports the proposal of the Polish People's Republic on setting up a denuclearized zone in Central Europe and on freezing nuclear weapons in that region, just as the proposals for denuclearized zones in other regions of the world." In addition, Kosygin declared, the USSR "is prepared to assume a commitment right away not to be the first to use nuclear weapons, provided other nuclear powers do the same."

First Conference Period

Lord Chalfont, the British delegate, and Gen. E. L. M. Burns, the Canadian delegate, announced Feb. 3 their support for a Swedish proposal for a seismic system to detect and identify underground nuclear tests.

The U.S. delegation Feb. 7 returned unread a note prepared by East Germany for presentation to the Disarmament Committee. East German Deputy Foreign Min. Georg Stibi had arrived in Geneva Feb. 6 and had presented a copy of the note to Soviet delegate Semyon K. Tsarapkin. Tsarapkin read the East German note at the conference Feb. 8. The note called on West Germany to join with East Germany in "renouncing nuclear weapons" as a step toward German reunification and toward a multilateral nonproliferation treaty.

Indian delegate Vishnu C. Trivedi Feb. 10 rejected a proposal by Tsarapkin that the conference move quickly from its general debate to a discussion of a non-proliferation treaty. Rumanian delegate Vasile Dumitrescu said a non-proliferation treaty would have to be a part of a broader set of measures to eliminate the nuclear threat and effect general disarmament.

Tsarapkin Feb. 17 said the U.S.' draft treaty attempted to leave open the possibility of giving West Germany "access to nuclear weapons . . . in the framework of a military alliance." But he admitted that the U.S. draft "blocks several channels for proliferation of nuclear weapons."

U.S. delegate Foster said Feb. 19 that "the conference has now moved forward to a stage where we might begin negotiation of such a [non-proliferation] treaty." Foster left for Washington to resume direction of the Arms Control & Disarmament Agency, and Clare H. Timberlake assumed control of the U.S. delegation, but he was replaced later by Adrian S. Fisher, the agency's deputy director.

The major development of the 3-month session was the presentation by the U.S. Mar. 22 of amendments to its Aug. 1965 draft treaty to bar the proliferation of nuclear weapons. The amended U.S. draft, Fisher said, "strikes at the heart of this threat [nuclear proliferation] by prohibiting any increase, even by one, in the number of power centers that have the right or ability to fire a nuclear weapon." The principal new element in the amendments was the "definition of control of nuclear weapons in terms of the right or ability to fire nuclear weapons." The original U.S. draft treaty would have barred the spread of nuclear weapons into the "national control of any non-nuclear state"; but it had not, Fisher said, "defined explicitly" what was meant by "control." The amended text stated: " 'Control' means right or ability to fire nuclear weapons without the concurrent decision of an existing nuclear-weapon state." Fisher cited testimony given to the Joint Congressional Committee on Atomic Energy by State Secy. Dean Rusk Feb. 23 and by Defense Secy. Robert S. McNamara Mar. 7 as evidence that the U.S. had no intention of reducing its "veto" on the use of nuclear weapons supplied to its allies. Fisher quoted McNamara as saying: "We have no plan to dilute our veto in any way, and our allies are not asking us for a dilution of that veto." Fisher asserted that the draft treaty the and Rusk-McNamara testimony demonstrated that the U.S. would not permit an allied non-nuclear-weapon state to acquire the "right or ability to fire such weapons on its own."

In another change, the amended draft substituted the terms "nuclear-weapon states" and "non-nuclear-weapon states" for "nuclear states" and "non-nuclear states," the terms used in the original U.S. draft. Fisher said the change recognized that there were "many states with important programs for peaceful uses of nuclear energy which have wisely chosen to refrain from manufacturing or acquiring nuclear weapons." "Our original draft," he said, "was therefore not accurate in defining such states as 'non-nuclear.' "

Under the amended U.S. draft treaty, "nuclear-weapon states" would pledge (1) "not to transfer nuclear weapons into the national control of any non-nuclear-weapon state, or into the control of any association of non-nuclear-weapon states" and (2) "not to provide any non-nuclear-weapon state or association of such states ... assistance in the manufacture of nuclear weapons, in preparations for such manufacture, or in the testing of nuclear weapons; or ... encouragement or inducement to manufacture or otherwise acquire its own nuclear weapons." In addition, "each of the non-nuclear-weapon states" would pledge (a) "not to manufacture nuclear weapons, and not to seek or to receive the transfer of nuclear weapons into its national control or into the control of any association of non-nuclear-weapon states of which it is a member" and (b) "not to seek or receive and not to provide, whether alone or in any association of non-nuclear-weapon states... assistance in the manufacture of nuclear weapons, in preparations for such manufacture or otherwise acquire its own nuclear weapons." Both "nuclear-weapon states" and "non-nuclear-weapon states" would pledge to take no "action which would cause an increase in the total number of states and associations of states having control of nuclear weapons." Finally, both "nuclear-weapon states" and "non-nuclear-weapon states" would pledge not to "take any... [action] prohibited" under the treaty "directly, or indirectly through 3d states or associations of states, or through units of... [their] armed forces of... military personnel, even if such units or personnel are under their command."

The amendments to the U.S. draft treaty were immediately repudiated by Tsarapkin, who told newsmen Mar. 22 that the U.S. proposal had not advanced negotiations "one inch." A "loophole" still existed that could permit nuclear weapons proliferation among NATO states, Tsarapkin declared. Aleksei A. Roshchin, who replaced Tsarapkin Mar. 24 as the USSR's chief disarmament negotiator (Tsarapkin became Soviet ambassador in Bonn), echoed this theme in a statement to the conference Mar. 29. Fisher replied Mar. 31 that the USSR's fears were "unfounded." The "real and immediate threat," Fisher said, was not proliferation of nuclear weapons among members of the Western and Communist alliances; the "great risk," rather, was that without a treaty barring such action, individual countries would decide unilaterally to make nuclear weapons.

Roshchin Apr. 5 criticized the U.S. for raising "the veto issue" in the amendments to its draft treaty. The U.S., he said, was "trying to create the impression that the association of its allies with nuclear weapons is not at all dangerous.... However, by raising the veto issue, the... [U.S.] in effect acknowledges that its draft leads to proliferation, because, had those weapons not fallen into the hands of non-nuclear powers, no question of veto would ever arise." Roshchin Apr. 28 charged that the U.S. still wanted "to leave the door open for nuclear proliferation among NATO partners," especially West Germany. Foster replied Apr. 28 that if Roshchin felt free to comment on NATO, the U.S. would request information concerning the nuclear arrangements among the USSR and its allies in the Warsaw Pact.

Among other issues discussed at the Jan. 27-May 10 meetings:

Test ban extension—Antonio Gomez Robledo, Mexican delegate, proposed Mar. 8 that a system of on-site inspection be established using scientists from non-aligned nations to verify compliance with a ban extended to underground testing. Tsarapkin rejected the proposal and called for a ban on underground testing without on-site inspection. Fisher Apr. 4 reiterated the U.S. stand that on-site inspection was required for positive identification of all underground nuclear tests. The U.S., he said, had developed a new system of on-site monitoring involving analysis of fission-produced gases that leak to the earth's surface following underground nuclear detonations.

Mrs. Alva Myrdal, speaking for Sweden, proposed Apr. 4 and 14 a system of "verification by challenge." Under the Swedish plan, a nation would be expected on demand to produce evidence that a suspicious seismic tremor on its territory had not been caused by a nuclear test. The challenged nation could invite on-site inspection if it believed inspection was the only way to dispel the suspicion that a test had occurred. Mrs. Myrdal said that the plan's ultimate deterrent against testing was the risk that other nations would abrogate the treaty in the event the "challenge" repeatedly was defied. UAR delegate Hussein Khallaf Apr. 26 suggested that the Swedish "verification-by-challenge" plan could be combined with his own nation's 1965 proposal for a ban on underground tests having a seismic magnitude above 4.75 on the Richter seismic scale. Under the UAR plan, a voluntary ban would exist for tests below 4.75. (The U.S. contended that underground tests above 4.75 on the Richter scale could be detected and distinguished from natural earth tremors by means of seismic instruments at a great distance from the test site. It held that smaller tests required on-site verification.)

Weapons & delivery systems—The USSR Mar. 8 rejected a U.S. proposal that the U.S. transfer 60,000 kilograms (132,000 pounds) and the USSR transfer 40,000 kilograms (88,000 pounds) of uranium-235 from military to peaceful uses. The U.S. plan, initially presented in 1965 at the 20th session of the UN General Assembly, had been repeated Jan. 27 when the Geneva disarmament committee reconvened. Tsarapkin Mar. 8 described the U.S. proposl as having "nothing in common with disarmament." He compared the plan to an earlier U.S. "bomber bonfire" plan (under which the U.S. and USSR each would destroy an agreed number of strategic bombers) as an attempt to pass off the destruction of outdated weapons as disarmament.

Explaining the U.S. plan, Fisher said Mar. 8 that each nation would be asked to make the transfer by destroying existing A-weapons. He said that a complete stoppage in the production of nuclear material for weapons would be necessary to prevent a replenishment of arms stockpiles. The destruction of U.S. and Soviet nuclear arms "would be demonstrated to nationals of both parties and to neutral observers" at depots on U.S. and Soviet territory. Fisher Mar. 15 asked the USSR to reconsider its rejection of Pres. Johnson's 1964 offer of a "verified freeze" on missile production. Fisher said that in the 2 years since Mr. Johnson had made the proposal, the U.S. arsenal of operational long-range missiles had grown from 750 to more than 1,300. This meant, he said, that an agreement to reduce missile stockpiles by half would only reduce the U.S. strategic missile force to the size it had been when the President initially made the offer. He said he was "sure" that the Soviet inventory of missiles had greatly increased in the previous 2 years. The U.S., Fisher said, believed that a production freeze was a "logical first step in the control of the growth of inventories of strategic nuclear vehicles." Tsarapkin Mar. 15 criticized the U.S. proposal for not setting a deadline for the destruction of all nuclear-armed weapons. Canadian delegate Burns said Mar. 17 that the Soviet Union's insistence on the destruction of all missiles in the first stage of disarmament was unrealistic; he proposed a step-by-step program.

Plant inspection—Foster announced Apr. 14 that the U.S. had developed a "safing tape" system able to detect whether a plutonium-producing reactor was being operated. The tape, in a tamper-proof tube, would register any operation of the reactor; inspectors could collect the tapes periodically to check on reactor operation. The device, Foster said, could be placed inside reactors that the U.S. and USSR had agreed to shut down. Soviet delegate Roshchin said that agreements to halt the production of fissionable material were "of no use in eliminating the menace" from existing stockpiles of nuclear weapons.

Foster Apr. 28 announced that the U.S. was opening to inspection by the International Atomic Energy Agency (IAEA) a newly built commercial nuclear-fuel reprocessing plant. The plant, owned by Nuclear Fuel Services, Inc. and located at West Valley, N.Y., was the first in the U.S. designed to recover plutonium and other nuclear materials from "spent" uranium fuel already used by a nuclear reactor. The IAEA, Foster said, had established procedures for control over electricity-producing nuclear reactors, and the U.S. already had opened to IAEA inspection a major atomic power station, the Yankee Atomic Power Station in Rowe, Mass. But IAEA, Foster explained, had yet to develop inspection procedures for nuclear-fuel reprocessing plants, and the purpose of submitting the West Valley facility to inspection was to permit IAEA to set up new inspection procedures and to give IAEA inspectors training in determing whether nuclear materials recovered at such plants were diverted to military purposes. (Dr. Glenn T. Seaborg, chairman of the U.S. Atomic Energy Commission, had announced Mar. 1 in Washington that the U.S. would offer IAEA limited access to the West Valley plant. Seaborg said the IAEA would be permitted to inspect the plant when it was reprocessing "spent" fuel from the Yankee Atomic Power Station. The U.S. Seaborg said, at first had considered placing the West Valley plant under full IAEA inspection but had decided upon limited access instead. He said that the U.S. wanted some "degree of reciprocity" from the USSR in the nuclear plant inspection field.)

General disarmament—Indian delegate Trivedi said May 3 that the committee had neglected the problem of general and complete disarmament. He proposed that when the committee reconvened in June, it devote one meeting a week to the subject of general disarmament—control of conventional as well as nuclear arms. Foster Apr. 19 had presented a formula of general principles for speeding economic and social development of non-nuclear states. The formula, an elaboration of Pres. Johnson's Jan. 27 message to the committee, which had proposed "regional" pacts to control arms races, included these principles: initiative for disarmament should come from members of various world regions; nations should pledge to abandon certain weapons by refusing to manufacture or import them; potential arms-supply nations should pledge to respect the regional agreements; the U.S. stood "ready to cooperate to the fullest" in assisting in the realization of such regional arms-control arrangements.

The Disarmament Committee adjourned its Geneva meetings May 10. At the closing session Soviet delegate Roshchin declared that the meetings had not been "fruitless." He said that they had helped to clarify each side's stand on disarmament. U.S. delegate Foster said the USSR was responsible for the committee's "impasse" on the nuclear proliferation issue. The USSR, he said, had refused to accept U.S. assurances that "any arrangements for nuclear defense in NATO will not involve the proliferation of its nuclear weapons." Foster said that the U.S. had gone to great trouble and expense to perfect electronic systems to assure that U.S. nuclear weapons supplied to allied nations could be fired only if the U.S. "decided that they are to be fired."

Before it recessed, the Disarmament Committee set June 14 as the date for the resumption of negotiations.

2d Conference Period

The UN Disarmament Committee met in Geneva, again June 14–Aug. 25 and then agreed to reconvene in Jan. 1967 after the 21st UN General Assembly session, which opened Sept. 20. Major issues discussed during the 2d conference period included the possibility of (1) extending the 1963 Moscow test ban treaty to include underground nuclear testing and (2) drafting a treaty against the proliferation of nuclear weapons to non-nuclear nations. Other issues included peaceful uses of atomic energy, atomic plant inspection, the imposition of a freeze on the production of nuclear weapons and general disarmament. No formal agreement was reached on any issue as the U.S. and USSR continued to maintain their previously-stated positions.

In closing speeches Aug. 25, delegates expressed guarded optimism about future success in the talks. Adrian S. Fisher, deputy director of the Arms Control & Disarmament Agency and chief U.S. delegate said

that more progress had been made than at any time since 1963 and that
he felt "we are getting very close to success." Fisher declared that "some
mutual adjustment" was necessary between the U.S. and USSR on a
non-proliferation treaty. Aleksei A. Roshchin, chief Soviet delegate,
referred to the talks as "fruitless" and "a waste of time," but he said "a
number of interesting and useful considerations, ideas and suggestions
have been introduced." Lord Chalfont, the British delegate, said the
talks had been successful to the extent that they had "refined ideas and
clarified issues that a year or so ago were still crued and often confused."

Among issues taken up at the June 14-Aug. 25 meetings:

Test-ban extension—William C. Foster, director of the U.S. Arms Control & Disarmament Agency, said June 14 that "hard evidence still points to the need for on-site inspection
to verify a comprehensive test ban." Roshchin asserted that the U.S. was advancing
"groundless demands" for on-site inspection in order to prevent an accord and thereby "have
a free hand for carrying on dangerous experiments with nuclear weapons."

Mrs. Alva Myrdal, the Swedish delegate, proposed Aug. 4 that the U.S. and USSR
agree in principle on how to verify the observance of an underground test ban so that the
committee in early 1967 could begin negotiating the details of a formal treaty outlawing
underground testing.

G. O. Ijewere of Nigeria Aug. 18 presented a memo, signed by the 8 non-aligned nations
at the conference, urging an immediate cessation of all nuclear testing without awaiting the
conclusion of a formal treaty banning underground testing.

Non-proliferation—In his opening statement June 14, Foster urged delegates not to
confuse the discussions on a non-proliferation treaty by an "obsession with any one country."
In reply, Roshchin asserted that the U.S. wanted to draft the treaty so as to extend to West
Germany the possibility of obtaining control over nuclear weapons. (Pres. Johnson had said
at a news conference in Johnson City, Tex. July 5: "We are doing everything we can to
reach an agreement on [a non-proliferation treaty]. . . . We hope the Soviet Union will
meet us and find an acceptable compromise in language which we can both live with."
Roshchin said July 13 that he was "very much disappointed" with Johnson's statement
in that it had disclosed no intention to introduce a "new basis of negotiation.")

Fisher July 26 proposed building a "bridge of agreement" by discussing issues that
"would be susceptible to useful and productive negotiation right now." But Roshchin rejected
the proposal on the ground that it would give only an "illusion of progress," whereas "what
is required are not appeals but concrete actions by the United States." Mieczyslaw Blusztajn,
the Polish delegate, said that what he defined as the U.S. position—"dissemination with safeguards equals non-proliferation"—was unacceptable to the Communist countries.

Fisher July 28 proposed an international monitoring arrangement under which all
nations would refrain from transferring nuclear materials or equipment to another nation
except under the safeguards of the International Atomic Energy Agency (IAEA) or
equivalent international controls. The aim of such an arrangement would be to assure that
peaceful nuclear activities were not being diverted to military ends.

Fisher said Aug. 9 that the non-proliferation treaty should cover nuclear explosives for
peaceful projects, *e.g.*, excavation. In this connection, he proposed that the nuclear powers
conduct any atomic blasting for peaceful purposes desired by non-nuclear states. The detonations would be conducted "under appropriate international observation, with the nuclear device remaining under the custody and control of the state which performs the service." Lt.
Gen. E. L. M. Burns, the Canadian delegate, indorsed the U.S. proposal Aug. 25 and announced that Canada would not develop atomic explosive devices for peaceful purposes.

Plant inspection—Britain June 20 and July 21 renewed its offer to open its A-power
station at Bradwell, Essex to inspection by the IAEA.

Fisher announced Aug. 11 that the U.S. was willing to demonstrate to representatives
of other nations the "safing tape" system designed to detect whether a plutonium-producing
reactor was being operated. Fisher said the demonstration, to be held at the idle Hanford nu-

clear reactor plant near Richland, Wash., would prove that the verification system "cannot be reasonably labeled espionage by anyone."

Weapons & delivery systems—Fisher called on the Soviet Union Aug. 2 to agree to a freeze on missile and strategic bomber production in order to "open all possible paths to reductions in all types of armaments." He included a call Aug. 17 for a freeze on the production of anti-ballistic-missile defense systems. Roshchin Aug. 17 called the U.S. proposals "fruitless" efforts and accused the U.S. of wasting time on "debates without a chance of success."

Nuclear guarantee—Roshchin announced June 23 that the Soviet Union's pledge not to use nuclear weapons against non-nuclear nations would be inapplicable unless the nations agreed to bar nuclear weapons from "their territory, territorial waters or air." Soviet Premier Aleksei N. Kosygin had made the pledge in February but had stipulated only that the states must bar nuclear weapons from their territory.

Progress Toward A-Arms Limitation

U.S. & Soviet Initiatives on Non-Proliferation

A resolution to express support for the Johnson Administration's efforts to achieve a non-proliferation treaty was introduced in the U.S. Senate Jan. 18 by Sen. John O. Pastore (D., R.I.) and 52 co-sponsors. It was passed by 84-0 vote May 17. In introducing the resolution, Pastore urged that any such treaty include a requirement for international inspection of nuclear facilities, including private plants. He also urged the inclusion of Communist China in disarmament talks. He suggested the possibility that the U.S. and Soviet Union might give non-nuclear states guarantees against "nuclear intimidation." He said special assistance in civilian nuclear technology could be given nations renouncing A-weapons development. Prior to the May 17 vote, the Administration was criticized for rejecting "out of hand" Communist China's 1965 proposal that both nations pledge that they would not be first to use nuclear weapons against each other. The criticism was made by Sens. Pastore, Robert F. Kennedy (D., N.Y.) and Joseph S. Clark (D., Pa.). The Administration action was defended by Sen. Jacob K. Javits (R., N.Y.), who suggested, however, that the U.S. should have "exploited" the Chinese offer by trying for more general arms talks.

Pres. Johnson submitted the 5th annual report of the U.S. Arms Control & Disarmament Agency to Congress Feb. 15. In a letter accompanying the report, Mr. Johnson warned that unless a non-proliferation treaty were negotiated soon, nuclear weapons would be "standard equipment in the world's arsenals." He said his Administration was committed "to the task of persuading the non-nuclear countries that it is neither in the interests of their security, nor of world peace, to develop nuclear weapons."

Following a meeting with Pres. Johnson Oct. 10, Soviet Foreign Min. Andrei A. Gromyko conferred at the State Department with State Secy. Dean Rusk. Gromyko reportedly said afterwards that disarmament had been discussed, and "it looks like both countries are striving to reach agreement and facilitate conclusion of an international agreement."

In a speech before a Polish government and party delegation visiting Moscow Oct. 15, Soviet CP Gen. Secy. Leonid Brezhnev "welcome[d] certain headway which has lately taken place" in the effort to negotiate a treaty to ban the proliferation of nuclear weapons. He pledged that the USSR "will try hard" to conclude such a tready.

(Gromyko and Canadian External Affairs Min. Paul Martin Nov. 13 issued a joint appeal for the early conclusion of a non-proliferation treaty. The appeal was made in a communique on a 5-day visit by Martin to the Soviet Union.)

UN Resolutions

The UN General Assembly Nov. 17 concluded its discussion on the non-proliferation of nuclear weapons for its current (21st) session by adopting 2 resolutions that had been approved Nov. 10 by the First (Political & Security) Committee. A 3d resolution had been approved by the First Committee Nov. 2 and adopted by the Assembly Nov. 4. The discussion took place amidst indications that the USSR was softening its opposition to Western positions on a non-proliferation agreement.

The Nov. 4 resolution, adopted by 110-1 (Albania) vote with Cuba abstaining, appealed "urgently" to all states, pending the conclusion of a non-proliferation treaty, to (a) "take all necessary steps to facilitate and achieve at the earliest possible time the conclusion of a treaty on the non-proliferation of nuclear weapons in accordance with the principles laid down in [the Assembly's Nov. 19, 1965] resolution" and (b) "refrain from any actions conducive to the proliferation of nuclear weapons or which might hamper the conclusion of an agreement on the non-proliferation of nuclear weapons." The resolution had been presented Oct. 20 in the First Committee by the Soviet Union; the U.S., Britain and 8 other nations were co-sponsors. It was approved in the committee Nov. 2 by 100-1 (Albania) vote with Cuba abstaining. (France was among those voting for the resolution.) In opening debate on the resolution Oct. 20, Soviet delegate Nikolai T. Federenko declared that there were "no insurmountable difficulties" in the way of concluding a treaty "in the near future." He said the USSR discerned and welcomed "some change for the better" in U.S. policy statements, and he expressed hope that this change "would be supported by concrete practical deeds." U.S. delegate Arthur J. Goldberg referred to the "new and promising situation" that had developed since Soviet Foreign Min. Andrei A. Gromyko's meeting with Pres. Johnson and State Secy. Dean Rusk Oct.

10. But he cautioned that discussions were still in an exploratory stage and that "important differences remain" between the U.S. and Soviet Union.

British Disarmament Min. Lord Chalfont said in committee Oct. 25: "After listening to the 2 statements [by the Soviet Union and U.S.]..., I believe we have reason to hope...that we can take in this Assembly the first real, positive steps twoards a disarmament agreement." Ismail Fahmy of the United Arab Republic said Oct. 25: The purpose of the treaty should not be to "freeze the option" of the non-nuclear states while permitting the nuclear powers to continue to increase their nuclear stockpiles; rather, the treaty should be considered a part of the over-all goal of general and complete disarmament; it also should state explicity that the nuclear powers renounced the use of nuclear weapons against non-nuclear states.

Indian delegate Vishnu C. Trivedi said Oct. 31 that the proposed treaty should not only prohibit the transfer of nuclear weapons to non-nuclear states but should ban the further production of nuclear arms by countries already possessing them. Citing the recent test of a nuclear-tipped missile by Communist China, Trivedi said that it was in the effort to perfect nuclear weapons that "proliferation...has its most catastrophic consequences." He suggested that the manufacture of nuclear weapons be placed under some form of international control similar to that exercised by the IAEA over some nuclear reactors. Trivedi rejected a U.S. proposal that would empower the nuclear powers to conduct any atomic blasting for peaceful purposes desired by non-nuclear states. He said such a plan would deny to the developing countries the benefits of technology currently enjoyed by a few. (Communist China declared Nov. 15 that it would never sign a non-proliferation treaty and that it would continue to develop its own nuclear weapons. The statement appeared in an article in *Jenmin Jih Pao,* the Chinese Communist Party daily. The paper said: The proposed non-proliferation treaty was a "monstrous fraud" "cooked up" by "the 2 nuclear overlords, the United States and the Soviet Union," so that they could maintain their nuclear monopoly and deny to others the right of defense; the treaty was "absolutely unjust and unfair to other countries of the world"; the total prohibition of nuclear weapons, which China advocated, would be possible "only when more or all countries possess them" and when the U.S.' "nuclear monopoly" had been broken completely.)

The 2d resolution, adopted by the Assembly Nov. 17 (a) asked the UN Disarmament Committee "to consider urgently the proposal that the nuclear powers...will not use, or threaten to use, nuclear weapons against non-nuclear states without nuclear weapons on their territories" and (b) called on the committee "to give high priority to the question of the non-proliferation of nuclear weapons." The resolution was adopted by 97-2 (Albania, Central African Republic) vote with 3 abstentions (the Congo [Kinshasa], France, Iceland). It had been approved by the First

Committee Nov. 10 by 103-1 (Albania) vote with 2 abstentions (Cuba, France).

The 3d resolution, adopted by the Assembly Nov. 17 called for the convening not later than July 1968 of a conference of non-nuclear states to consider such matters as security from nuclear threat, cooperation to prevent the proliferation of nuclear weapons and the development of nuclear energy for peaceful purposes. It was adopted by 48-1 (India) vote with 59 abstentions. It had been approved by the First Committee Nov. 10 by 46-1 (India) vote with 56 abstentions. Pakistan had submitted the resolution Oct. 31.

The Assembly Dec. 5 adopted 5 resolutions on disarmament and nuclear-test suspension. 3 of the resolutions, dealing with general and complete disarmament, had been adopted by the First Committee Nov. 23: (1) The first, adopted unanimously, requested that the Secretary General submit, before the 1967 Assembly session, a study on the effects of the possible use of nuclear weapons and on the security and economic implications for states acquiring and developing such weapons. (2) The 2d resolution, passed by 91-0 vote (4 abstentions), declared that mass-destruction weapons endangered mankind and were incompatible with the norms of civilization. It called on all states to observe the 1925 Geneva Protocol on the "Prohibition of the Use of Asphyxiating, Poisonous & Other Gases & Bacteriological Methods of Warfare." (3) The 3d resolution asked the Geneva Disarmament Committee to exert greater effort in drafting international treaties to prevent (a) the proliferation of nuclear weapons and (b) underground nuclear tests. The resolution was passed by 98-0 vote (France and Cuba abstaining). The 4th resolution, passed by 100-1 vote (Albania) with Cuba and France abstaining, called all states possessing nuclear weapons "to suspend nuclear weapon tests in all environments." It expressed "great concern" over the fact that all states had not abided by the 1963 limited nuclear test ban treaty. (The resolution had been adopted by the First Committee Nov. 24.) The 5th resolution, passed by 80-0 vote (23 abstentions), had been approved by the First Committee Nov. 28. It proposed that a potential world disarmament conference give serious consideration to establishing a convention on the prohibition of the use of nuclear and thermonuclear weapons.

It stated that such a convention "would greatly facilitate negotiations on general and complete disarmament under effective international control."

Space-Weapon Ban Drafted

In December, the UN General Assembly indorsed a draft treaty barring mass destruction weapons from space. The draft was the product of efforts by both the U.S. and USSR. Pres. Johnson had announced May 7 that the U.S. would propose through the UN a treaty barring any nation from asserting sovereignty over the moon or other celestial bodies. Among the "essential elements" of the proposed treaty was the demand that "no country should be permitted to station weapons of mass destruction on a celestial body. Weapons tests and military maneuvers should be forbidden."

The Legal Subcommittee of the 28-member UN Committee on the Peaceful Uses of Outer Space met in Geneva July 12-Aug. 4 and at UN headquarters in New York Sept. 12-16 to consider draft treaties on space exploration proposed by the U.S. and the Soviet Union. The Soviet draft, circulated to all UN delegations June 16, called for (1) a prohibition on national claims for "sovereignty" over celestial bodies or space, (2) a ban on placing military weapons on celestial bodies and against weapons testing in space and (3) a ban on "orbit[ing] around the earth any vehicles with nuclear weapons or other mass destruction weapons on board." Soviet Foreign Min. Andrei A. Gromyko had requested in a letter to UN Secy. Gen. U Thant May 30 that the problem of space exploration be included in the agenda of the 21st session of the General Assembly.

U.S. Amb.-to-UN Arthur J. Goldberg spoke in the UN General Assembly Sept. 22 about the proposed space treaty. He said: "Major progress had been made in the negotiation of this treaty, but several issues remain." "The outer space treaty is too important and too urgent to be delayed. This treaty offers us the opportunity to establish, in the unlimited realm of space beyond this planet, a rule of peace and law—before the arms race has been extended into that realm."

Soviet Amb.-to-UN Nikolai T. Fedorenko said Oct. 5: "I think we are getting closer and closer [to an agreement]."

The final text of the treaty, to ban mass destruction weapons in space, was drafted primarily in negotiations between the U.S. and the USSR, with the assistance of the UN Committee on the Peaceful Uses of Outer Space. The space treaty was agreed on by U.S. and Soviet officials at the UN Dec. 8 and approved unanimously by the Assembly's First Committee Dec. 9. In announcing the agreement from Austin, Tex., Pres. Johnson Dec. 8 termed it "the most important arms control development since the limited test ban treaty of 1963." Mr. Johnson said that he planned to present the treaty to the U.S. Senate at the next session of Congress and hoped that the U.S. would "be one of the first countries to ratify it."

The draft treaty was unanimously indorsed by the UN General Assembly Dec. 19, one day before its 21st session adjourned. The resolution asked the treaty's depository countries (Britain, the U.S. and the USSR) to open it for "ratification at the earliest possible date."

Major provisions of the "Treaty on Principles Governing the Activities of States in the Exploration & Use of Outer Space, including the Moon & Other Celestial Bodies":

● "Outer space...shall be free for exploration and use by all states without discrimination of any kind,...and there shall be free access to all areas of celestial bodies."

● Celestial bodies shall not be "subject to national appropriation" by claim, occupation or any other means.

● No state "may place in orbit around the earth any objects carrying nuclear weapons or any other kinds of weapons of mass destruction" or install such weapons on any celestial body. Military bases, weapons testing and military maneuvers shall be forbidden on celestial bodies.

● All parties to the treaty shall assist each other's astronauts "in the event of accident, distress or emergency landing" and shall promptly return the astronauts to their countries or origin.

● States launching space vehicles, whether from the earth or from celestial bodies, are liable for damages caused by their vehicles.

● States shall consider requests "on the basis of equality" made by other states "to observe the flight of space objects" they launch.

● "All stations, installations, equipment and space vehicles on the moon and other celestial bodies shall be open to representatives of other states, parties to the treaty on a basis of reciprocity. Such representatives shall give reasonable advance notice of a projected visit."

● The treaty shall enter into force on the ratification of 5 governments, including Britain, the U.S. and the USSR.

UN Secy. Gen. U Thant congratulated the Assembly after the resolution had been adopted. He added, however: "I note with regret that the door is not yet barred against military activities in space."

OTHER DEVELOPMENTS

H-Bomb Lost Off Spain

An atomic device was lost Jan. 17 from a U.S. Air Force B-52 that crashed near Palomares, Spain following a collision with a KC-135 jet tanker while refueling. The crash, approximately 230 miles southeast of Madrid on Spain's Mediterranean coast, killed 7 men, including the entire KC-135 crew; 4 men from the B-52 parachuted to safety. An intensive search for the nuclear device, later reported to be a 20-kiloton termonuclear (hydrogen) bomb, was begun by the U.S. Air Force and Spanish officials, but it was not recovered until Apr. 7.

A U.S. 16th Air Force spokesman had admitted Jan. 20 in Almeria, Spain that the B-52 had carried "unarmed nuclear armament" on its training flight from its home base, Seymour Johnson Air Force Base, N.C. (The KC-135 had been based near Austin, Tex. at Bergstom Air

Force Base.) The spokesman said built-in safety mechanisms had prevented an atomic blast; but he declined to tell whether all "nuclear armament" aboard the B-52 had been located. Spanish sources asserted the same day that 3 of the B-52's 4 bombs had been found and that a search for the 4th was in process. The AP reported Jan. 21 that 1,000 Spanish and U.S. military personnel, some equipped with Geiger counters, were combing the crash area near the coastal towns of Garrucha, Cuevas de Almanzora and Vera. It was reported Jan. 23 that the search had narrowed to an area 500 yards offshore midway between Garrucha and the village of Aguilas and that the U.S. 6th Fleet had dispatched 2 minesweepers to the vicinity. The UPI reported Jan. 25 that the 6th Fleet had sent a destroyer leader and a repair ship there. The *N.Y. Herald Tribune* said Jan. 27 that a bathysphere was at the search site.

The AP had reported Jan. 21 that doctors assigned to the crash area by the Spanish Nuclear Energy Board had said they had discovered "slight traces" of radioactive "contamination" on Spanish civil guardsmen who had been with the search party. But a U.S. Defense Department spokesman in Washington said Jan. 21 that Defense Secy. Robert S. McNamara had received word through the 16th Air Force that the Spanish Nuclear Energy Board had found no radioactivity among Spaniards searching the area. Reuters reported Jan. 21 that U.S. Air Force nuclear experts in Cuevas de Alamzora had temporarily declared thousands of dollars worth of vegetables untouchable; according to the report, one Spanish family had been quarantined at home.

The U.S. acknowledged officially Mar. 2 that the crash had resulted in the loss of an H-bomb. In statements released by the State and Defense Departments and the Atomic Energy Commission, it was explained that one bomb had been recovered intact, that 2 bombs had broken open on impact with the ground, scattering "some plutonium and uranium," and that search for the 4th bomb was still in process. A Defense Department spokesman explained that the radioactive material from 2 bombs had been scattered when "some" of the TNT detonators inside the bombs had exploded on impact with the ground and had ruptured the bombs' casings. He insisted that there was no possibility of an accidental nuclear explosion because a termonuclear reaction could be precipitated only if all the TNT segments detonated with precise timing, thereby squeezing the plutonium into a critical mass.

The plutonium and uranium from the 2 bombs had been spread over 2 areas (each several hundred feet in diameter) near Palomares. One of the spots had no vegetation, the other was planted with alfalfa and tomatoes. The AEC statement said: "Approximately 1,500 cubic yards of earth and vegetation were collected in southeastern Spain to preclude any possibility, however remote, of public health or safety hazard....The material will be shipped to the AEC's Savannah River Plant, near Aiken, S.C., where it will be buried in the same manner as other low-level radioactive waste material is routinely disposed of....

The levels of radioactivity are being carefully monitored to be sure they are well within the standard limits for such shipments."

The State Department statement Mar. 2 said: "Some plutonium and uranium" had been scattered and the removal was being carried out "to eliminate the chance of hazard, to set at rest unfounded fears and thus to restore normal life and livelihood to the people of Palomares." Radiological tests conducted in the area "throughout the 44 days since the accident" indicated "no evidence of a health hazard."

Dr. Jose Maria Otero Navascues, president of the Spanish Nuclear Energy Board, said in Madrid Mar. 2 that 1,800 of the 2,000 people potentially affected by radioactive contamination had been examined and the results were "practically negative." He said there was no risk in eating fish, meat or vegetables from the area since vegetation and earth "contaminated by the accident" had been removed. (The completion of the clean-up operation in the Palomares area—with more than 1,000 tons of topsoil and vegetation removed for disposal in the U.S.—was reported Mar. 24.)

The U.S. replied Feb. 26 to a Soviet protest that the crash of the B-52 loaded with nuclear weapons constituted a violation of the 1963 limited test ban treaty. Soviet Foreign Min. Andrei A. Gromyko Feb. 16 had given U.S. Amb.-to-USSR Foy D. Kohler a note demanding that the U.S. "discontinue flights by aircraft carrying atomic and nuclear bombs beyond national borders." In a diplomatic note delivered in Moscow Feb. 26, the U.S. said: "The government of the USSR must be aware—or could easily have ascertained— that no nuclear explosion of any kind" occurred. The Mediterranean Sea in the area was not contiminated by radioactivity. U.S. flights were made "for the express purpose of reinforcing...[the free world's] collective security against the threat posed by the huge nuclear forces of the Soviet Union."

The U.S. embassy in Madrid announced Apr. 7 that the missing bomb had been brought to the surface after an intensive search under the direction of U.S. Naval Task Force 65, which included 16 ships. The bomb was displayed to newsmen on the recovery ship Apr. 8; it was the first time the U.S. had displayed a nuclear weapon publicly.

Newsmen and officials aboard the *U.S.S. Albany,* flagship of the task force, viewed the 10-foot long silvery-colored bomb Apr. 8 from a distance of about 35 yards. The bomb was displayed from the fantail of the submarine rescue ship *U.S.S. Petrel.* Rear Adm. William S. Guest, commander of the task force, said that the bomb had been raised Apr. 7 in a 4-hour operation.

2 attempts to raise the bomb had failed Mar. 24 and 25 when cables attached to it by the research submersible vessel *Alvin* snapped. Then, it was reported, contact with the bomb had been lost by the search vessels Mar. 26. The *Alvin* relocated the bomb Apr. 2 at a depth of 2,310 feet. It was buried in mud, with only its parachute exposed. It was brought to the surface by a torpedo recovery device, the CURV (cable-controlled

un-manned recovery vehicle), an electronically controlled retrieving apparatus equipped with sonar and claws. Throughout the recovery operation, it was reported, U.S. officials feared that the "object," which was resting on a steep 70° slope, might slide into a narrow trench 4 feet wide and 10 feet deep—too narrow for *Alvin* to enter.

Bonn 'Peace Note'

In a major diplomatic initiative, the West German government Mar. 25 transmitted to 115 nations and to UN Secy. Gen. U Thant a note containing a 6-point series of disarmament proposals. These proposals were specifically addressed to the U.S. government "in its capacity as a member of the Geneva 18-Nation Disarmament Committee." 6 governments did not receive the note: Communist China, Nationalist China, North Korea, North Vietnam, Albania and Cuba. The note said:

West Germany "renounced the production of...nuclear weapons [in 1954 in the Paris agreement] and...subjected itself to international control by the Western European Union." "Within the framework of...[NATO] it advocates...that all parties to it [the alliance] should have a share in the responsibility for nuclear defense. It does not, however, as it has repeatedly declared, seek national possession of nuclear weapons."

The 6 points of the disarmament proposal:

(1) West Germany, having renounced nuclear arms production in 1954, "appeals to all non-nuclear states who are members of military alliances in East or West to express the same renunciation and submit to a similar international control. This should be followed by further steps concerning the non-aligned states." In addition, "the Federal [West German] government suggests that the nuclear powers come to an agreement not to transfer any nuclear weapons to the national control of other countries."

(2) West Germany "is prepared to consent to any agreement...[under which countries] pledge themselves not to increase the number of nuclear weapons in Europe but to reduce them in stages. Such an agreement...would have to extend to the whole of Europe, preserve the overall balance of power, provide for effective control and be linked with essential progress in the solution of political problems in Central Europe."

(3) West Germany, having already accepted international controls for the "fissionable material" it receives, "is prepared...to demand similar controls by the [UN] International Atomic Energy Agency" in supplying fissionable material to countries "outside the Euratom area." "Its attitude is based on the assumption that other supplying countries impose the same condition."

(4) "The Federal government proposes that formal declarations be exchanged...with the governments of the Soviet Union, Poland, Czechoslovakia and any other East European state, in which either side gives an undertaking to the other people not to use force to settle international disputes."

(5) "To dispel the mistrust with regard to alleged German aggressive intentions, the Federal government also proposes bilaterial agreements with the Soviet, Polish, Czechoslovak, Hungarian, Rumanian and Bulgarian governments concerning the exchange of military observers to attend maneuvers of armed forces."

(6) "The Federal government is prepared to participate and to cooperate in a constructive spirit in a world disarmament conference, or in any disarmament conference, promising success."

Other Initiatives

About 60 disarmament officials and specialists from 25 countries attended the International Assembly on Nuclear Weapons (a private disarmament conference) in Toronto, Canada June 23-26. In a report June 26, they called for an "experimental suspension" for "a limited trial period" of underground nuclear testing in order to determine whether a system of "verification by challenge or invitation" could work in enforcing a ban on underground testing. Among those attending the conference were Adrian S. Fisher, Chief U.S. delegate at the Geneva disarmament talks, his British counterpart, Lord Chalfont, and Prof. Vasily S. Yemelyanov, chairman of the Soviet Academy of Sciences' Commission on Scientific Problems of Disarmament. The conference was sponsored by the Canadian Institute of International Affairs, the Institute for Strategic Studies of London, the Carnegie Endowment for International Peace and the American Assembly (Columbia University).

The leftist 12th World Conference Against Atomic & Hydrogen Bombs convened in Tokyo July 30. 46 delegates from 20 countries and 4 international organizations attended the conference, which was sponsored by the Japanese Socialist Party and the General Confederation of Japanese Trade Unions (Sohyo). In a message read to the conference July 30, Communist Chinese Premier Chou En-lai referred to proposals for a nuclear non-proliferation treaty as "the U.S.-Soviet scheme to deprive peace-loving countries of the right to develop nuclear weapons." A conference declaration Aug. 7 scored U.S. action in Vietnam as "posing the danger of nuclear conflagration."

Representatives of 5 Latin American nations met in Bogota, Colombia Aug. 14-16 for discussions considered preparatory to the proposed meeting of Western Hemisphere presidents. A "Declaration of Bogota," signed at the conclusion of the talks Aug. 16, called for world disarmament, particularly with respect to nuclear weapons, and the channeling of military expenditures into the economic development of poor countries.

The 16th Pugwash Conference met in Sopot, Poland Sept. 11-16 with 80 scientists from 22 countries attending. Issues discussed included disarmament and nuclear testing.

1966's NUCLEAR TESTS

U.S. Explosions

All U.S. nuclear tests conducted during 1966 were underground. The dates, force and sites of the tests:

Date	Force	Site
Jan. 13	Low yield	Nevada test site
Jan. 18	Low-intermediate	Nevada test site
Jan. 21	Low yield	Nevada test site
Feb. 3	Low yield	Nevada test site
Feb. 24	Low yield	Nevada test site
Mar. 5	Low yield	Nevada test site
Mar. 7	Low yield	Nevada test site
Mar. 12	Low yield	Nevada test site
Mar. 18	Low-intermediate	Nevada test site
Mar. 24*	Low yield	Nevada test site
Apr. 1	Low yield	Nevada test site
Apr. 6	Low yield	Nevada test site
Apr. 7	Low yield	Nevada test site
Apr. 14	Low-intermediate	Nevada test site
Apr. 25	Low yield	Nevada test site
May 4	Low yield	Nevada test site
May 5	Low yield	Nevada test site
May 6	Low-intermediate	Nevada test site
May 12	Low yield	Nevada test site
May 13	Low-intermediate	Nevada test site
May 19	Low-intermediate	Nevada test site
May 27	Low yield	Nevada test site
June 2	Low-intermediate	Nevada test site
June 3	Low-intermediate	Nevada test site
June 10	Low yield	Nevada test site
June 25*	Low yield	Nevada test site
June 30	Intermediate	Nevada test site
July 28*	Low yield	Nevada test site
Aug. 10	Low yield	Nevada test site
Sept. 12	Low yield	Nevada test site
Sept. 23	Low-intermediate	Nevada test site
Sept. 29	Low yield	Nevada test site
Nov. 7*	Low yield	Nevada test site
Nov. 14	Low yield	Nevada test site
Nov. 18	Low yield	Nevada test site
Dec. 5**	700 Kiloton	Hattiesburg, Miss.
Dec. 13	Low yield	Nevada test site
Dec. 20§	Intermediate	Nevada test site

Soviet Explosions

Feb. 13***	Low-intermediate	Semipalatinsk
Mar. 20***	Low-intermediate	Semipalatinsk
Apr. 20***	Low yield	Semipalatinsk
Aug. 5***	Medium force	Semipalatinsk

* Test was part of Project Plowshare Program to develop peaceful uses of atomic explosives (other tests were presumably weapons related).
** Test conducted in spherical 110-foot cavity formed by 5-kiloton Project Salmon nuclear explosion in Oct. 1964. Test's purpose was to determine the extent to which a large cavity could decouple (reduce) seismic force of underground explosion.
*** Underground test.
§ Purpose of test was to further development of warhead for anti-missile missile.

Date	Force	Site
Sept. 30***		
Oct. 19***	Low-intermediate	
Oct. 27***	"Intermediate to high"	Novaya Zemlya
Dec. 18***	Low-intermediate	Semipalatinsk
Dec. 19***		Semipalatinsk

French Explosions

Date	Force	Site
July 2★●	"Tactical range"	Muruora Atoll
July 19★●	60 kiloton	Muruora Atoll
Sept. 11★●	100 kiloton	Muruora Atoll
Sept. 24★		Fangatanfa Atoll
Oct. 4★	100 kiloton	Muruora Atoll

Chinese Explosions

Date	Force	Site
May 9★‡	Intermediate	Lob Nor
Oct. 27★¶		Lob Nor
Dec. 28★†		Lob Nor

● "Plutonium fission devices"

‡ According to Hsinhua, Chinese Communist news agency, the explosion "contained thermonuclear material." Test's size taken to indicate that it combined fission and fusion reactions.

¶ Guided missile delivered weapons. The U.S. estimated that the missile was fired 400 miles to its target.

† Test thought to be of a triple-stage fission-fusion-fission device. The device tested "involved thermonuclear material" and utilized normally non-fissionable uranium-238.

★ Atmospheric test.

1967

The treaty banning weapons of mass destruction from outer space became effective Oct. 10. The Geneva Disarmament Committee met Feb. 21-Mar. 23 and May 18-Dec. 14. Its most important accomplishment was a draft treaty on the nonproliferation of nuclear weapons, presented Aug. 24 by the U.S. and USSR. The draft was criticized by Communist China and France as designed to preserve the nuclear monopoly of the superpowers and to give them undue political leverage in dealing with other countries. West Germany raised objections to the draft because of restrictions it allegedly placed on the peaceful development of nuclear energy by non-nuclear countries. Red China exploded its first hydrogen bomb June 17. The armament race threatened to take a new dangerous turn as both the USSR and the U.S.—in an apparent shift from an offensive to a defensive nuclear strategy—began considering the use of anti-ballistic missiles.

NON-PROLIFERATION

Geneva Talks Resume

In a new effort to work out a treaty to prevent the proliferation of atomic weapons, the UN 18-Nation Disarmament Committee (ENDC) reconvened in Genva Feb. 21. It had been in recess since Aug. 25, 1966. Highlighting the opening session were messages from Pres. Johnson, British Prime Min. Harold Wilson and UN Secy. Gen. U Thant. In his message, Wilson declared that "we have now reached the point at which, given the political will, a treaty to prevent the spread of nuclear weapons can be negotiated soon." Wilson urged that work in this area be joined with efforts to ban underground nuclear tests and to achieve general disarmament. U Thant's message also urged efforts in all 3 areas.

Mr. Johnson's message was read to the committee by William C. Foster, director of the U.S. Arms Control & Disarmament Agency and co-chairman (with the Soviet delegate) of the conference. The message was intended to assure the non-nuclear nations that a non-proliferation treaty would not hinder the development of peaceful uses of atomic energy. The President's message said:

"A non-proliferation treaty must be equitable as between the nuclear and the non-nuclear-weapon powers.... Such a treaty will help free the non-nuclear nations from the agonizing decision of whether to pursue a search for security through nuclear arms. Freed from the fear that non-nuclear neighbors may develop such weapons, nations can devote their efforts in the field of atomic energy to developing strong, peaceful programs.

"I have instructed our negotiators to exercise the greatest care that the treaty not hinder the non-nuclear powers in their development of nuclear energy for peaceful purposes. We believe in sharing the benefits of scientific progress.... We have shared—and will continue to share—the knowledge we have gained about nuclear energy....

"...A non-proliferation treaty should not contain any provisions that would defeat its major purpose. The treaty must, therefore, cover nuclear explosive devices for peaceful as well as military purposes. The technology is the same. A peaceful nuclear explosive device would, in effect, also be a highly sophisticated weapon. However, this will not impose any technological penalty on the participating nations. The U.S. is prepared to make available nuclear explosive services for peaceful purposes on a nondiscriminatory basis under appropriate international safeguards. We are prepared to join other nuclear states in a commitment to do this.

"More generally, we recommend that the treaty clearly state the intention of its signatories to make available the full benefits of peaceful nuclear technology—including any benefits that are the by-product of weapons research."

Mr. Johnson's message called for "a broad international system of safeguards satisfactory to all concerned" and for "further cooperative steps to reduce nuclear armaments." (Pres. Johnson had submitted the 6th annual report of the Arms Control & Disarmament Agency to Congress Feb. 17. In a letter accompanying the report Mr. Johnson expressed hope that the "long effort" to prevent the proliferation of nuclear weapons "will soon be crowned with success." At the same time, however, Mr. Johnson warned that the buildup of Soviet strategic forces and the deployment of an anti-ballistic missile defense system around Moscow indicated that "our hard-won accomplishments can be swept away overnight by still another costly and futile escalation of the arms race." The paradox of such a situation, the President said, was that "this should be happening at a time when there is abundant evidence that our mutual antagonism is beginning to ease."

Aleksei A. Roshchin, the chief Soviet delegate to the ENDC, said during the opening session that "at present in some countries, particularly in the German Federal Republic, statements are made . . . against the conclusion of a treaty on non-proliferation of nuclear weapons. . . . Allegations are being spread to the effect that a non-proliferation treaty would hinder peaceful use of scientific discoveries in the sphere of nuclear energy by the states not possessing nuclear weapons." Such statements, Roshchin asserted, "do not help at all." He also charged that "the aggressive war unleashed by the U.S. in Vietnam" was complicating the conclusion of a non-proliferation treaty.

There had been speculation that the U.S. and the Soviet Union would present at the committee's opening session those parts of the secret draft treaty on which they were said to have reached an "understanding" since the ENDC recessed in 1966. But it was reported from Geneva Feb. 20 that the Soviet Union had raised last-minute objections to announcing any part of the treaty in advance of an agreement on its full text.

The committee held almost daily sessions on the subject of non-proliferation except for the period Mar. 23—May 18, when it was in recess.

Much of the debate centered on the 3 basic positions taken by the ENDC members with respect to the inspection issue: (1) The Soviet Union held to its position that the non-nuclear members of the European Atomic Energy Community (Euratom)—West Germany, Italy, Belgium, the Netherlands and Luxembourg—must be subject to inspection by the International Atomic Energy Agency (IAEA) rather than by Euratom inspectors. (2) The Euratom countries, particularly West Germany and Italy, maintained their reservations about IAEA inspection since they believed that such inspection would be tantamount to legalized espionage by Communist countries that were members of the agency; they held that internal inspection by Euratom was sufficient. (3) The U.S., in general agreement with the Soviet Union but also concerned that it do nothing to impair its alliance with Euratom members, sought to obtain agreement on a compromise course that would permit Euratom inspectors to insure the Euratom countries' compliance with the treaty for a transitional period of 3 years, during which IAEA inspectors would be gradually worked in so that they could assume full inspection responsibility at the end of the transitional period.

Other basic aspects of the discussion involved (1) the concern of some non-nuclear states, particularly West Germany, Italy, India and Japan, that the proposed treaty would deprive them of the opportunity to develop atomic energy for peaceful purposes and (2) the demand by certain countries, notably India and Japan, that the treaty guarantee to the non-nuclear states that the nuclear powers would protect them against nuclear attack, presumably from Communist China, who was not expected to sign the treaty.

Among other developments in the effort to work out a non-proliferation treaty:

●Lord Chalfont, the British delegate, said Feb. 23 that, with respect to the technological question, he believed the nuclear powers gained very little "spin-off," *i.e.*, "immediate technological advantage in the civil field from a military program." "If there is any significant spin-off, or if any should emerge in the future," Chalfont said, "it is only right that we should devise a way to share it equally among nuclear–weapon powers and the rest." With respect to enforcing the treaty once it came into effect, Chalfont said that "my clear impression is that if there are to be safeguards, they must be international and the treaty must not be the subject of self–policing." He referred to the safeguards exercised by the IAEA as "the type of thing that one has in mind." But Chalfont did not "rule out the possibility" of adopting the "extremely effective and stringent" safeguards system employed by Euratom. On the disarmament issue, Chalfont said that "what the neutrals seek is a declaration of intent [by the nuclear powers to disarm] coupled with or following a non–proliferation treaty," rather than a comprehensive treaty that would both ban the spread of nuclear weapons and provide for arms reduction by the nuclear powers.

●In her opening remarks to the committee Feb. 23, Mrs. Alva Myrdal, the Swedish delegate, called for "firm assurances" from the nuclear powers that, in addition to concluding a non-proliferation treaty, they would adopt "concrete measures" for achieving a comprehensive nuclear test-ban treaty and a suspension of the production of fissionable materials for weapons. She said that all 3 issues were "technically interdependent."

●Italian delegate Francesco Cavalletti announced Feb. 28 that Italy would not sign the proposed treaty if it would impede the scientific and technological development of countries without nuclear capability. He said non-nuclear states were entitled to some form of compensation for the "sacrifices" that they would have to make in signing the treaty. He indicated that one of these compensations should be a pledge by the nuclear powers to reduce and eventually to abolish their nuclear stockpiles.

●India indicated Mar. 7 that it would seek joint action with other non-nuclear states, particularly Japan, West Germany and Sweden, in attempting to forestall any "discrimination" against the non-nuclear states in the proposed treaty. The Japanese Foreign Ministry indicated Mar. 8 that it considered the proposed consultation a favorable step. Speaking in the Japanese Diet (parliament) Mar. 14, Japanese Foreign Min. Takeo Miki said that Japan had "no intention at this time to develop nuclear explosive devices," but he added that "our future generations should not be deprived of the opportunity to take part" in peaceful atomic development. Indian Foreign Min. M. C. Chagla told his parliament Mar. 27 that India would not sign the proposed treaty until it had received a guarantee against "nuclear attack or nuclear blackmail." He said India had come "under the continuing menace of a country [Communist China] which has already exploded an atom bomb, and we will certainly bear in mind this vital factor." Noting that India was "in the unique position of having the capability of exploding an atom bomb but, at the same time, of placing itself under a self-imposed ordinance of not making the bomb," Chagla asserted that India expected the nuclear powers "to assume certain responsibilities either by reducing their stockpiles or banning further tests."

●It was reported Apr. 10 that all the foreign ministers of Euratom except the French had agreed in Brussels to seek a compromise solution on the inspection issue that would be acceptable both to Euratom and to the Soviet Union. The foreign ministers of Belgium and the Netherlands, reportedly offered to take the initiative in working out a compromise along the lines that had been proposed by the U.S. in memos submitted to Euratom and the Soviet Union Feb. 22, i.e. the 3-year transitional period during which IAEA inspectors would gradually take over the work of the Euratom inspection teams. It was reported Apr. 11, however, that West Germany and Italy had insisted at the meeting that they be permitted to withdraw from the treaty once the IAEA had assumed full inspection responsibilities. The 2 countries reportedly urged that the 3-year transitional period serve instead as a "trial period." Lord Chalfont had warned Euratom members Mar. 21 that "a long delay" in obtaining agreement on the proposed treaty might mean "no treaty at all." He urged them to accept a compromise on the inspection issue since the lack of agreement on non-proliferation would cause political damage far in excess of "any sacrifice of regional interests which may be needed to achieve a treaty."

●After a 2-hour meeting of the NATO Permanent Council Apr. 20, the U.S. announced that it had received "a green light" from its allies to press its negotiations with the Soviet Union on the proposed treaty. A U.S. official noted that the international controls article of the treaty had been "rewritten completely." It was reported Apr. 25 that the U.S. had altered its compromise solution to the inspection issue in an effort to gain the support of the Euratom members. Under the terms of the U.S. revision, IAEA inspectors would be barred from Euratom countries throughout the 3-year period, rather than assuming joint inspection responsibility as the earlier draft had stipulated. State Department officials reported Apr. 28, however, that the Soviet Union had objected to this plan. Soviet delegate Roshchin reportedly had charged that such a formula amounted to "self-inspection" and was unacceptable.

●West German government officials reported May 4 that the U.S. and Britain had agreed to subject their peaceful atomic energy projects to the same inspection controls that would be imposed on non-nuclear states. West German Foreign Min. Willy Brandt said May 11: "The states with nuclear weapons must be willing to make available to the other countries any industrial knowledge gained from their nuclear experiments. There is reason to believe that the U.S. and the Soviet Union are willing to make this concession." Brandt, speaking in Tokyo following a conference with Japanese Foreign Min. Miki, said the 2 countries had reached agreement on most aspects of the proposed treaty. He denied that West Germany had sought to obtain a privileged position with respect to the inspection clause, as he said Japan had charged.

●Brazilian delegate Sergio Correa da Costa told ENDC May 18 that his country would not sign the proposed treaty unless it permitted non-nuclear nations to carry out atomic explosions for "great engineering works." The U.S. had sought to have the nuclear powers carry out such excavation services for the non-nuclear states. Foster warned June 8 that the U.S. would not perform such services for any country that refused to sign the treaty.

●Rumanian delegate Nicolae Ecobesco asserted Aug. 8 that Rumania would not support the proposed treaty unless the nuclear powers (1) ended the production of nuclear weapons, (2) stopped underground nuclear testing for military purposes and (3) destroyed existing stockpiles of nuclear weapons.

●U.S. delegate Foster returned to Washington Aug. 9, apparently because of a stalemate that had developed in the negotiations with the Soviet Union. But he announced at a news conference in Washington Aug. 11 that the Soviet Union had requested him to return to Geneva "urgently." In Geneva Aug. 13, Foster expressed the hope that the U.S. and the Soviet Union would be able to agree on submitting a draft treaty "very soon."

●It was reported Aug. 23 that the U.S. and the Soviet Union had reached final agreement to submit the draft treaty minus the inspection clause. Final difficulties reportedly had been cleared away after Rumania had indicated to the USSR Aug. 22 that it would approve the submission of the draft.

West German Opposition

During a visit to Washington Feb. 8-9, West German Foreign Min. Willy Brandt had expressed fear that the proposed non-proliferation treaty might handicap West Germany in peaceful atomic development. Brandt told newsmen Feb. 10 that West Germany was a small country and, as such, "we don't need [nuclear] explosions on our soil." But, he said, his country was interested "in research [and] industrial development." At a speech in Chicago Feb. 10, Brandt indorsed the proposed non-proliferation treaty by saying that "we shall be among the first to say yes to this development."

At a televised news conference in London Feb. 9, visiting Soviet Premier Aleksei N. Kosygin criticized the West German position: "We take a stand for non-proliferation of nuclear weapons and firmly believe that the time has come when further proliferation of such weapons should be banned.... [West Germany] will have to join the agreement on non-proliferation, whether it wants it or not. We will not allow the FRG [West Germany] to have nuclear weapons, and we will take all measures to prevent its getting nuclear weapons." "The ruling circles of this country must...give up the hope of...ever obtaining nuclear weapons.... [They] must realize that the frontiers now existing in Europe are to stay.... Our people detest German fascism and are fully resolved not to tolerate its resurgence."

Speaking in Bonn Feb. 11, West German Chancellor Kurt-Georg Kiesinger charged that Kosygin's remarks were "a slander against the will for peace of the German people and their government." Although West Germany could not be forced to relinquish its "inalienable national interests," Kiesinger said, "we want no vengeance. We want equal rights for our people." With respect to the proposed nuclear non-proliferation treaty, Kiesinger declared: "If we sign such a treaty, no one will force us to do it except our own opinions and our own concepts."

In a statement issued Feb. 20, West Germany indorsed the principle of the non-proliferation of nuclear weapons but had insisted that any treaty respect "justified vital interests in security" and in "peaceful atomic research." The statement called on the nuclear powers to carry out "substantial" disarmament in conjunction with the treaty. Kiesinger said in Bonn Feb. 21 that a non-proliferation treaty was not a real advance toward disarmament. "The nuclear powers do not only keep their terrible potential," he said, "they can even enlarge it at will."

The West German government Apr. 7 sent to other governments a memo criticizing the limited non-proliferation efforts of the great powers. According to the memo, the renunciation of the nuclear option by non-nuclear powers should be accompanied by nuclear disarmament by the nuclear powers, if the possibility of blackmail was to be avoided. The memo said: "In a limited non-proliferation treaty the non-nuclear-weapon powers, in contrast to the nuclear-weapon powers, would be giving up something specific and agreeing to restrictions in the cause of the universal aim of disarmament. Initially, the nuclear-weapon powers would not balance the preliminary contributions by the non-nuclear-weapon powers with far-reaching restrictions of their own. The existing mass-destruction weapons would continue to threaten humanity."

It was reported Apr. 13 that West Germany had sent the ENDC a note outlining its position on the proposed non-proliferation treaty. The note set forth these basic positions: (1) The treaty should provide for disarmament by those nations with nuclear weapons so as to provide "a guarantee of peace in a nuclear age." (2) The treaty should provide the framework for the establishment of better relations among its signatories. (3) The treaty should insure the security of non-nuclear states against an attack by the nuclear powers. (4) The treaty should not discriminate against the use of nuclear energy for peaceful purposes. (5) There should be a "general system of controls" that would not "impair the effectiveness of control systems already existing."

West German Science Min. Gerhard Stoltenberg said in Bonn July 28 that the revised draft treaty before ENDC had "decidedly lessened" West German reservations about the treaty. He said the draft indicated that West Germany would have no difficulty in obtaining long-term supplies of enriched uranium for its atomic reactors. He also pointed out that the draft would permit Euratom inspection of West Germany's nuclear activity.

At a press conference at the National Press Club in Washington Aug. 16, Chancellor Kiesinger explained that West Germany sought the conclusion of a nuclear non-proliferation treaty, but "we must take note that countries which sign the treaty and have no atomic weapons cannot be objects of political blackmail by a power which possesses those nuclear weapons."

At a press conference in Bonn Aug. 21, Kiesinger reiterated that the treaty should provide safeguards against "political blackmail" of the non-nuclear states by the nuclear powers and that it should guarantee to the non-nuclear states the right to "proceed with their peaceful atomic development."

U.S. & USSR Submit Draft Treaty

The U.S. and the Soviet Union submitted to the 18-Nation UN Disarmament Commitee (ENDC) in Geneva Aug. 24 their revised draft treaty to prevent the further spread of nuclear weapons. Identical but separate texts were presented by U.S. delegate Foster and Soviet delegate Roshchin. The draft, similar in language to the one presented by the U.S. to the ENDC in 1965, left blank Article 3, dealing with international control—the method of inspection to ensure compliance with the terms of the treaty by the non-nuclear nations. The draft nonetheless represented a major milestone in the 18-nation disarmament negotiations that had begun at Geneva in 1962.

On the controversial issue of international controls, the Soviet Union had insisted that the IAEA conduct all inspections. The U.S., while in basic agreement with the Soviet position, had sought to obtain a 3-year grace period for the non-nuclear members of Euratom. During this period, Euratom's inspectors would have been solely responsible for ensuring the compliance of these countries. The U.S. had adopted this position after West Germany and Italy had indicated their objections to IAEA inspection, which they viewed as a possible source of espionage since the agency included both Communist and non-Communist members.

Foster said Aug. 24 that a final agreement on the non-proliferation treaty was "within reach" and could, hopefully, be concluded by the beginning of 1968. He urged the cooperation of the other members of the ENDC while he sought to work out a compromise with the USSR on inspection. Roshchin reaffirmed the Soviet position on the question of international controls by referring to the preamble to the draft treaty, which stated that the parties would "cooperate in facilitating the application of International Atomic Energy Agency safeguards on peaceful nuclear activities."

The basic provisions of the draft treaty:

(1) The nuclear-weapon states that were a party to the treaty would be barred from transferring nuclear weapons or other nuclear explosive devices to non-nuclear nations or from giving them control over such devices or aiding them in their manufacture. A nuclear-weapon state was defined as one that had manufactured and exploded a nuclear device prior to Jan. 1, 1967. (5 nations satisfied this criterion—the U.S., the Soviet Union, Great Britain, France and Communist China. But France and Communist China were not expected to sign the treaty.)

(2) The non-nuclear states would undertake not to receive, obtain control over or manufacture nuclear weapons or other nuclear explosive devices.

(3) The treaty would not affect the right of all nations to develop nuclear energy for peaceful purposes.

(4) Any party could propose amendments to the treaty. If requested by 1/3 or more of the signatories to the treaty, a conference would be convened to consider such amendments. Approval of an amendment required a majority of the votes of all parties to the treaty, including the votes of all nuclear-weapon states party to the treaty and of all states party to the treaty who were members of the IAEA Board of Governors at the time the amendment had been circulated.

(5) 5 years after the treaty had become effective, a conference of all parties would be convened in Geneva to review the provisions of the treaty.

(6) The treaty would be open to all states for signature and would enter into force after all signatories had ratified it.

(7) The treaty would be of unlimited duration, but any signatory could withdraw from the treaty if it felt that its national interests had been placed in jeopardy.

Pres. Johnson Aug. 24 hailed the draft treaty as a significant step toward freeing the world from the threat of nuclear destruction. Excerpts from the President's remarks:

"... For more than 20 years, the world has watched with growing fear as nuclear weapons have spread. Since 1945, 5 nations have come into possession of these dreadful weapons. We believe now—as we did then—that even one such nation is too many. But the issue now is not whether some have nuclear weapons while others do not. The issue is whether the nations will agree to prevent a bad situation from becoming worse. Today, for the first time, we have within our reach an instrument which permits us to make a choice.

"The submission of a draft treaty brings us to the final and most critical stage of this effort....

"The treaty must reconcile the interest of nations with our interest as a community of human beings on a small planet. The treaty must be responsive to the needs and problems of all the nations of the world....

"It must add to the security of all.

"It must encourage the development and use of nuclear energy for peaceful purposes.

"It must provide adequate protection against the corruption of the peaceful atom to its use for weapons for war.

"I am convinced that we are today offering an instrument that will meet these requirements.

"If we now go forward to completion of a worldwide agreement ... we shall demonstrate that—despite all his problems, quarrels, and distractions—man still retains a capacity to design his fate, rather than be engulfed by it.

"Failure to complete our work will be interpreted by our children and grandchildren as a betrayal of conscience, in a world that needs all of its resources and talents to serve life, not death...."

Among other international reaction to the draft treaty:

●The West German Foreign Ministry referred to the treaty Aug. 24 as "an important step in a new and improved phase in the efforts to control the spread of nuclear weapons." It said the treaty could serve as a major step toward obtaining general and complete disarmament, thereby relaxing international tensions.

●Agence France-Presse, the French press agency, Aug. 25 quoted "responsible circles" as saying that France had not participated in the Geneva talks and thus had "no intention of signing this treaty." (France, though technically a member of the ENDC, had boycotted its sessions since 1962.)

●UN Secy. Gen. U Thant Aug. 25 expressed his gratification over the breakthrough in the non-proliferation negotiations.

●Izvestia, the Soviet government newspaper, hailed the treaty Aug. 26 as an "important forward step." An Izvestia commentator, V. A. Matveyev, said the controversial issue of inspection procedures could be worked out "without long procrastination."

●Hsinhua, the Chinese Communist press agency, assailed the treaty Aug. 26 as a fraud perpetrated by the U. S. and the Soviet Union in order to maintain their nuclear monopoly.

●Dr. Sigvard Eklund, director general of the International Atomic Energy Agency (IAEA), said Sept. 26 that the IAEA had the "inherent capacity" to police the proposed treaty and that it was the organization "most capable of undertaking this important task." He said the treaty should provide for international rather than regional inspection procedures if it were "to be credible and give assurance to the people of the world."

●Joachim Prepsch, a high official in the West German Ministry of Science, told members of the IAEA Sept. 29 that the inspection procedures of the proposed treaty should be "automatic as far as possible." He elaborated by saying that checking "the flow of fissionable material from one nuclear plant to another would be enough to prevent diversion for weapons production." For this reason, he said, on-the-spot checks by inspectors would become "more and more dispensable."

●Meeting in Brussels Oct. 27, the 5 non-nuclear members of Euratom (Belgium, Italy, Luxembourg, the Netherlands and West Germany) agreed on a set of 5 principles concerning the safeguards to be employed in the proposed non-proliferation treaty. The 5 principles were: (1) the negotiation of an agreement between Euratom and IAEA concerning the control procedure to be adopted, (2) "verification" of the Euratom control system by the IAEA but not direct IAEA control over Euratom programs, (3) no "guillotine clause" providing automatic IAEA controls after a fixed period of time, (4) restriction of controls to fissionable materials with no controls over nuclear reactors or other facilities, (5) an assurance that the supply of fissionable materials to all Euratom members, including France, would not be endangered.

Text of Draft Treaty

This is the complete text of the "Draft Treaty on the Non-Proliferation of Nuclear Weapons":

The states concluding this treaty, hereinafter referred to as the 'parties to the treaty,'

Considering the devastation that would be visited upon all mankind by a nuclear war and the consequent need to make every effort to avert the danger of such a war and to take measures to safeguard the security of peoples,

Believing that the proliferation of nuclear weapons would seriously enhance the danger of nuclear war,

In conformity with resolutions of the United Nations General Assembly calling for the conclusion of an agreement on the prevention of wider dissemination of nuclear weapons,

Undertaking to cooperate in facilitating the application of International Atomic Energy Agency safeguards on peaceful nuclear activities,

Expressing their support for research, development and other efforts to further the application, within the framework of the International Atomic Energy Agency safeguards system, of the principle of safeguarding effectively the flow of source and special fissionable materials by use of instruments and other techniques at certain strategic points,

Affirming the principle that the benefits of peaceful applications of nuclear technology, including any technological by-products which may be derived by nuclear-weapon states from the development of nuclear-explosive devices, should be available for peaceful purposes to all parties to the treaty, whether nuclear-weapon or non-nuclear-weapon states,

Convinced that in furtherance of this principle, all parties to this treaty are entitled to participate in the fullest possible exchange of scientific information for, and to contribute, alone or in cooperation with other states, to the further development of the applications of atomic energy for peaceful purposes,

Declaring their intention that potential benefits from any peaceful applications of nuclear explosions should be available through appropriate international procedures to non-nuclear-weapon states party to this treaty on a non-discriminatory basis and that the charge to such parties for the explosive devices used should be as low as possible and exclude any charge for research and development,

Declaring their intention to achieve at the earliest possible date the cessation of the nuclear arms race,

Urging the cooperation of all states in the attainment of this objective,

Desiring to further the easing of international tension and the strengthening of trust between states in order to facilitate the cessation of the manufacture of nuclear weapons, the liquidation of all their existing stockpiles and the elimination from national arsenals of nuclear weapons and the means of their delivery pursuant to a Treaty on General and Complete Disarmament under strict and effective international control,

Noting that nothing in this treaty affects the right of any group of states to conclude regional treaties in order to assure the total absence of nuclear weapons in their respective territories,

Have agreed as follows:

Article I. Each nuclear-weapon state party to this treaty undertakes not to transfer to any recipient whatsoever nuclear weapons or other nuclear explosive devices or control over such weapons or explosive devices directly, or indirectly; and not in any way to assist, encourage, or induce any non-nuclear-weapon state to manufacture or otherwise acquire nuclear weapons or other nuclear explosive devices, or control over such weapons or explosive devices.

Article II. Each non-nuclear-weapon state party to this treaty undertakes not to receive the transfer whatsoever from any transferor of nuclear weapons or other nuclear explosive devices or of control over such weapons or explosive devices directly, or indirectly; not to manufacture or otherwise acquire nuclear weapons or other nuclear explosive devices; and not to seek or receive any assistance in the manufacture of nuclear weapons or other nuclear explosive devices.

Article III. [This article, dealing with international controls, was left blank because of disagreement over the method of inspection to adopt.]

Article IV. Nothing in this treaty shall be interpreted as affecting the inalienable right of all the parties to the treaty to develop research, production and use of nuclear energy for peaceful purposes without discrimination and in conformity with Articles 1 and 2 of this treaty, as well as the right of the parties to participate in the fullest possible exchange of information for, and to contribute alone or in cooperation with other states to the further development of the applications of nuclear energy for peaceful purposes.

Article V. 1. Any party to this treaty may propose amendments to this treaty. The text of any proposed amendment shall be submitted to the depositary government which shall circulate it to all parties to the treaty. Thereupon, if requested to do so by 1/3 or more of the parties to the treaty, the depositary governments shall convene a conference, to which they shall invite all the parties to the treaty, to consider such an amendment.

2. Any amendment to this treaty must be approved by a majority of the votes of all the parties to the treaty, including the votes of all nuclear-weapon states party to this treaty and all other parties which, on the date the amendment is circulated, are members of the Board of Governors of the International Atomic Energy Agency. The amendment shall enter into force for all parties upon the deposit of instruments of ratification by a majority of all the parties, including the instruments of ratification of all nuclear-weapon states party to this treaty and all other parties which, on the date the amendment is circulated, are members of the Board of Governors of the International Atomic Energy Agency.

3. 5 years after the entry into force of this treaty, a conference of parties to the treaty shall be held in Geneva, Switzerland, in order to review the operation of this treaty with a view to assuring that the purposes and provisions of the treaty are being realized.

Article VI. 1. This treaty shall be open to all states for signature. Any state which does not sign the treaty before its entry into force in accordance with Paragraph 3 of this article may accede to it at any time.

2. This treaty shall be subject to ratification by signatory states. Instruments of ratification and instruments of accession shall be deposited with the governments of————, which are hereby designated the depositary governments.

3. This treaty shall enter into force after its ratification by all nuclear-weapon states signatory to this treaty, and———— other states signatory to this treaty, and the deposit of their instruments of ratification. For the purposes of this treaty, a nuclear-weapon state is one which has manufactured and exploded a nuclear weapon or other nuclear explosive device prior to Jan. 1, 1967.

4. For states whose instruments of ratification or accession are deposited subsequent to the entry into force of this treaty, it shall enter into force on the date of the deposit of their instruments of ratification or accession.

5. The depositary governments shall promptly inform all signatory and acceding states of the date of each signature, the date of deposit of each instrument of ratification or of accession, the date of the entry into force of this treaty and the date of receipt of any requests for convening a conference or other notices.

6. This treaty shall be registered by the depositary governments pursuant to Article 102 of the Charter of the United Nations.

Article VII. This treaty shall be of unlimited duration.

Each party shall in exercising its national sovereignty have the right to withdraw from the treaty if it decides that extraordinary events, related to the subject matter of this treaty, have jeopardized the supreme interests of its country. It shall give notice of such withdrawal to all other parties to the treaty and to the United Nations Security Council 3 months in advance. Such notice shall include a statement of the extraordinary events it regards as having jeopardized its supreme interests.

Article VIII. This treaty, the English, Russian, French, Spanish and Chinese texts of which are equally authentic, shall be deposited in the archives of the depositary governments. Duly certified copies of this treaty shall be transmitted by the depositary governments to the governments of the signatory and acceding states.

In witness whereof the undersigned, duly authorized, have signed this treaty.

U.S. Inspection Offer

Pres. Johnson announced Dec. 2 that, on the successful conclusion of the nuclear non-proliferation treaty currently under discussion in Geneva, the U.S. would open up to inspection by the IAEA "all nuclear activities in the U.S." with the exception of those "with direct national security significance." Mr. Johnson said this offer would enable the IAEA "to inspect a broad range of U.S. nuclear activities, both governmental and private, including the fuel in nuclear-power reactors owned by utilities for generating electricity and the fabrication and chemical reprocessing of such fuel." The offer was viewed as an attempt by the U.S. to demonstrate to some of the non-nuclear states that the inspection article in the proposed non-proliferation treaty would not (1) be applied discriminately to only the non-nuclear states, (2) inhibit the development of peaceful applications of atomic energy or (3) pose the threat of industrial espionage. The U.S. had opened up 2 of its plants to IAEA inspection in 1964 and 1967.

Mr. Johnson made the offer while speaking in commemoration of the 25th anniversary of the first controlled nuclear chain reaction, conducted by Enrico Fermi at the University of Chicago in 1942. *Among his remarks:*

"Giant nuclear reactors, direct descendants of Fermi's first atomic pile, are producing millions of kilowatts of power for peaceful purposes [throughout the world].... Today, a single reactor can, while generating electricity, produce enough plutonium to make dozens of bombs every year. And scores of these reactors are now being built all over the world. Their purpose is peaceful. Yet ... the secret diversion of even a small part of the plutonium they create could soon give every nation power to destroy civilization—if not life on this earth. We cannot permit this to happen. Nor can mankind be denied the unlimited benefits of the peaceful atom. We must find a way to remove the threat while preserving the promise.... [The U.S. is] trying to assure that the peaceful benefits of the atom will be shared by all mankind without increasing the threat of nuclear destruction. We do not believe that safeguards we propose in ... [the non-proliferation] treaty will interfere with the peaceful activities of any country. And I want to make it clear to the world that we in the U.S. are not asking any country to accept safeguards that we are unwilling to accept ourselves."

Italian Pres. Giuseppe Saragat welcomed the U.S. inspection offer and expressed the hope that other nuclear powers, including the Soviet Union, would follow suit.

British State Min. (for foreign affairs) Fred Mulley welcomed Johnson's announcement and said Dec. 4 that Britain was prepared "to offer an opportunity for the application of similar [IAEA] safeguards in the United Kingdom, subject to exclusions for national security reasons only," "at such time as international safeguards are put into effect in the non-nuclear weapon states in implementation of the provisions of a [non-proliferation] treaty."

The U.S. and British initiatives on the inspection issue were praised by Brazil, Italy, India and Canada at the Geneva disarmament discussions Dec. 5.

Draft Discussed at Geneva Sessions

During meetings held between August and December the ENDC discussed the draft non-proliferation treaty. Much of the discussion related to the article on inspection (Article 3), which had been omitted from the draft treaty because of disagreement over the kind of inspection safeguards to adopt.

Italian delegate Roberto Coracciolo proposed Aug. 29 that the draft treaty be adopted without provisions for inspection if controversy over the latter were to hold up an agreement on the other provisions of the treaty. He noted that "certain of our suggestions have not yet found a place in the text of the treaty" as presented by the U.S. and USSR. He said these related to (1) non-discrimination between nuclear and non-nuclear states concerning application of the provisions of the treaty, (2) the security of the non-nuclear states and (3) the danger of damaging European unity through the attempt to achieve unanimity on the inspection issue.

Swedish delegate Alva Myrdal presented to the ENDC Aug. 30 a draft proposal for the blank inspection article. The major attempt of the proposal was to prevent the signatories to the treaty, whether nuclear or non-nuclear, from aiding the nuclear development programs of nuclear states that were not expected to sign the treaty (France and Communist China). Under the Swedish proposal, the IAEA would maintain a check on all transfers of nuclear materials or equipment from the treaty signatories to any other state, nuclear or non-nuclear, whether or not such a state was a signatory to the treaty.

Brazilian delegate A. F. A. da Silveira was joined by the Nigerian delegate in proposing Aug. 30 that the treaty permit non-nuclear signatories to conduct nuclear explosions for earth-moving purposes.

Lt. Gen. E. L. M. Burns, the Canadian delegate, said Sept. 12 that only a world body like the IAEA could supervise nuclear explosions for civil engineering purposes. He suggested that the nuclear signatories to the treaty issue separate declarations in conjunction with the treaty pledging (1) to go to the aid of non-nuclear signatories who were threatened by or subjected to a nuclear attack and (2) to refrain from the use of nuclear weapons against non-nuclear signatories who were not allied with a nuclear power.

Adrian S. Fisher, deputy director of the U.S. Arms Control & Disarmament Agency and deputy U.S. delegate to the ENDC, told the conferees Sept. 19 that the U.S.' decision to deploy a "limited" anti-ballistic missile (ABM) defense system was aimed at protecting the U.S. from a possible Communist Chinese nuclear attack and "should not in any way decrease the desirability" of the nuclear non-proliferation treaty to other nations. He explained that the ABM deployment would "foreclose any possibility of a successful Chinese nuclear attack on the U.S." and would therefore "provide further assurance of our determination to support our Asian friends against Chinese nuclear blackmail."

Soviet delegate Aleksei A. Roshchin said Sept. 27 that there could be a "transition period" during which the non-nuclear members of Eruatom could continue to operate under their own safeguards before coming under IAEA inspection.

Swedish delegate Myrdal asserted Oct. 3 that the U.S.' decision to deploy an ABM system, as well as the absence of any big-power accord banning the deployment of such systems, "leads us in a pessimistic direction." She called for the inclusion in the proposed treaty of a firm commitment by the nuclear powers to pursue other disarmament measures.

The U.S. and Canada Oct. 5 scored proposals for the inclusion of other disarmament or arms control measures in the draft treaty. U.S. delegate Fisher said: "We should not alter our course in a direction that will put the treaty further from our grasp." Canadian delegate Burns warned that, without an accord on nuclear non-proliferation, there was "little hope of any other disarmament agreement."

Soviet delegate Roschchin charged Oct. 10 that West Germany was impeding progress toward the conclusion of a non-proliferation treaty by attempting to exempt itself from the "unified and generally recognized" safeguards systems of the IAEA and thereby leaving a "loophole to nuclear weapons." Roschchin read to the ENDC and East German government statement accepting the IAEA controls system. The statement also accused West Germany of having concluded "far-reaching agreements with the Republic of South Africa on the production and testing of atomic weapons on South African territory."

The Rumanian delegate Oct. 19 submitted proposed treaty amendments that called for (1) a review of the treaty at the end of 5 years if the nuclear signatories had not destroyed their stocks of nuclear weapons and delivery systems by that time, (2) conferences every 5 years to review compliance with the treaty and (3) a commitment by the nuclear signatories not to use nuclear weapons against non-nuclear signatories.

Italian delegate Coracciolo proposed Oct. 24 that the treaty be valid for only a fixed (unspecified) number of years. He said a treaty of unlimited duration would be an "iron corset" on the non-nuclear signatories and could not be "adjusted to changing conditions."

Brazilian delegate da Silveira Oct. 31 submitted a series of proposed treaty amendments that would (1) eliminate the ban on nuclear explosions by non-nuclear signatories for peaceful purposes, (2) state the "inalienable right" of all signatories to develop nuclear explosive devices for peaceful uses, (3) require the nuclear signatories to conclude a treaty halting the nuclear arms race and (4) make it easier for the non-nuclear signatories to withdraw from the treaty.

The British delegate Nov. 23 tabled a proposed treaty amendment that would subject the treaty to review after 5 years so as to determine whether its provisions, including those of the preamble, were being realized. The preamble specified that, in addition to preventing the proliferation of nuclear weapons, the signatories would seek the institution of other disarmament measures.

Failing to obtain agreement on the inspection article, the conferees agreed Nov. 30 to submit an interim report to the UN General Assembly.

The ENDC adjourned Dec. 14 until Jan. 18, 1968. In closing remarks, both Soviet delegate Roshchin and U.S. delegate Foster said progress had been made toward resolving the remaining differences on the non-proliferation treaty.

PROGRESS IN ARMS LIMITATION

Space A-Ban Treaty Effective

Representatives of 60 countries Jan. 27 signed a treaty banning mass destruction weapons in space. The signing took place at separate ceremonies in Washington, London and Moscow. Representatives of the treaty's depositary countries (Britain, the USSR and the U.S.) signed copies at all 3 locations. But the treaty, which had been approved by the UN General Assembly Dec. 19, 1966, did not go into effect until Oct. 10 since it required the ratification of at least 5 states, including the 3 depositary countries.

Speaking at the Washington ceremony Jan. 27, Pres. Johnson hailed the signing as an "inspiring moment in the history of the human race." He voiced the hope that U.S. and Soviet astronauts "will meet someday on the surface of the moon as brothers and not as warriors," and he added that the treaty represented a "very hopeful sign" for further East-West agreements. Soviet Amb.-to-U.S. Anatoly F. Dobrynin declared: "Let us hope we shall not wait long for similar approval of other urgent problems."

State Secy. Dean Rusk and U.S. Amb.-to-UN Arthur J. Goldberg signed for the U.S., Dobrynin for the USSR and UK Amb.-to-U.S. Sir Patrick Dean for Britain. Among states not signing were France, Communist China, Cuba and Albania. (Hsinhua, the official Communist Chinese press agency, accused the USSR Jan. 28 of betraying the Vietnamese people by cooperating with the U.S. in the treaty.)

The treaty was ratified by the U.S. Apr. 25 and by the Soviet Union May 19. The U.S. Senate voted unanimously (88-0) Apr. 25 in favor of ratification. Military leaders had assured Senators earlier that the pact would not endanger national security.

The French cabinet Aug. 9 authorized France's signing of the treaty. The government had been hesitant to sign the treaty because of legal objections to parts of the text.

The treaty came into force Oct. 10 when 13 nations deposited their instruments or notices of ratification in Washington. (84 governments had signed the treaty by Oct. 10.) In addition to the depositary nations, the following states deposited their ratifications Oct. 10: Bulgaria, Niger, Czechoslovakia, Hungary, Finland, Sierra Leone, Denmark, Canada, Japan and Australia.

The treaty's full title was: Treaty on Principles Governing the Activities of States in the Exploration & Use of Outer Space,* Including the Moon & Other Celestial Bodies." *Full text of the Treaty:*

The states parties to this treaty,

Inspired by the great prospects opening up before mankind as a result of man's entry into outer space,

Recognizing the common interest of all mankind in the progress of the exploration and use of outer space for peaceful purposes,

Believing that the exploration and use of outer space should be carried on for the benefit of all peoples, irrespective of the degree of their economic or scientific development,

Desiring to contribute to broad international co-operation in the scientific as well as the legal aspects of the exploration and use of outer space for peaceful purposes,

Believing that such co-operation will contribute to the development of mutual understanding and to the strengthening of friendly relations between States and peoples,

Recalling resolution 1962 (XVIII), entitled 'Declaration of Legal Principles Governing the Activities of States in the Exploration & Use of Outer Space,' which was adopted unanimously by the United Nations General Assembly on 13 Dec. 1963,

Recalling resolution 1884 (XVIII), calling upon states to refrain from placing in orbit around the earth any objects carrying nuclear weapons or any other kinds of weapons of mass destruction or from installing such weapons on celestial bodies, which was adopted unanimously by the United Nations General Assembly on 17 Oct. 1963,

---

* The UN Scientific & Technical Subcommittee on the Peaceful Uses of Outer Space reported Sept. 6 that it had failed in efforts to produce an agreed definition of the term "outer space." The subcommittee concluded that it was "not possible at the present time to identify scientific or technical criteria which would permit a precise and lasting definition of outer space."

Taking account of United Nations General Assembly resolution 110(II) of 3 Nov. 1947, which condemned propaganda designed or likely to provoke or encourage any threat to the peace, breach of the peace or act of aggression, and considering that the aforementioned resolution is applicable to outer space,

Convinced that a Treaty on Principles Governing the Activities of States in the Exploration & Use of Outer Space, including the Moon & Other Celestial Bodies, will further the purposes and principles of the Charter of the United Nations,

Have agreed on the following:

Article I. The exploration and use of outer space, including the moon and other celestial bodies, shall be carried out for the benefit and in the interests of all countries, irrespective of their degree of economic or scientific development, and, and shall be the province of all mankind.

Outer space, including the moon and other celestial bodies, shall be free for exploration and use by all states without discrimination of any kind, on a basis of equality and in accordance with international law, and there shall be free access to all areas of celestial bodies.

There shall be freedom of scientific investigation in outer space, including the moon and other celestial bodies, and States shall facilitate and encourage international co-operation in such investigation.

Article II. Outer space, including the moon and other celestial bodies, is not subject to national appropriation by claim of sovereignty, by means of use of occupation or by any other means.

Article III. States parties to the treaty shall carry on activities in the exploration and use of outer space, including the moon and other celestial bodies, in accordance with international law, including the Charter of the United Nations, in the interest of maintaining international peace and security and promoting international co-operation and understanding.

Article IV. States parties to the treaty undertake not to place in orbit around the earth any objects carrying nuclear weapons or any other kinds of weapons of mass destruction, install such weapons on celestial bodies, or station such weapons in outer space in any other manner.

The moon and other celestial bodies shall be used by all states parties to the treaty exclusively for peaceful purposes. The establishment of military bases, installations and fortifications, the testing of any type of weapons and the conduct of military maneuvers on celestial bodies shall be forbidden. The use of military personnel for scientific research or for any other peaceful purposes shall not be prohibited. The use of any equipment or facility necessary for peaceful exploration of the moon and other celestial bodies shall also not be prohibited.

Article V. States parties to the treaty shall regard astronauts as envoys of mankind in outer space and shall render to them all possible assistance in the event of accident, distress, or emergency landing on the territory of another state party or on the high seas. When astronauts make such a landing, they shall be safely and promptly returned to the state of registry of their space vehicle.

In carrying on activities in outer space and on celestial bodies, the astronauts of one state party shall render all possible assistance to the astronauts of other states Parties.

States parties to the treaty shall immediately inform the other states parties to the treaty or the Secretary General of the United Nations of any phenomena they discover in outer space, including the moon and other celestial bodies, which could constitute a danger to the life or health of astronauts.

Article VI. States parties to the treaty shall bear international responsibility for national activities in outer space, including the moon and other celestial bodies, whether such activities are carried on by governmental agencies or by non-governmental entities, and for assuring that national activities are carried out in conformity with the provisions set forth in the present treaty. The activities of non-governmental entities in outer space, including the moon and other celestial bodies, shall require authorization and continuing supervision by the appropriate state party to the treaty. When activities are carried on in outer space, including the moon and other celestial bodies, by an international organization, responsibility for compliance with this treaty shall be borne both by the international organization and by the states parties to the treaty participating in such organization.

Article VII. Each state party to the treaty that launches or procures the launching of an object into outer space, including the moon and other celestial bodies, and each state party from whose territory or facility an object is launched, is internationally liable for damage to another state party to the treaty or to its natural or juridical persons by such object or its component parts on the earth, in air space or in outer space, including the moon and other celestial bodies.

Article VIII. A state party to the treaty on whose registry an object launched into outer space is carried shall retain jurisdiction and control over such object, and over any personnel thereof, while in outer space or on a celestial body. Ownership of objects launched into outer space, including objects landed or constructed on a celestial body, and of their component parts, is not affected by their presence in outer space or on a celestial body or by their return to the earth. Such objects or component parts found beyond the limits of the state party to the treaty on whose registry they are carried shall be returned to that state party, which shall, upon request, furnish identifying data prior to their return.

Article IX. In the exploration and use of outer space, including the moon and other celestial bodies, states parties to the treaty shall be guided by the principle of co-operation and mutual assistance and shall conduct all their activities in outer space, including the moon and other celestial bodies, with due regard to the corresponding interests of all other states parties to the treaty. States parties to the treaty shall pursue studies of outer space, including the moon and other celestial bodies, and conduct exploration of them so as to avoid their harmful contamination and also adverse changes in the environment of the earth resulting from the introduction of extraterrestrial matter and, where necessary, shall adopt appropriate measures for this purpose. If a state party to the treaty has reason to believe that an activity or experiment planned by it or its nationals in outer space, including the moon and other celestial bodies, would cause potentially harmful interference with activities of other states parties in the peaceful exploration and use of outer space, including the moon and other celestial bodies, it shall undertake appropriate international consultations before proceeding with any such activity or experiment. A state party to the treaty which has reason to believe that an activity or experiment planned by another state party in outer space, including the moon and other celestial bodies, would cause potentially harmful interference with activities in the peaceful exploration and use of outer space, including the moon and other celestial bodies, may request consultation concerning the activity or experiment.

Article X. In order to promote international cooperation in the exploration and use of outer space, including the moon and other celestial bodies, in conformity with the purposes of this treaty, the states parties to the treaty shall consider on a basis of equality any requests by other states parties to the treaty to be afforded an opportunity to observe the flight of space objects launched by those states.

The nature of such an opportunity for observation and the conditions under which it could be afforded shall be determined by agreement between the states concerned.

Article XI. In order to promote international cooperation in the peaceful exploration and use of outer space, states parties to the treaty conducting activities in outer space, including the moon and other celestial bodies, agree to inform the Secretary General of the United Nations as well as the public and the international scientific community, to the greatest extent feasible and practicable, of the nature, conduct, locations and results of such activities. On receiving the said information, the Secretary General of the United Nations should be prepared to disseminate it immediately and effectively.

Article XII. All stations, installations, equipment and space vehicles on the moon and other celestial bodies shall be open to representatives of other states parties to the treaty on a basis of reciprocity. Such representatives shall give reasonable advance notice of a projected visit, in order that appropriate consultations may be held and that maximum precautions may be taken to assure safety and to avoid interference with normal operations in the facility to be visited.

Article XIII. The provisions of this treaty shall apply to the activities of states parties to the treaty in the exploration and use of outer space, including the moon and other celestial bodies, whether such activities are carried on by a single state party to the treaty or jointly with other states, including cases where they are carried on within the framework of international inter-governmental organizations.

Any practical questions arising in connection with activities carried on by international inter-governmental organizations in the exploration and use of outer space, including the moon and other celestial bodies, shall be resolved by the states parties to the treaty either with the appropriate international organization or with one or more states members of that international organization, which are parties to this treaty.

Article XIV. 1. This treaty shall be open to all states for signature. Any state which does not sign this treaty before its entry into force in accordance with paragraph 3 of this article may accede to it at any time.

2. This treaty shall be subject to ratification by signatory states. Instruments of ratification and instruments of accession shall be deposited with the governments of the United States of America, the United Kingdom of Great Britain & Northern Ireland and the Union of Soviet Socialist Republics, which are hereby designated the depositary governments.

3. This treaty shall enter into force upon the deposit of instruments of ratification by 5 governments including the governments designated as depositary governments under this treaty.

4. For states whose instruments of ratification or accession are deposited subsequent to the entry into force of this treaty, it shall enter into force on the date of the deposit of their instruments of ratification or accession.

5. The depositary governments shall promptly inform signatory and acceding states of the date of each signature, the date of deposit of each instrument of ratification of and accession to this treaty, the date of its entry into force and other notices.

6. This treaty shall be registered by the depositary governments pursuant to Article 102 of the Charter of the United Nations.

Article XV. Any state party to the treaty may propose amendments to this treaty. Amendments shall enter into force for each state party to the treaty accepting the amendments upon their acceptance by a majority of the states parties to the treaty and thereafter for each remaining state party to the treaty on the date of acceptance by it.

Article XVI. Any state party to the treaty may give notice of its withdrawal from the treaty one year after its entry into force by written notification to the depositary governments. Such withdrawal shall take effect one year from the date of receipt of this notification.

Article XVII. This treaty, of which the English, Russian, French, Spanish and Chinese texts are equally authentic, shall be deposited in the archives of the depositary governments. Duly certified copies of this treaty shall be transmitted by the depositary governments to the governments of the signatory and acceding states.

In Witness Whereof the undersigned, duly authorized, have signed this treaty. Done in triplicate, at the cities of Washington, London and Moscow, this 27th day of January 1967.

Latin American Nuclear-Free Zone

14 Latin American nations Feb. 14 signed a treaty banning nuclear weapons from Central and South America and the Caribbean and thereby establishing the first nuclear-free zone in an inhabited area of the world. (Antarctica had been made a nuclear-free zone in 1959, and a treaty banning nuclear weapons from space had been signed in 1966.) The signatories of the treaty were Bolivia, Chile, Colombia, Costa Rica, Ecuador, El Salvador, Guatemala, Haiti, Honduras, Mexico, Panama, Peru, Uruguay and Venezuela.

The accord, entitled the "Treaty for the Prohibition of Nuclear Weapons in Latin America," outlawed, in the area covered: (1)the "testing, use, manufacture, production or acquisition by any means whatsoever of any nuclear weapons," (2) the "receipt, storage, installation, deployment and any form of possession of any nuclear weapon," (3) the "engaging in, encouraging or authorizing...or in any way participating in the testing, use, manufacture, production, possession or control of any nuclear weapons." The treaty did not prohibit the use of nuclear energy for peaceful purposes, particularly for "economic development and social progress." It provided that, on the fulfillment of certian notification prodedures, the treaty signatories could "carry out explosions of nuclear devices for peaceful purposes—including explosions which involve devices similar to those used · in nuclear weapons—or collaborate with 3d parties for the same purpose."

Among the treaty's provisions:

●An "Agency for the Prohibition of Nuclear Weapons in Latin America" was to be established in Mexico City to administer the treaty. Its principal organs would be a General Conference, a Council and a Secretariat.

●"Each contracting party shall negotiate multilateral or bilateral agreements with the [UN] International Atomic Energy Agency [IAEA] for the application of its safeguards to its nuclear activities.... The IAEA and the Council...have the power of carrying out special inspections."

●"Unless the parties concerned agree on another mode of peaceful settlement, any question or dispute concerning the interpretation of this treaty which is not settled shall be referred to the International Court of Justice with the prior consent of the parties to the controversy."

●The treaty "shall be open indefinitely for signature by [a] all the Latin American Republics; [b] all other sovereign states situated in their entirety south of latitude 35 degrees north in the Western Hemisphere."

●The treaty "shall remain in force indefinitely, but any party may denounce it" if it considered "its supreme interests and the peace and security of one or more contracting parties" to be affected by the treaty; the denunciation would take effect 3 months after notification.

●Treaty languages: Spanish, Chinese, English, French, Portuguese and Russian.

Brazil signed the treaty in Mexico City May 9.

British Amb.-to-UN Lord Caradon announced Oct. 26 that Britain would uphold the Latin American A-ban treaty by signing a protocol attached to the treaty calling for respect for the treaty's provisions by the nuclear powers. The U.S. announced in the UN General Assembly's First (Policial & Security) Committee that it was giving "careful and sympathetic consideration" to signing the protocol. Cuba reiterated its opposition to the treaty and asserted that it had the right to use "any weapon" in self-defense.

EFFECTS OF A-WEAPONS USE

Report Warns of Widespread Damage

An international committee of experts, commissioned by UN Secy. Gen. U Thant as a result of the Dec. 5, 1966, General Assembly resolution, submitted Oct. 6 a report on the effects of the possible use of nuclear weapons. The report concluded that the use of such weapons would cause widespread damage not confined to the warring nations. The report concluded:

"Nuclear weapons constitute one of the dominant facts of modern world politics. They are at present deployed in thousands by the nuclear-weapon powers, with warheads ranging from kilotons to megatons. We have already witnessed the experimental explosion of a 50- to 60-megaton bomb, *i.e.* of a weapon with about 3,000 times the power of the bomb used in 1945 against Japan. Hundred-megaton devices, weapons about 5,000 times the size of those used in 1945, are no more difficult to devise. They could be exploded just outside the atmosphere of any country, in order utterly to destroy hundreds, even thousands, of square kilometers by means of blast and spreading fire. It has been suggested on good authority that in certain geographical circumstances multi-megaton weapons could also be exploded in ships near coastlines in order to create enormous tidal waves which would engulf the coastal belt.

"The effects of all-out nuclear war, regardless of where it started, could not be confined to the powers engaged in that war. They themselves would have to suffer the immediate kind of destruction and the immediate and more enduring lethal fall-out whose effects have already been described. But neighboring countries, and even countries in parts of the world remote from the actual conflict, could soon become exposed to the hazards of radioactive fallout precipitated at great distances from the explosion, after moving through the atmosphere as a vast cloud. Thus, at least within the same hemisphere, an enduring radio-active hazard could exist for distant as well as close human populations, through the ingestion of foods derived from contaminated vegetation and the external irradiation due to fallout particles deposited on the ground. The extent and nature of the hazard would depend upon the numbers and type of bomb exploded. Given a sufficient number, no part of the world would escape exposure to biologically significant levels of radiation. To a greater or lesser degree, a legacy of genetic damage could be incurred by the world's population.

"It is to be expected that no major nuclear power could attack another without provoking a nuclear counter-attack. It is even possible that an aggressor could suffer more in retaliation than the nuclear power it first attacked. In this lies the concept of deterrence by the threat of nuclear destruction. Far from an all-out nuclear exchange being a rational action which could ever be justified by any set of conceivable political gains, it may be that no country would, in the pursuit of its political objectives, deliberately risk the total destruction of its own capital city, leave alone the destruction of all its major centers of population; or risk the resultant chaos which would leave in doubt a government's ability to remain in control of its people. But the fact that a state of mutual nuclear deterrence prevails between the super powers does not, as we know all too well, prevent the outbreak of wars with conventional weapons involving both nuclear and non-nuclear weapon nations; the risk of nuclear war remains as long as there are nuclear weapons.

"The basic facts about the nuclear bomb and its use are harsh and terrifying for civilization; they have become lost in a mass of theoretical verbiage. It has been claimed that the world has learnt to live with the bomb; it is also said there is no need for it to drift unnecessarily into the position that it is prepared to die for it. The ultimate question for the world to decide in our nuclear age—and this applies both to nuclear and non-nuclear powers—is what short-term interests it is prepared to sacrifice in exchange for an assurance of survival and security."

NEW WEAPONS DEVELOPMENTS

Soviet Anti-Missile Defense & Orbital Bomb

In his State-of-the-Union message Jan. 10, Pres. Johnson noted that the Soviet Union had started to build "a limited antimissile defense" system near Moscow. He said Russia and the U.S. had "the solemn duty to slow down the arms race between us, if that is at all possible, in both conventional and nuclear weapons and defenses." "Any additional race," Mr. Johnson said, "would impose on our peoples, and on all mankind for that matter, an additional waste of resources with no gain in security to either side."

U.S. Defense Secy. Robert S. McNamara told reporters Nov. 3 that the USSR might be developing a method of nuclear attack from orbit. McNamara said in a press conference statement that "a fractional orbital bombardment system, or FOBS," apparently was the method being perfected in Russia. In such a system, he reported, a missile "is fired into a very low orbit about 100 miles above the earth" and is brought out of orbit—"generally before the first orbit is complete"—by the firing of a retro-rocket. McNamara based his announcement on "certain intelligence information we have collected on a series of space system flight tests being conducted by the Soviet Union." He estimated that a Soviet FOBS might be operational by as early as 1968. But he conceded that the tests might be for "some re-entry program" other than a FOBS. McNamara said the U.S. had "examined the desirability of the FOBS" several years previously but had decided not to develop it because "it would not improve our strategic offensive power."

McNamara said: The FOBS had both advantages and disadvantages when compared with "the traditional intercontinental ballistic missile," or ICBM. An ICBM "normally does not go into orbit" but "reaches a peak altitude of perhaps 800 miles," or 700 miles more than the FOBS. "Because of the low altitude of their orbits, some trajectories of a FOBS would avoid detection by some early warning radars, including our BMEWS [Ballistic Missile Early Warning System]"; "the impact point cannot be determined until [retro-rocket] ignition," and "the flight path can be as much as 10 minutes shorter than an ICBM." But a FOBS would be "significantly less" accurate than an ICBM, and its payload "would be but a fraction" of the ICBM's. A FOBS payload could be one to 3 megatons (equal in explosive force to one to 3 million tons of TNT), or about the same as a Polaris missile warhead. (The U.S. had deployed 650 of the latter submarine-launched weapons.) The FOBS "would not be accurate enough for a satisfactory attack upon United States Minutemen missiles, protected in their silos," but it might "provide a surprise nuclear strike against . . . soft land targets such as bomber bases." "Several years ago," however, the U.S. "initiated the deployment of equipment to deny" the Soviets the latter capability. "Already we are beginning to use operationally over-the-horizon [OTH] radars which possess a greater capability of detecting FOBS than do the

BMEWS." OTH radars, the first of which had gone into service 2 months previously, "will give us more warning time [about 15 minutes] against a full-scale attack using FOBS than BMEWS does against the ICBM launch."

"With 3-minute warning, 15-minute warning or no warning at all, we could still absorb a surprise attack and strike back with sufficient power to destroy the attacker."

It was reported that 2 unannounced Soviet satellite launchings of Sept. 17 and Nov. 2, 1966 and perhaps 9 of the Cosmos satellites launched by the USSR on short-duration flights (one orbit or less) beginning Jan. 25, 1967 were assumed to be FOBS development shots. The suspected Cosmos satellites were *Cosmos 139, 160, 169, 170, 171, 178, 179, 183 and 187.* The FOBS, in which nuclear warheads were not stationed in orbit, was not considered a violation of the treaty banning nuclear weapons in space.

Sen. Henry M. Jackson (D. Wash.) disclosed Nov. 4 that he had heard previously about the USSR's "new device" and that his Military Applications Subcommittee of the Joint Congressional Committee on Atomic Energy had scheduled hearings on it.

The 1968-9 edition of *Jane's All the World's Aircraft* reported Oct. 31 that the Soviet Union had launched at least 12 space-bomb rockets in 1967-8. The space bomb was described as a FOBS for use on ground targets.

American ABM System

Defense Secy. McNamara announced Sept. 18 that the U.S. would deploy a network of missiles capable of defending the nation against the sort of limited missile attack that Communist China was believed capable of mounting within a decade. The creation of a "light" Nike-X network, expected to cost $5 billion, was to be started by the end of 1967, and full deployment of the missiles was expected within 5 years. Under the Nike-X system, Spartan missiles would be used to intercept enemy missiles within 400 miles of the target, and Sprint missiles would be fired within 50 miles of the target at missiles penetrating the Spartan line. McNamara's announcement of the missile-defense decision was made in a speech in San Francisco before editors and publishers of United Press International. (A disclosure that the decision had been made and would be announced by McNamara in San Francisco had been made Sept. 15.)

McNamara asserted that the decision was taken because of the nuclear-attack threat from Communist China. He said: "It is important to understand that none of the systems at the present or foreseeable future would provide an impenetrable shield" over the U.S. against an all-out attack by the Soviet Union. Although "it would be insane and suicidal" for China to launch a missile attack against the U.S., "one can conceive conditions under which China might miscalculate," and "we wish to reduce such possibilities to a minimum."

McNamara stressed that the U.S. relied primarily on its ability to launch a lethal nuclear counterattack against an aggressor. "Our alert forces alone," he said, "carry more than 2,200 weapons, averaging more than one megaton [equal in explosive force to one million tons of TNT] each. A mere 400 one-megaton weapons, if delivered on the Soviet Union, would be sufficient to destroy over 1/3 of her population and 1/2 of her industry." To those who called for a "heavy" missile defense system in the event the nuclear deterrent did not deter, McNamara retorted that the Soviet Union would merely expand its striking power to assure penetration of such a defense. Similarly, McNamara said, the U.S. would augment its offensive power if the Soviet Union expanded its limited antimissile defense system.

"The blunt fact is," McNamara said, that neither the Soviet Union nor the U.S. "can attack the other without being destroyed in retaliation; nor can either of us attain a first-strike capability in the foreseeable future. The further fact is that both the Soviet Union and the United States presently possess an actual and credible 2d-strike capability against one another—and it is precisely this mutual capability that provides us both with the strongest possible motive to avoid a nuclear war." McNamara said both nations had "a deterrent in excess of our individual needs," and "both of our nations would benefit from a properly safeguarded agreement first to limit and later to reduce both our offensive and defensive strategic nuclear forces." Such an agreement, he said, "is fully feasible, since it is clearly in both our nations' interests." Neither nation would "risk the other's obtaining a first-strike capability," he asserted, and each, therefore, would "maintain a maximum effort to preserve an assured destruction capability." Furthermore, he said, "it would not be sensible for either side to launch a maximum effort to achieve a first strike capability . . . because the intelligence-gathering capability of each side being what it is, and the realities of lead-time from technological breakthrough to operational readiness being what they are, neither of us would be able to acquire a first-strike capability in secret."

State Secy. Dean Rusk had warned at a news conference Sept. 8 that the U.S. would feel compelled to deploy an antimissile defense network unless the Soviet Union agreed to begin talks soon on limiting nuclear missiles. "Time is becoming urgent," Rusk said. "We'd like to have discussions about both offensive and defensive missiles just as soon as possible."

The decision to deploy a limited missile defense system was criticized Sept. 16 by Chairman J. William Fulbright (D., Ark.) of the Senate Foreign Relations Committee. "Once this is started," he declared, "there will be no stopping it, and its cost will be astronomical, comparable to the space program. I also have very grave doubts about its effectiveness."

Other Senators, however, had called for the deployment of a missile defense. Sen. John G. Tower (R., Tex.) said Sept. 3 that the issue was "at least as important as Vietnam." Sen. John O. Pastore (D., R.I.), chairman of the Joint Atomic Energy Committee, asserted Sept. 9 that the U.S. "should move full speed ahead on building an antiballistic missile system." If the nation was able to spend $24 billion a year in Vietnam, he said, it "can certainly spend as much to insure the life and security of our American society."

Ex-Vice Pres. Richard M. Nixon, in an AP interview, also called on the U.S. to "go ahead at all costs" to build an anti-missile system.

(At the opening session of the UN General Assembly Sept. 19, Secy. Gen. U Thant warned that there was "a very grave danger that the nuclear arms race may be pushed to unimaginable levels by a new race for anti-missile missiles... and the whole new armory of weapons and counter-weapons." In reply, U.S. Amb.-to-UN Arthur J. Goldberg explained that the U.S. had recently decided that "our security, including particularly security against the threat of a missile attack by mainland China, required us to embark upon the construction of a limited anti-ballistic-missile system—and I emphasize the word 'limited'." No nation, Goldberg stressed, should feel threatened by this U.S. decision.)

First Chinese H-Bomb

Communist China announced June 17 that it had successfully tested its first hydrogen bomb. A communique broadcast by Hsinhua, the Chinese Communist news agency, said: "Today, on June 17, 1967, after the 5 nuclear tests in 2 years and 8 months, China successfully exploded its first hydrogen bomb, over the western region of the country." China's last previous nuclear test, conducted Dec. 28, 1966, had included some thermonuclear material. The communique continued:

"The success of this hydrogen bomb test represents another leap in the development of China's nuclear weapons. It marks the entry of the development of China's nuclear weapons into an entirely new stage.... With happiness and elation, we hail this fresh great victory of Mao Tse-tung's thought, this fresh splendid achievement of the great proletarian cultural revolution.... Warmest congratulations to all the commanders of the Chinese People's Liberation Army, the workers, engineers, technicians and scientists and other personnel who have been engaged in the research, manufacture and testing of the nuclear weapons.... It is hoped that...[these persons], following the teachings of Chairman Mao and the call of Comrade [Defense Min.] Lin Piao,... will guard against conceit and impetuosity, continue to exert themselves and win new and still greater merit in accelerating the development of our country's national defense, science and technology.... China has got atom bombs and guided missiles, and she now has the hydrogen bomb.... The success of...[the] test has further broken the nuclear monopoly of U.S. imperialism and Soviet revisionism and dealt a telling blow at their policy of nuclear blackmail. It is a very great encouragement and support to the Vietnamese people in their heroic war against U.S. aggression and for national salvation, to the Arab people in their resistance to aggression by the U.S. and British imperialists and their tool, Israel, and to the revolutionary people of the whole world.... The conducting of necessary and limited nuclear tests and the development of nuclear weapons by China are entirely for the purpose of defense, with the ultimate aim of abolishing nuclear weapons.

"We solemnly declare once again that at no time and in no circumstances will China be the first to use nuclear weapons. We always mean what we say...."

The communique gave no details of the magnitude of the test or of its location, but the U.S. Atomic Energy Commission reported June 17 that the test had been conducted at China's Lob Nor test site in Sinkiang Province and that it had produced a yield "in the range of several megatons." (One megaton was equivalent to the explosive force of one million tons of TNT.) It was reported June 17 that, on the basis of seismic measurements, U.S. officials had estimated the explosive yield of the test to be 3 megatons; this was 10 times greater than the estimated yield of the previous Chinese test and was equivalent to the explosive force of the U.S.' largest ICBM warhead.

Rep. Craig Hosmer (R., Calif.), the senior Republican on the Joint Congressional Atomic Energy Committee, reported to House Republicans June 19 that the Chinese test had produced a yield in the range of 2-7 megatons. Hosmer, who had access to intelligence information, said that the Chinese had carried out a "proof test" of an actual hydrogen bomb rather than of an experimental prototype. He said the device had been detonated atop a tower at the Lob Nor test site.

The speed with which China had been able to produce a thermonuclear bomb, coupled with its simultaneous development of a ballistic missile system, was taken as evidence of the Chinese leadership's determination to acquire an operational nuclear arsenal in the shortest possible time. Observers pointed out that it had taken the U.S. 8 years and the USSR and Britain about 4 years after their first atomic tests to develop a hydrogen weapon but it had taken Peking only 2 years 8 months to achieve the same success.

Sen. Henry M. Jackson (D., Wash.), chairman of the Military Applications Subcommittee of the Joint Congressional Committee on Atomic Energy, said June 17 that Red China's latest test made it imperative that the U.S. deploy a "light cover" missile defense system as quickly as possible. (Central Intelligence Agency Director Richard Helms had briefed the committee Jan. 11 on China's nuclear capabilities. After the briefing, Jackson told reporters that, while Peking was giving "highest priority" to the development of thermonuclear weapons, it was "going full blast and really pushing hard on missiles" as well. He said the Chinese were doing "quite well" in coordinating their nuclear weapon and delivery systems. He predicted that China "shortly would begin deploying medium-range ballistic missiles capable of striking targets within 1,000 miles of its borders and that it would have ICBMs capable of striking the U.S. by the early 1970s.)

Among other reaction to the test:

●UN Secy. Gen. U Thant said June 17 that "any explosion of an atomic or hydrogen bomb by any country anywhere is to be regretted in the context of the General Assembly resolutions on the matter."

●The French high commissioner for atomic energy, Francis Perrin, said June 17 that the test was a "very remarkable performance" but that it had "greater impact from the propaganda viewpoint than from the military viewpoint, at least in the near future."

●The Japanese Foreign Ministry denounced the test June 18 as a "reckless act" that defied world opinion.

●Indian Prime Min. Indira Gandhi referred to the test June 18 as "a matter for anxiety" and said it indicated China's "continued defiance of world public opinion."

●North Vietnamese Pres. Ho Chi Minh and other government officials congratulated Peking June 18 and asserted that the test aided their struggle against U.S. "imperialism."

The U.S. Joint Congressional Committee on Atomic Energy reported Aug. 2 that Communist China had made "rapid progress" in its development of a thermonuclear warhead and that it would be able to launch a limited missile attack on the U.S. by the 1970s. The report, entitled "The Impact of Chinese Communist Nuclear Weapons Progress on United States National Security," was based on secret testimony given to the committee earlier in the year by officials of the State Department, Defense Department, Central Intelligence Agency, Atomic Energy Commission and various laboratories involved in atomic weapons research. According to the committee, China's progress had been "more rapid and surprisingly more effective than had been expected or indeed predicted." It said that China currently had the capability of developing a multi-megaton thermonuclear weapon for delivery by an airplane and that by about 1970 it would probably be able to design a warhead in the megaton range for delivery by an intercontinental ballistic missile. Since the Chinese bomber force consisted only of several hundred short-range jets and a few longer-range bombers, the committee said, China appeared to be concentrating on the development of a missile delivery system. The committee noted that China had already tested a missile with a range of about 800 miles.

It was reported Aug. 29 that the Soviet information service had been distributing leaflets in Asian capitals warning of the danger of a Chinese nuclear attack in that area. The leaflets, made available by U.S. sources in Washington, said: "Even 8 to 10 years from now, the Chinese nuclear warheads will hardly be able to deal a 'retaliatory' blow and hit overseas targets. No doubt Peking understands this. Nevertheless, it hastily builds up its own nuclear weapons. Why? This is not a rhetorical question. For many Asian countries it is of vital importance."

French Nuclear & Weapons Programs

France completed the first stage of its missile-testing program Mar. 2 with the launching of a solid-fueled rocket from the Landes firing range in southwestern France. While French defense officials said they were satisfied with the results of the first series of tests, they admitted that they had encountered difficulties in the use of solid fuels.

France Mar. 29 launched its first nuclear-powered submarine, *Le Redoutable.* The submarine was scheduled to begin its sea trials in 1968 and to become fully operational by 1970, the date set for the final development and installation of its nuclear armament system—16 sea-to-land ballistic missiles, each with a range of 1,700-2,000 miles and an atomic payload of 500 kilotons. The submarine, entirely French-built was lauded by French Pres. Charles de Gaulle as a major milestone for "our navy, our defense and our independence." Specifications of *Le Redoutable:* weight—7,900 tons; length—423 feet; width at beam—34 feet; draft—60 feet; underwater displacement—9,000 tons; speed—greater than 20 knots; cruising depth—up to 600 feet; cruising range without refueling—200,000 miles; duration of average cruise—2 months; crew—2 crews of 135 men each; cost without armament—$140 million, with armament—over $250 million.

The French Armed Forces Ministry announced Apr. 19 that the French navy had successfully conducted its first test-firing of the M-122 sea-to-land intercontinental ballistic missile intended for use by the French nuclear submarine fleet. The missile was fired from a submerged submarine in the Mediterranean.

French Armed Forces Min. Pierre Messmer announced Aug. 3 that France's first hydrogen bomb, to be tested at the Mururoa test site in July 1968, would be in the 500-kiloton range. Messmer outlined this timetable for development of the *force de frappe:* (1) The first stage of French atomic weaponry had already become operational. It consisted of 62 Mirage-4 bombers, each of which carried one 60-kiloton atomic bomb. (The Mirage-4 had a top cruising range of 2,500 miles but could be refueled in flight.) (2) The 2d stage, to be completed by 1969, would consist of 25 medium-range ground-to-ground ballistic missiles, each of which would carry a 240-kiloton atomic warhead. The missiles would be installed in "hardened" underground silos in Provence in southeastern France. (Estimates on the range of the missile: 1,800-2,600 miles.) (3) The 3d and last stage would comprise "at least 3" nuclear-powered submarines, each of which would be outfitted with 16 intermediate-range (1,700-2,000 miles) ballistic missiles designed to carry a 500-kiloton hydrogen warhead. The submarines would become operational in 1970, 1972 and 1974 respectively. Messmer also noted that by 1972 France would have tactical nuclear weapons, to be delivered by planes or rockets, that could repel any conventional (non-nuclear) attack.

NATO Defense

Plans for defending NATO members with and against nuclear weapons were discussed by NATO's 7-nation Nuclear Planning Group at a meeting in Ankara, Turkey Sept. 28-29. The group's previous meeting had been held in Washington Apr. 6-7. Participating in the talks were U.S. Defense Secy. McNamara and Defense Mins. Denis Healey of Britain, Gerhard Schroeder of West Germany, Roberto Tremelloni of Italy, Ahmet Topaloglu of Turkey, Paul Hellyer of Canada and Willem den Toom of the Netherlands. NATO Secy. Gen. Manlio Brosio chaired the meeting.

While no communique was issued at the conclusion of the talks, the major issues discussed reportedly dealt with (1) the U.S.' decision to deploy a limited ABM defense system to guard against Communist China's potential nuclear threat to the U.S., (2) the possible deployment of an ABM system by the European members of NATO and (3) Turkey's request for nuclear land mines to guard against a possible land invasion by the Soviet Union.

It was reported Sept. 29 that the planning group had agreed to instruct the NATO military command to prepare a detailed study of the tactical usefulness of deploying nuclear land mines on NATO soil. A NATO source said that "Turkey made a *prima facie* case for the use of the mines on her border with the Soviet Union." "After a detailed plan for their deployment is drawn up," the official said, "then the military advantages will have to be weighed against the political considerations."

McNamara reportedly had argued during the meeting that the U.S.' proposed ABM system would not upset the balance of power between the U.S. and the Soviet Union since it was designed to protect the U.S. from a Communist Chinese rather than a Soviet nuclear attack. He also asserted that the U.S.' decision would not jeopardize the Geneva discussions on a nuclear non-proliferation treaty.

Healey reportedly argued that European deployment of an ABM system would be prohibitive in cost and ineffective in meeting a Soviet attack. But the defense ministers did not rule out the possibility of such a European system and agreed to study the matter further.

Following the Oct. 21 Paris meeting of the NATO Permanent Council, the U.S. announced that it had received "the green light to resume negotiations with the USSR on our own responsibility on a no-commitment basis ... with a view to establishing a generally acceptable text for the nuclear treaty."

MILITARY SPENDING

According to U.S. Arms Control & Disarmament Agency statistics, the U.S. ranked first and the USSR 2d in both total gross national product (GNP) and in military expenditures among all countries during 1967. While the U.S. also ranked first in per capita

GNP and per capita military expenditures, the Soviet Union ranked 2d in per capita military spending but only 19th in per capita GNP. The rankings and the military expenditures (in 1969 dollars) of the 30 countries with the highest GNP during 1967:

	Gross national product				Military expenditures			
	Total		Per Capita		Total		Per Capita	
	Rank	Billion dollars	Rank	Dollars	Rank	Billion dollars	Rank	Dollars
U.S.	1	793.5	1	3,985	1	75.5	1	379
USSR	2	384.0	19	1,630	2	52.0	2	221
West Germany..	3	121.0	11	2,097	6	5.3	10	93
France	4	115.9	8	2,323	4	5.9	5	117
Japan	5	115.7	25	1,158	13	1.1	58	11
Britain	6	110.9	15	2,014	5	6.4	7	117
Mainland China..	7	85.0	97	108	3	7.0	62	9
Italy	8	67.0	23	1,280	7	2.2	21	42
Canada	9	57.3	5	2,803	8	1.8	11	89
India	10	43.7	105	85	10	1.5	89	3
Poland	11	33.9	27	1,061	9	1.7	18	53
Brazil	12	29.7	53	347	15	.9	56	11
East Germany...	13	28.8	18	1,780	18	.8	18	56
Spain	14	26.9	32	837	17	.8	34	25
Czechoslovakia ..	15	26.3	16	1,839	11	1.3	9	94
Australia	16	25.2	10	2,145	12	1.2	8	87
Mexico	17	24.1	44	528	45	.2	78	4
Sweden	18	23.9	3	3,037	14	.9	4	120
Netherlands	19	22.7	17	1,802	16	.9	14	70
Belgium	20	19.5	14	2,035	22	.6	17	59
Rumania	21	18.8	29	975	20	.6	29	32
Switzerland	22	16.0	6	2,645	31	.4	16	62
Argentina	23	14.9	37	649	39	.3	55	9
Pakistan	24	13.7	96	113	25	.5	77	4
South Africa....	25	13.1	36	698	32	.4	38	20
Hungary	26	12.6	24	1,234	42	.2	33	28
Denmark	27	12.2	7	2,521	36	.3	15	62
Turkey	28	10.6	55	324	23	.5	48	16
Austria	29	10.6	22	1,447	47	.1	44	20
Yugoslavia	30	9.7	46	487	30	.4	43	20

1967's NUCLEAR TESTS

U.S. Explosions

All U.S. nuclear tests conducted during 1967 were underground. The dates, force and sites of the tests:

Date	Force	Site
Jan. 19	Low-intermediate	Nevada test site
Feb. 8	Low yield	Nevada test site
Feb. 20	Low yield	Nevada test site
Feb. 23	Low yield	Nevada test site
Feb. 23	Low-intermediate	Nevada test site
Mar. 2	Low yield	Nevada test site
Apr. 7	Low yield	Nevada test site
Apr. 21	Low yield	Nevada test site
Apr. 27	Low yield	Nevada test site
May 10	Low-intermediate	Nevada test site
May 22	Intermediate	Nevada test site
May 23	Intermediate	Nevada test site
May 26	Low-intermediate	Nevada test site
June 22*	Low yield	Nevada test site
June 26	Low yield	Nevada test site
June 29**	Low yield	Nevada test site
Aug. 10	Low yield	Nevada test site
Aug. 18	Low yield	Nevada test site
Aug. 31	Low yield	Nevada test site
Sept. 7	Low-intermediate	Nevada test site
Sept. 22*	Low yield	Nevada test site
Sept. 27	Low-intermediate	Nevada test site
Oct. 18	Intermediate	Nevada test site
Oct. 25	Low yield	Nevada test site
Nov. 8	Low yield	Nevada test site
Dec. 10§*	Low-intermediate	New Mexico
Dec. 25	Low yield	Nevada test site

Soviet Explosions

Feb. 26***	Intermediate	Semipalatinsk
Apr. 20***	Low-intermediate	Semipalatinsk
Mar. 26***	Low yield	Semipalatinsk
July 16***		Semipalatinsk
Oct. 17***	Low-intermediate	Semipalatinsk
Oct. 23***	Lower end intermediate	Novaya Zemlya

* Test was part of Plowshare Program for developing peaceful uses of nuclear explosives.
** The AEC announced that the June 29 test had resulted in a "small release of radio-activity" into the atmosphere but that fallout had been confined to the test site and that the radioactive level presented no health hazard.
*** Underground test.
§ This test was conducted in cooperation with the Bureau of Mines and the El Paso Natural Gas Co. in an effort to free a deposit of natural gas trapped in a tight sandstone formation. Dubbed Project Gasbuggy, it was part of the Plowshare Program.

Date	Force	Site

French Explosions

June 5★†		Muruora Atoll
June 27★†		Muruora Atoll
July 24★†		Muruora Atoll

Chinese Explosions

June 17★‡	3 megatons	Lob Nor
July 3★¶	Low yield	Lob Nor
Dec. 24★	Low yield	Lob Nor

---

† Tests aimed at developing an atomic triggering device for the detonation of thermonuclear weapons.

‡ Hydrogen explosion.

¶ Test reported in Tokyo by Japanese news agency Jiji, which quoted unidentified Chinese sources but had no seismological or meteorological evidence to substantiate the report of a nuclear explosion.

★ Atmospheric test.

1968

Little progress toward disarmament was made in 1968 despite the UN approval June 12 of the final text of the non-proliferation treaty. The pledges by the USSR, U.S. and Britain to guarantee the security of non-nuclear nations were considered insufficient by most of these nations. The efforts in the UN by non-nuclear powers to present a security plan of their own failed. The ratification of the nonproliferation treaty was delayed, especially after the Aug. 21 invasion of Czechoslovakia by the USSR encouraged U.S. mistrust of the Soviet Union. Reports about the progress of anti-ballistic missiles (ABMs) and multiple independently targeted re-entry vehicles (MIRVs) further increased the fear of a costly new acceleration of the armaments race. The Geneva conference was in session Jan. 18-Mar. 14 and July 16-Aug. 28.

NON-PROLIFERATION TREATY

Revised Draft Submitted in Geneva

The U.S. and the Soviet Union submitted to the 18-Nation UN Disarmament Committee (ENDC) in Geneva Jan. 18 a revised and complete draft treaty to prevent the further spread of nuclear weapons. The most significant feature of the revised draft was the inclusion of an article (Article 3) providing for an international inspection and controls system designed to insure compliance with the terms of the treaty. The U.S. and USSR had submitted the original draft to the ENDC Aug. 24, 1967 but had left blank the article on inspection because of disagreement over the kinds of controls to adopt. Agreement on Article 3 was reached only after long negotiating sessions between American and Soviet representatives.

The inspection article stipulated that each non-nuclear-weapon state that became a party to the treaty would negotiate an agreement with the International Atomic Energy Agency (IAEA), either individually or together with other states, concerning the acceptance of suitable safeguards for verifying the fulfillment of its obligations under the treaty. Negotiations were to begin within 180 days from the date the treaty entered into force and were to be completed not later than 18 months after the date negotiations had begun. By stipulating that the type of safeguards system to be employed would be an issue negotiable with the IAEA, the article skirted what had proved to be a major stumbling block in the negotiations on the inspections issue: the unwillingness of the non-nuclear members of the European Atomic Energy Community (Euratom) to subordinate their own inspection system to that of the IAEA, primarily out of fear that inspection by the IAEA would be tantamount to legalized espionage since the IAEA, a UN organization, included Communist as well as non-Communist members. While the inspection article, as finally worded, did not mention Euratom by name, it nonetheless held open the possibility that Euratom and IAEA could work out a mutually acceptable arrangement concerning the suitability of the Euratom controls system. U.S. ENDC delegate Adrian S. Fisher interpreted the article in this light when he noted Jan. 18 that the IAEA would be empowered to conclude an agreement with "another international organization" in the atomic energy field. He also said that, in order to avoid "unnecessary duplication," the IAEA should make "appropriate use of existing records and safeguards" if agreement could be reached on a mutually acceptable arrangement.

Soviet delegate Aleksei A. Roshchin did not object to this interpretation of Article 3.

In addition to the inspection article, the revised draft made these changes: (1) It stipulated that the treaty would enter into force once it had been ratified by all the nuclear-weapon signatories as well as by 40 non-nuclear-weapon signatories; the original draft had not stipulated how many non-nuclear-weapon signatories would have to ratify the treaty for it to enter into force. (2) It stipulated that a conference would be convened 25 years from the date the treaty had gone into force to determine whether the treaty was to be extended indefinitely or only for a fixed period or periods of time; the original draft had stipulated that the treaty would be of unlimited duration. (3) It stipulated that any amendment to the treaty would be binding only on parties that ratified it; the original draft had stipulated that any amendment would be binding on all treaty signatories, whether or not they ratified it. (4) It strengthened the commitment of the signatories to pursue negotiations on effective means of ending the nuclear arms race and achieving a treaty on general and complete disarmament. (5) It strengthened the commitment of the nuclear-weapon signatories to provide nuclear devices for peaceful purposes to the non-nuclear-weapon signatories.

U.S. delegate Fisher said Jan. 18 that the submission of the revised draft represented a "major advance" in efforts to develop a "widely acceptable treaty." Soviet delegate Roshchin said the event marked an "important step forward that opens the way toward a speedy conclusion of the treaty." Delegates from Britain, Canada, India, Italy and Mexico welcomed the development. The British, Canadian and Czechoslovak delegates urged Jan. 23 that the draft be adopted quickly.

Among international reaction to the Geneva development:

● Pres. Johnson said Jan. 18: "The draft treaty text submitted today clearly demonstrates an important fact. In the face of the differences that exist in the world, the 2 nations which carry the heaviest responsibility for averting the catastrophe of nuclear war can, with sufficient patience and determination, move forward." It was his "fervent hope" that he would be able to submit the treaty to the Senate "for its advice and consent this year."

● West German Press Secy. Gunter Diehl Jan. 19 "greeted" the revised draft treaty as representing "very important progress." He expressed hope that the ENDC could now "find a treaty for the other countries to negotiate on that can find worldwide acceptance." When asked if West Germany considered the draft acceptable in its current form, Diehl said: "I think that it is still capable of being improved."

● French Armed Forces Min. Pierre Messmer denounced the draft Jan. 22 as "dangerous and doomed to failure." He charged that, if adopted, the treaty would "lead to tensions and create new, dangerous situations." (France and Communist China, 2 of the world's 5 nuclear powers, had consistently voiced their opposition to the treaty and were not expected to sign it.)

New Draft Debated

The UN 18-nation Disarmament Committee (ENDC) Mar. 15 forwarded its draft non-proliferation treaty to the UN General Assembly to be debated at a special session scheduled to begin in late April. The draft had been amended, and the final version was tabled Mar. 11.

A U.S.-USSR-British security pledge was extended Mar. 7 to the non-nuclear-weapon members of the ENDC. The pledge, spelled out in identical draft resolutions submitted by the U.S. and USSR and indorsed by Britain, was to be transmitted to the UN Security Council for its consideration. The resolution promised that the nuclear-weapon states that signed the non-proliferation treaty would act "immediately" through the Security Council to "provide or support immediate assistance" to any non-nuclear-weapon signatory of the treaty that came under nuclear attack or threat of nuclear attack. The agreement sought to assure the non-nuclear states (particularly India) that they would not forfeit their security by signing the proposed treaty and thereby foregoing the possibility of developing their own nuclear-weapon potential. U.S. delegate William C. Foster said Mar. 7 that the big-power pledge would "enhance the security of all parties to the treaty, and in particular of those who find themselves confronted by a direct nuclear threat to their security." Soviet delegate Roshchin said the resolution "properly solved" the question of assurances to the non-nuclear-weapon states that signed the treaty.

The text of the draft resolution:

"The Security Council, noting with appreciation the desire of a large number of states to subscribe to the treaty on the nonproliferation of nuclear weapons, and thereby to undertake not to receive the transfer whatsoever of nuclear weapons or other nuclear explosive devices or of control over such weapons or explosive devices directly, or indirectly, not to manufacture or otherwise acquire nuclear weapons or other nuclear explosive devices, and not to seek or receive any assistance in the manufacture of nuclear weapons or other nuclear explosive devices;

"Taking into consideration the concern of certain of these states that, in conjunction with their adherence to the treaty on the non-proliferation of nuclear weapons, appropriate measures be undertaken to safeguard their security;

"Bearing in mind that any aggression accompanied by the use of nuclear weapons would endanger the peace and security of all states;

"[1] Recognizes that aggression with nuclear weapons or the threat of such aggression against a non-nuclear-weapon state would create a situation in which the Security Council, and above all its nuclear-weapon-state permanent members, would have to act immediately in accordance with their obligations under the United Nations Charter.

"[2] Welcomes the intention expressed by certain states that they will provide or support immediate assistance in accordance with the Charter, to any non-nuclear-weapon state party to the treaty on the non-proliferation of nuclear weapons that is a victim of an act or an object of a threat of aggression in which nuclear weapons are used.

"[3] Reaffirms in particular the inherent right, recognized under Article 51 of the Charter, of individual and collective self-defense if an armed attack occurs against a member of the United Nations, until the Security Council has taken measures necessary to maintain international peace and security."

Among international reaction to the ENDC development:

● Communist China charged Mar. 9 that the "United States-Soviet 'nuclear umbrella' project is mainly directed against China."

● In a statement transmitted to the ENDC Mar. 8 and made public Mar. 10, West Germany greeted the security pledge as an "important step" but warned that the draft treaty still did not meet all objections of the non-nuclear states. The statement said in part: "A ban against threats, political pressure or political blackmail against non-atomic powers should be in the treaty. Such a provision would be just and reasonable compensation to the renunciation of atomic weapons by the non-nuclear powers." The statement also urged that the preamble to the treaty state unequivocally that the final goal of nuclear non-proliferation was "general, complete and controlled disarmament."

● Indian Prime Min. Indira Gandhi told the Lok Sabha (parliament) Mar. 14 that India was not satisfied with the proposed treaty. She said that a nuclear security guarantee "cannot be made a *quid pro quo* for signing the nuclear non-proliferation treaty in its present form."

In previous ENDC debate, Rumania had charged Feb. 6 that the proposed treaty still "discriminates profoundly" against the non-nuclear states. Rumanian delegate Nicolae Ecobesco introduced 12 amendments, including proposals that would (1) extend a "precise" security guarantee to the non-nuclear signatories and (2) stipulate that the U.S. and Soviet Union would be subject to the same inspection controls as the non-nuclear parties to the treaty. In reference to the security guarantee, Ecobesco said: "We would like to know if the nuclear powers are disposed to take on a solemn undertaking, by means of the non-proliferation treaty, never and in no circumstances to use nuclear arms against states not possessing them and not to threaten these states with their use in any case or in any way." U.S. delegate Samuel DePalma replied that the non-nuclear states were not entitled to "compensation" since they would receive more "security benefits" from the proposed treaty than would the nuclear powers.

Brazil charged Feb. 8 that the proposed treaty would impose "a new form of dependence [on the non-nuclear signatories] which is certainly inconsistent with our aspirations for development." As in the past, Brazil sought to obtain a guarantee that the non-nuclear states could acquire nuclear devices for peaceful purposes, particularly for large earthmoving projects. Brazilian delegate J. A. de Araujo Castro described the pledge of the nuclear powers to conduct such explosions for the non-nuclear signatories as "the institutionalization of a status of dependence" since it would serve to freeze "all technological development that might be connected, even remotely, with the specific technology of nuclear explosive devices intended for civil use."

Swedish delegate Alva Myrdal urged Feb. 8 that the Soviet Union place its peaceful nuclear activities under international inspection controls so as to "wipe out this quite unnecessary lack of equal treatment in regard to controls." While the proposed treaty exempted the nuclear powers from inspection controls, the U.S. and Britain had announced in Dec. 1967 that they would permit inspection of their civil nuclear plants in the event of the successful conclusion of the non-proliferation treaty.

The Soviet Union warned Feb. 16 that the non-nuclear states that did not sign the proposed treaty would lose the benefits of international cooperation in peaceful nuclear development. Soviet delegate Roshchin said: "It is quite natural that the states that are not parties to the treaty on non-proliferation will not be in the same favorable position, as the participation both in the international exchange of information and in other forms of international cooperation is concerned, since they will not be able to use the opportunities that will be open for the parties to the treaty.... It is also natural that those who will adopt a positive attitude toward the treaty and adhere to it will enjoy a wide measure of trust. These states will be given assistance and cooperation in the nuclear field."

In its first comment of the revised treaty since its presentation Jan. 18, India asserted Feb. 27 that the draft failed to meet "some of the more fundamental and basic requirements" of the non-nuclear states. Indian delegate Azim Husain accused the U.S. and USSR of ignoring "many of the important ideas and suggestions put forward by a number of delegations, including my own."

In the first Italian reaction to the revised draft, delegate Roberto Caracciolo called Feb. 20 for an amendment that would guarantee the right of all signatories, nuclear or non-nuclear, to obtain nuclear devices for peaceful purposes.

Following the presentation of their security pledge, the U.S. and Soviet Union Mar. 11 tabled a final revised draft treaty. In contrast to previous practice, the 2 powers submitted a single document rather than separate but identical ones. The sponsors barred any major changes in the final draft but did accept 3 amendments that had been proposed by Sweden and that had received wide support among ENDC members. The amendments (1) authorized treaty signatories to conduct periodic review of the treaty every 5 years instead of only after the first 5 years, (2) stipulated that new efforts would be made to achieve agreement on the banning of underground nuclear testing and (3) strengthened the clause on efforts to halt the nuclear arms race by stating that negotiations toward that end should begin "at an early date."

In committee debate Mar. 12, the Soviet Union rejected West German and Rumanian proposals that controls be placed on the peaceful nuclear activities of the nuclear powers. Soviet delegate Roshchin said: "The nuclear non-proliferation treaty does not envisage the banning of nuclear weapons and their production—though it is a step towards this objective—and therefore as far as the treaty is concerned the question does not arise of controlling the nuclear powers' activities in the atomic field."

As the ENDC concluded its discussions Mar. 14, only 5 of the members—Britain, Bulgaria, Canada, Czechoslovakia and Poland—had indorsed the U.S.-Soviet draft treaty. Brazil, India and Italy reserved their position but were known to have strong objections to the treaty, as had Rumania. Of the remaining 6 active members of the ENDC, Mexico, Sweden and the United Arab Republic were viewed as favoring the treaty, while Burma, Ethiopia and Nigeria remained undecided. France, the 18th ENDC member, had not participated in the discussions and was considered opposed to the treaty. West Germany was not a member of the ENDC, but the acceptance of the treaty by the nuclear powers was known to be contingent on Bonn's tacit agreement to adhere to it.

UN Approves Final Draft

The UN General Assembly June 12 adopted a resolution commending the draft nuclear non-proliferation treaty submitted to it Mar. 15 by the ENDC. The vote was 95-4 with 21 abstentions and 4 absent. UN indorsement of the treaty completed 4 years of intensive negotiations on measures to halt the proliferation of nuclear weapons and fulfilled a UN General Assembly resolution adopted in 1960. The resolution commending the treaty had been adopted by the First (Political & Security) Committee June 10 by 92-4 vote with 22 abstentions.

The resolution (1) requested that the depositary governments "open the treaty for signature and ratification at the earliest possible date," (2) expressed hopes for "the widest possible adherence to the treaty by both nuclear-weapon and non-nuclear-weapon states," (3) urged the ENDC and the nuclear-weapon states "urgently to pursue negotiations on effective measures relating to the cessation of the nuclear arms race at an early date and to nuclear disarmament, and on a treaty on general and complete disarmament under strict and effective international control" and (4) requested that the ENDC "report on the progress of its work to the General Assembly at its 23d session."

The U.S. and Soviet Union, as the 2 sponsors of the treaty, had agreed May 31 to revisions in the treaty to overcome objections raised by a number of smaller countries. As outlined by U.S. Amb.-to-UN Arthur J. Goldberg, the changes were designed to (1) "strengthen the provisions of the treaty for sharing in the benefits of the peaceful uses of nuclear energy," (2) "strengthen the provisions of the treaty calling for further and prompt measures to halt the nuclear arms race and to limit existing nuclear arsenals" and (3) "enhance the security of the signatories by reaffirming the principles of the UN Charter regarding the use of force and threats of force in international relations."

The 95-4 vote by which the Assembly adopted the resolution:

In favor—Afghanistan, Australia, Austria, Barbados, Belgium, Bolivia, Botswana, Britain, Bulgaria, Byelorussia, Cameroon, Canada, Ceylon, Chad, Chile, China (Nationalist), Colombia, Congo (Kinshasa), Costa Rica, Cyprus, Czechoslovakia, Dahomey, Denmark, Ecuador, Ethiopia, Finland, Ghana, Greece, Guatemala, Guyana, Honduras, Hungary, Iceland, Indonesia, Iran, Iraq, Ireland, Israel, Italy, Ivory Coast, Jamaica, Japan, Jordan, Kenya, Kuwait, Laos, Lebanon, Lesotho, Liberia, Libya, Luxembourg, Madagascar, Malaysia, Maldive Islands, Malta, Mauritius, Mexico, Mongolia, Morocco, Nepal, Netherlands, New Zealand, Nicaragua, Nigeria, Norway, Pakistan, Panama, Paraguay, Peru, Philippines, Poland, Rumania, Salvador, Senegal, Singapore, Somalia, South Africa, Southern Yemen, Sudan, Sweden, Syria, Thailand, Togo, Trinidad & Tobago, Tunisia, Turkey, Ukraine, USSR, UAR, U.S., Upper Volta, Uruguay, Venezuela, Yemen, Yugoslavia.

Opposed—Albania, Cuba, Tanzania, Zambia.

Abstaining—Algeria, Argentina, Brazil, Burma, Burundi, Central African Republic, Congo (Brazzaville), France, Gabon, Guinea, India, Malawi, Mali, Mauritania, Niger, Portugal, Rwanda, Saudi Arabia, Sierra Leone, Spain, Uganda.

Absent—Cambodia, Dominican Republic, Gambia, Haiti.

France abstained because of its view that disarmament could not be made effective in the absence of a "true *dentente*" between East and West. However, French Amb.-to-UN Armand Berard said June 12 that France would abide by the treaty's major provision, which barred the nuclear-weapon states from providing such arms or the means of manufacturing them to the non-nuclear-weapon states.

In an address to the Assembly following the adoption of the resolution, Pres. Johnson hailed the treaty as "the most important international agreement in the field of disarmament since the nuclear age began." He pledged U.S. compliance with the treaty and stressed that the U.S. would "give particular attention to the needs of developing nations" by sharing "our technical knowledge and experience in peaceful nuclear research." He urged speedy ratification of the treaty as a "first step toward ending the peril of nuclear war." He expressed his belief that the treaty could lead to further arms control measures and he affirmed that the U.S. urgently desired "to begin early discussion on the limitation of strategic offensive and defensive nuclear weapons systems." "We shall search for an agreement that will not only avoid another costly and futile escalation of the arms race, but will de-escalate it," the President pledged. He also called for "new ways to eliminate the threat of conventional conflicts that might grow into nuclear disasters."

As a follow-up to the UN indorsement of the treaty, the U.S., USSR and Britain called June 12 for a meeting of the UN Security Council to consider a parallel resolution drafted by the 3 powers in the course of the ENDC negotiations. The text pledged the treaty's nuclear-weapon signatories to come to the aid of the non-nuclear-weapon signatories in the event of an atomic attack or threat of such an attack on their territory. The Council began debate on the draft security pledge June 17.

Final Text of Non-Proliferation Treaty

This is the complete text of the final and approved draft of the "Treaty on the Non-Proliferation of Nuclear Weapons" (new language is indicated in italics; deletions are noted in brackets where they occur):

The states concluding this treaty, hereinafter referred to as the "parties of the treaty,"

Considering the devastation that would be visited upon all mankind by a nuclear war and the consequent need to make every effort to avert the danger of such a war and to take measures to safeguard the security of peoples,

Believing that the proliferation of nuclear weapons would seriously enhance the danger of nuclear war,

In conformity with resolutions of the United Nations General Assembly calling for the conclusion of an agreement on the prevention of wider dissemination of nuclear weapons,

Undertaking to cooperate in facilitating the application of International Atomic Energy Agency safeguards on peaceful nuclear activities,

Expressing their support for research, development and other efforts to further the application, within the framework of the International Atomic Energy Agency safeguards system, of the principle of safeguarding effectively the flow of source and special fissionable materials by use of instruments and other techniques at certain strategic points,

Affirming the principle that the benefits of peaceful applications of nuclear technology, including any technological by-products which may be derived by nuclear-weapon states from the development of nuclear explosive devices, should be available for *peaceful purposes to all parties to the treaty, whether* nuclear-weapon or non-nuclear-weapon states,

Convinced that, in furtherance of this principle, all parties to the treaty are entitled to participate in the fullest possible exchange of scientific information for, and to contribute alone or in cooperation with other states to, the further development of the applications of atomic energy for peaceful purposes,

[One paragraph deleted]

Declaring their intention to achieve at the earliest possible date the cessation of the nuclear arms race *and to undertake effective measures in the direction of nuclear disarmament,*

Urging the cooperation of all states in the attainment of this objective,

Recalling the determination expressed by the parties to the 1963 treaty banning nuclear weapon tests in the atmosphere, in outer space and under water in its preamble to seek to achieve the discontinuance of all test explosions of nuclear weapons for all time and to continue negotiations to this end,

Desiring to further the easing of international tension and the strengthening of trust between states in order to facilitate the cessation of the manufacture of nuclear weapons, the liquidation of all their existing stockpiles, and the elimination from national arsenals of nuclear weapons and the means of their delivery pursuant to a treaty on general and complete disarmament under strict and effective international control.

[One paragraph deleted]

Recalling that, in accordance with the Charter of the United Nations, states must refrain in their international relations from the threat or use of force against the territorial integrity or political independence of any state, or in any other manner inconsistent with the purposes of the United Nations, and that the establishment and maintenance of international peace and security are to be promoted with the least diversion for armaments of the world's human and economic resources,

Have agreed as follows:

Article I. Each nuclear-weapon state party to the treaty undertakes not to transfer to any recipient whatsoever nuclear weapons or other nuclear explosive devices or control over such weapons or explosive devices directly, or indirectly; and not in any way to assist, encourage or induce any non-nuclear-weapon state to manufacture or otherwise acquire nuclear weapons or other nuclear explosive devices, or control over such weapons or explosive devices.

Article II. Each non-nuclear-weapon state party to the treaty undertakes not to receive the transfer from any transferor whatsoever of nuclear weapons or other nuclear explosive devices or of control over such weapons or explosive devices directly, or indirectly; not to manufacture or otherwise acquire nuclear weapons or other nuclear explosive devices;

and not to seek or receive any assistance in the manufacture of nuclear weapons or other nuclear explosive devices.

Article III. 1. Each non-nuclear-weapon state party to the treaty undertakes to accept safeguards, as set forth in an agreement to be negotiated and concluded with the International Atomic Energy Agency in accordance with the Statute of the International Atomic Energy Agency and the Agency's safeguards system, for the exclusive purpose of verification of the fulfilment of its obligations assumed under this treaty with a view to preventing diversion of nuclear energy from peaceful uses to nuclear weapons or other nuclear explosive devices. Procedures for the safeguards required by this article shall be followed with respect to source or special fissionable material whether it is being produced, processed or used in any principal nuclear facility or is outside any such facility. The safeguards required by this article shall be applied on all source or special fissionable material in all peaceful nuclear activities within the territory of such state, under its jurisdiction, or carried out under its control anywhere.

2. Each state party to the treaty undertakes not to provide: (a) source or special fissionable material or (b) equipment or material especially designed or prepared for the processing, use or production of special fissionable material, to any non-nuclear-weapon state for peaceful purposes, unless the source or special fissionable material shall be subject to the safeguards required by this article.

3. The safeguards required by this article shall be implemented in a manner designed to comply with article IV of this treaty, and to avoid hampering the economic or technological development of the parties or international cooperation in the field of peaceful nuclear activities, including the international exchange of nuclear material and equipment, for the processing, use or production of nuclear material for peaceful purposes in accordance with the provisions of this article and the principle of safeguarding set forth in the preamble.

4. Non-nuclear-weapon states party to the treaty shall conclude agreements with the International Atomic Energy Agency to meet the requirements of this article either individually or together with other states in accordance with the Statute of the International Atomic Energy Agency. Negotiation of such agreements shall commence within 180 days from the original entry into force of this treaty. For states depositing their instruments of ratification or accession after the 180-day period, negotiation of such agreements shall commence not later than the date of such deposit. Such agreements shall enter into force not later than 18 months after the date of initiation of negotiations.

Article IV. 1. Nothing in this treaty shall be interpreted as affecting the inalienable right of all the parties to the treaty to develop research, production and use of nuclear energy for peaceful purposes without discrimination and in conformity with articles I and II of this treaty.

2. All the parties to the treaty undertake to facilitate, and have the right to participate in, the fullest possible exchange of equipment, materials and scientific and technological information for the peaceful uses of nuclear energy. Parties to the treaty in a position to do so shall also cooperate in contributing alone or together with other states or international organizations to the further development of the applications of nuclear energy for peaceful purposes, especially in the territories of non-nuclear-weapon states party to the treaty, with due consideration for the needs of the developing areas of the world.

Article V. Each party to this treaty undertakes to [word "cooperate" deleted] take appropriate measures to ensure that, in accordance with this treaty, under appropriate international observation and through appropriate international procedures, potential benefits from any peaceful applications of nuclear explosions will be made available [words "through appropriate international procedures" deleted] to non-nuclear-weapon states party to this treaty on a non-discriminatory basis and that the charge to such parties for the explosive devices used will be as low as possible and exclude any charge for research and development. [One sentence deleted] Non-nuclear-weapon states party to the treaty shall be able to obtain such benefits, pursuant to a special international agreement or agreements, through an appropriate international body with adequate representation of non-nuclear-weapon states. Negotiations on this subject shall commence as soon as possible after the treaty enters into force. Non-nuclear-weapon states party to the treaty so desiring may also obtain such benefits pursuant to bilateral agreements.

Article VI. Each of the parties to the treaty undertakes to pursue negotiations in good faith on effective measures [word "regarding" deleted] relating to cessation of the nuclear arms race at an early date and to nuclear disarmament, and on a treaty on general and complete disarmament under strict and effective international control.

Article VII. Nothing in this treaty affects the right of any group of states to conclude regional treaties in order to assure the total absence of nuclear weapons in their respective territories.

Article VIII [formerly Article V]. 1. Any party to the treaty may propose amendments to this treaty. The text of any proposed amendment shall be submitted to the depositary governments which shall circulate it to all parties to the treaty. Thereupon, if requested to do so by 1/3 or more of the parties to the treaty, the depositary governments shall convene a conference, to which they shall invite all the parties to the treaty, to consider such an amendment.

2. Any amendment to this treaty must be approved by a majority of the votes of all the parties to the treaty, including the votes of all nuclear-weapon states party to the treaty and all other parties which, on the date amendment is circulated, are members of the Board of Governors of the International Atomic Energy Agency. The amendment shall enter into force for [words "all parties" deleted] *each party that deposits its instrument of ratification of the amendment* upon the deposit of such instruments of ratification of all nuclear-weapon states party to the treaty and all other parties which, on the date the amendment is circulated, are members of the Board of Governors of the International Atomic Energy Agency. *Thereafter, it shall enter into force for any other party upon the deposit of its instrument of ratification of the amendment.*

3. 5 years after the entry into force of this treaty, a conference of parties to the treaty shall be held in Geneva, Switzerland, in order to review the operation of this treaty with a view to assuring that the purposes *of the preamble* and the provisions of the treaty are being realized. *At intervals of 5 years thereafter, a majority of the parties to the treaty may obtain, by submitting a proposal to this effect to the depositary governments, the convening of further conferences with the same objective of reviewing the operation of the treaty.*

Article IX [formerly Article VI]. 1. This treaty shall be open to all states for signature. Any state which does not sign the treaty before its entry into force in accordance with paragraph 3 of this article may accede to it at any time.

2. This treaty shall be subject to ratification by signatory states. Instruments of ratification and instruments of accession shall be deposited with *the governments of the Union of Soviet Socialist Republics, the United Kingdom of Great Britain and Northern Ireland and the United States of America,* which are hereby designated the depositary governments.

3. This treaty shall enter into force after its ratification by [words "all nuclear-weapon states signatory to this treaty" deleted] *the states, the governments of which are designated depositaries of the treaty,* and *40* other states signatory to this treaty and the deposit of their instruments of ratification. For the purpose of this treaty, a nuclear-weapon state is one which has manufactured and exploded a nuclear weapon or other nuclear explosive device prior to Jan. 1, 1967.

4. For states whose instruments of ratification or accession are deposited subsequent to the entry into force of this treaty, it shall enter into force on the date of the deposit of their instruments of ratification or accession.

5. The depositary governments shall promptly inform all signatory and acceding states of the date of each signature, the date of deposit of each instrument of ratification or of accession, the date of the entry into force of this treaty, and the date of receipt of any requests for convening a conference or other notices.

6. This treaty shall be registered by the depositary governments pursuant to Article 102 of the Charter of the United Nations.

Article X [formerly Article VII]. [One sentence ("This treaty shall be of unlimited duration.") deleted.] *1.* Each party shall, in exercising its national sovereignty, have the right to withdraw from the treaty if it decides that extraordinary events, related to the subject-matter of this treaty, have jeopardized the supreme interests of its country. It shall give notice of such withdrawal to all other parties to the treaty and to the United Nations

Security Council 3 months in advance. Such notice shall include a statement of the extraordinary events it regards as having jeopardized its supreme interests.

2. 25years after the entry into force of the treaty, a conference shall be convened to decide whether the treaty shall continue in force indefinitely, or shall be extended for an additional fixed period or periods. This decision shall be taken by a majority of the parties to the treaty.

Article XI [formerly Article VIII]. This treaty, the English, Russian, French, Spanish and Chinese texts of which are equally authentic, shall be deposited in the archives of the depositary governments. Duly certified copies of this treaty shall be transmitted by the depositary governments to the governments of the signatory and acceding states.

In witness whereof the undersigned, duly authorized, have signed this treaty.

3 Powers Pledge Security of Non-Nuclear Nations

The UN Security Council June 19 adopted a resolution welcoming pledges by the U.S., USSR and Britain to act "immediately" through the Council in the event of a nuclear attack or threat of such an attack on non-nuclear-weapon states. The vote on the resolution was 10-0 with 5 abstentions. Those abstaining were Algeria, Brazil, France, India and Pakistan. The intention of the pledge was to assure the non-nuclear-weapon states that they would not jeopardize their security by signing the treaty.

In submitting the pledge for the U.S., Amb.-to-UN Goldberg noted that the security guarantee "introduces a powerful element of deterrence against aggression with nuclear weapons" and "lay[s] a firm political, moral and legal basis for assuring the security of non-nuclear-weapon parties" to the non-proliferation treaty. Soviet First Deputy Foreign Min. Vasily V. Kuznetsov, submitting the Soviet pledge, said the guarantee was a "logical and natural" demand of the non-nuclear-weapon states since "there still remains in the world the possibility of unleashing a nuclear war against non-nuclear countries." Lord Caradon submitted the pledge for Britain and declared that it should be clear "to everyone" that any country considering nuclear aggression against a non-nuclear-weapon signatory of the treaty "would be deterred by these assurances." Caradon described the "common determination of East and West in this issue of supreme international concern" as a "development of the utmost significance and importance in world affairs."

The text of the U.S. pledge, identical to the ones submitted by the Soviet Union and Britain:

The government of the U.S. notes with appreciation the desire expressed by a large number of states to subscribe to the treaty on the non-proliferation of nuclear weapons.

We welcome the willingness of these states to undertake not to receive the transfer from any transferrer whatsoever of nuclear weapons or other nuclear explosive devices or of control over such weapons or explosive devices directly, or indirectly; not to manufacture or otherwise acquire nuclear weapons or other nuclear explosive devices; and not to seek or receive any assistance in the manufacture of nuclear weapons or other nuclear explosive devices.

The U.S. also notes the concern of certain of these states that, in conjunction with their adherence to the treaty on the non-proliferation of nuclear weapons, appropriate measures be undertaken to safeguard their security. Any aggression accompanied by the use of nuclear weapons would endanger the peace and security of all states.

Bearing these considerations in mind, the U.S. declares the following:

Aggression with nuclear weapons, or the threat of such aggression, against a non-nuclear-weapon state would create a qualitatively new situation in which the nuclear-weapon states which are permanent members of the UN Security Council would have to act immediately through the Security Council to take the measures necessary to counter such aggression or to remove the threat of aggression in accordance with the UN Charter, which calls for taking "effective collective measures for the prevention and removal of threats to the peace, and for the suppression of acts of aggression or other breaches of the peace."

Therefore, any state which commits aggression accompanied by the use of nuclear weapons or which threatens such aggression must be aware that its actions are to be countered effectively by measures to be taken in accordance with the UN Charter to suppress the aggression or remove the threat of aggression.

The U.S. affirms its intention, as a permanent member of the UN Security Council, to seek immediate Security Council action to provide assistance, in accordance with the Charter, to any non-nuclear-weapon state party to the treaty on the non-proliferation of nuclear weapons that is a victim of an act of aggression or an object of a threat of aggression in which nuclear weapons are used.

The U.S. reaffirms in particular the inherent right, recognized under Article 51 of the Charter, of individual and collective self-defense if an armed attack, including a nuclear attack, occurs against a member of the UN, until the Security Council has taken measures necessary to maintain international peace and security.

The U.S. vote for the resolution before us and this statement of the way in which the U.S. intends to act in accordance with the Charter of the UN are based upon the fact that the resolution is supported by other permanent members of the Security Council who are nuclear-weapon states and are also proposing to sign the treaty on the non-proliferation of nuclear weapons, and that these states have made similar statements as to the way in which they intend to act in accordance with the Charter.

Security Plan of Non-Nuclear States Defeated

Communist China refused June 27 to accept an invitation by UN Secy. Gen. U Thant to attend, as an observer, a conference in Geneva Aug. 29-Sept. 28 of the world's non-nuclear-weapon states. This was the first time that China had been invited to attend a UN-sponsored conference. Thant had extended invitations June 25 to the non-nuclear members of the UN and, as observers, to the UN specialized agencies, the International Atomic Energy Agency and "those powers possessing nuclear weapons, including the People's Republic of China." (Thant specified that the invitation to Peking had "no relation to the question of the representation of China in the United Nations.") But a message transmitted June 27 by the Peking Telegraph Office asserted that China had "no relations whatsoever with the United Nations" and thus would "refuse to accept the June 25 telegram of U Thant."

The conference had been called by the UN General Assembly to discuss the security of the non-nuclear states in a nuclear-armed world. Representatives of 92 non-nuclear states attended. In a message read Aug. 29 at the opening session in Geneva, Thant called for cooperation between nuclear and non-nuclear powers to develop peaceful uses of nuclear energy. Mian Arshad Husain of Pakistan, president of the conference, said the meeting was "the first concerted attempt by the lesser powers to make their voice felt by the great powers in the establishment of an arrangement for collective security."

The conference adjourned Sept. 28 after failing to conclude a firm draft on the major issue—protection of non-nuclear powers from nuclear attack or blackmail by nuclear powers. A Latin American proposal for an international convention to provide security guarantees for non-nuclear powers failed by one vote to obtain the required 2/3 majority. Most non-nuclear nations felt that the security guarantees tied to the new nuclear-weapons non-proliferation treaty were inadequate because they could be invoked only with the authorization of the Security Council.

The conference's final declaration stressed "the necessity of further steps for an early solution of the question of security assurances in the nuclear era," but it offered no specific recommendations. The weakness of the declaration resulted partly from a split between the potential nuclear nations and the other members of the conference and partly from the opposition of the U.S. and the Soviet Union, whose representatives were present (along with Britain and France) as non-voting observers. Differences also arose concerning the needs and security of quarreling neighbors, such as Pakistan and India, particularly since India borders nuclear-armed Communist China, with which India had also had border conflict.

It was reported that 6 of the potential nuclear nations—India, Brazil, West Germany, Italy, Switzerland and Japan—had tried unsuccessfully to get the conference to support their desire to obtain advantages in acquiring nuclear material and equipment from nuclear powers without having to sign the non-proliferation treaty. Many of the more permanently non-nuclear nations, most of whom had already signed the treaty, were interested in meeting the objections expressed by the 6 nations as reasons for not signing the treaty. (81 countries had signed the treaty.)

Resolutions adopted at the conference urged the UN, the International Atomic Energy Agency (IAEA) and the World Bank to help non-nuclear nations share in the benefits of nuclear development. Expressing concern at "the imminent danger of a renewal of the strategic nuclear arms race and its escalation to new levels which become uncontrollable," the conference urged that the USSR and the U.S. begin early bilateral discussions on nuclear arms limitation. The conference also advocated nuclear-weapon-free zones in halting proliferation and recommended that the members study the possibility of establishing a treaty to form denuclearized zones under the proper political and security conditions.

The conference rejected a Latin American draft calling for the eventual establishment of an "international service for nuclear explosions for peaceful purposes within the framework of the IAEA, through which the nuclear states would undertake to provide states which have renounced nuclear weapons" with services required for specific projects.

Treaty Ratification Delayed

62 nations, including the U.S., the Soviet Union and Britain, signed the nuclear non-proliferation treaty July 1 as it was opened for signature in Washington, Moscow and London. The July 1 signatories were: Afghanistan, Austria, Barbados, Bolivia, Botswana, Britain, Bulgaria, Ceylon, Chad, Colombia, Costa Rica, Cyprus, Czechoslovakia, Dahomey, Denmark, Dominican Republic, East Germany, El Salvador, Finland, Ghana, Greece, Haiti, Honduras, Hungary, Iceland, Iran, Iraq, Ireland, Ivory Coast, Kenya, Laos, Lebanon, Liberia, Malaysia, Mauritius, Mongolia, Morocco, Nationalist China, Nepal, New Zealand, Nicaragua, Nigeria, Norway, Panama, Paraguay, Peru, Philippines, Poland, Rumania, San Marino, Senegal, Somalia, South Korea, South Vietnam, Syria, Togo, Tunisia, USSR, UAR, U.S., Uruguay, Venezuela.

Pres. Johnson, Soviet Premier Aleksei N. Kosygin and British Prime Min. Harold Wilson, attending the signing ceremonies in their respective capitals, lauded the treaty as a major advance toward a safer world and expressed the hope that it would lead to further arms control and disarmament measures.

A notable absentee from the list of signatories was West Germany. Gunter Diehl, West German press secretary, said July 1 that there was a "whole series of world political problems" that had to be resolved before Bonn could initial the treaty. Diehl referred specifically to "massive Soviet political pressure" against Bonn and said that the "manifestations of Soviet policy in recent days have activated the federal government's considerations of the treaty." Diehl said Bonn would await the outcome of the Geneva meeting Aug. 29-Sept. 28 of the non-nuclear nations before making a decision on whether to sign the treaty.

Canada signed the treaty July 22.

White House sources confirmed Nov. 27 that Pres. Johnson, following a meeting with the National Security Council Nov. 25, was considering calling the Senate into special session in December to ratify the treaty. The President had directed Senate majority leader Mike Mansfield (D., Mont.) to sound out the sentiments of Democratic Senators. The poll indicated Nov. 27 that although the Senators overwhelmingly approved ratification of the treaty, there was strong sentiment against a special session unless Richard M. Nixon, the new President-elect, concurred. During the Presidential election campaign Mr. Nixon, while generally favoring the ratification of the treaty, had opposed its immediate passage "as long as Soviet troops are on Czechoslovak soil." Nixon press spokesman Ronald Ziegler said Nov. 27 that while Mr. Nixon had "no reason" to oppose the session, "nothing has occurred" to alter his position on the treaty.

Republican Senate leaders were in general agreement that ratification of the treaty should wait until Congress reconvened Jan. 3, 1969. Chrmn. J. William Fulbright (D., Ark.) of the Senate Foreign Relations Committee said Nov. 27 that the Senate "should come back next week" to ratify the treaty.

(According to a Louis Harris poll conducted in October-November and published Dec. 9, 73% of 5,553 persons polled favored ratification of the non-proliferation treaty while 18% opposed ratification. By 66% to 23% the people polled favored a U.S.-Soviet agreement to limit nuclear weapons systems, particularly ABM complexes; and there was 57%-to-33% support for a final summit meeting between Mr. Johnson and Soviet Premier Aleksei N. Kosygin. But only 40% thought that Soviet-U.S. collaboration to prevent war was possible.)

Britain Nov. 27 became the first nuclear power to ratify the non-proliferation treaty.

New Weapons

U.S. Missiles

In a message introducing the budget for fiscal year 1969, Pres. Johnson said Jan. 29 that "while we stand ready to enter meaningful discussions with the Soviet Union on the limitation of strategic forces, it is necessary to assure that our defense capabilities remain equal to any challenge or threat." To do this, he requested funds to: (a) maintain the strategic deterrent force; (b) begin procurement of the Sentinel missile defense system and revamp air defenses; (c) buy new fixed-wing aircraft and helicopters and other "new weapon systems" to augment the mobility and readiness of the general purpose forces; (d) buy C-5A aircraft and begin procurement of the fast-deployment logistics ships to improve airlift-sealift capability.

Maintenance of the strategic deterrent, the President asserted, included continued conversion of the missile force to the Minuteman-3 (for emplacement in "silos") and Poseidon (for Polaris submarines) missiles; provision of multiple, independently targeted warheads for these missiles; modernizing the manned bomber force with additional FB-111 aircraft and improved short-range attack missiles. Major fund requests included $1.2 billion for the Sentinel program, an additional $269 million for research on missile defense, about $2 billion for various versions of the F-111 (Air Force fighter-bombers and strategic bombers, Navy fighter-interceptors).

In its annual report submitted to Congress Jan. 31, the Atomic Energy Commission said it was undertaking a "major effort" to design, test and produce new nuclear warheads for the U.S. missile defense system. The AEC listed these aspects of its program: (a) The modernization and expansion of plants for producing the new warheads, (b) the development of techniques for the underground testing of increasingly large weapons, (c) the establishment of new test sites at Hot Creek Valley in Nevada and on Amchitka Island in Alaska. AEC Chairman Glenn T. Seaborg had told the Joint Committee on Atomic Energy Jan. 30 that the tests conducted by the AEC in 1967 were "considerably" smaller than the ones the AEC hoped to conduct in the near future. Seaborg said the cost of developing the Sentinel system would be $840.8 million in 1968, an increase of $118.3 million over 1967. He said $40 million of the increase was earmarked for development of the Hot Creek valley and Amchitka test sites.

2 new U.S. long-range missiles—the Navy's Poseidon and the Air Force's Minuteman Space-3—were test-fired at Cape Kennedy, Fla. Aug. 16 and pronounced successes. Both missiles were designed to carry clusters of nuclear warheads capable of individual guidance. Such cluster systems were designated MIRV—for multiple independently targeted re-entry vehicle. The Poseidon was designed to be launched by submerged submarine and to carry a cluster of up to 10 warheads. Its range was about 2,900 miles. The Minuteman-3 was designed to be launched from underground silos, to handle a 3-warhead load and to have an 8,000-mile range. Both systems were expected to be ready for deployment by the early 1970s.

After an unusual 2-1/2-hour secret session (censored details of which were published in the *Congressional Record* Nov. 1), the Senate Oct. 2, by 45—25 vote (25 D. & 20 R. vs. 17 D. & 8 R.), rejected a proposal to delete from the defense appropriations bill (HR 18707) $387.4 million in initial funds for the construction, operation and maintenance of a "thin" Sentinel ABM system. The anti-ABM amendment was introduced by Sen. John Sherman Cooper (R., Ky.) and Philip A. Hart (D., Mich.) with 10 co-sponsors.

Soviet Arms Reduce U.S. Superiority

The London-based Institute for Strategic Studies, in a 61-page report issued Sept. 12, asserted that the Soviet Union had rapidly developed its intercontinental missile system and was expected to match the current U.S. force (estimated to total 1,054) by the end of 1968. The report, entitled *The Military Balance,* said that although the USSR currently had fewer missiles than the U.S., its rockets carried larger warheads. The U.S. was said to have kept its superiority in submarine-launched missiles (625 to 125), but the USSR reportedly had expanded its fleet of nuclear-powered ballistic missile submarines, similar to the

U.S. Polaris submarine. The U.S. use of quick-firing solid fuels in its estimated 1,000 Minuteman missiles was said to far exceed Soviet use of such propellents. The study reported evidence of an increasing diversification in Soviet military forces to include both conventional and nuclear war preparations.

The study, written prior to the Aug. 21 invasion of Czechoslovakia, estimated the number of Warsaw Pact troops at 990,000 (of which 1/2 million were Soviet), compared to 875,000 NATO troops. Warsaw Pact forces reportedly had twice the number of tanks that NATO had, but the Atlantic forces were credited with "greater superiority" in antitank defenses.

Spokesmen for the institute denied that the Czechoslovak invasion had upset the "balance of power" in Europe. ISS Deputy Director Kenneth Hunt said at a news conference Sept. 12 that the "same number of NATO forces still face the same number of Warsaw Pact forces." Rather, what has changed, Hunt said, "is the political environment. NATO may now want to change its deployment of forces in Europe."

The study also reported that the development of Communist China's nuclear weapons had been retarded by internal political problems.

First French H-Test

France exploded its first thermonuclear bomb Aug. 24 and became the world's 5th thermonuclear nation. (The other 4: the U.S., USSR, Britain and Communist China.) Suspended from a balloon 1/3 mile over Fangataufa Lagoon in the Mururoa Atoll test site in the Pacific Ocean, the fusion device was detonated after 8 years of preparation and 15 atmospheric tests of fission devices. Research Min. Robert Galley said at a news conference in Paris Aug. 27 that the blast had released 2 megatons of force-energy, equal to that produced by the explosion of 2 million tons of TNT (or about 100 bombs of the kind dropped on Hiroshima). "It can be considered equal to the best American efforts of 1965," he noted, and was an exceptionally "clean" explosion as it had been limited to reduce fallout and damage to ground installations. The device used an enriched uranium bomb as a detonator and lithium and deuterium for the fusion fuel. Galley admitted that the device was not an operational H-bomb.

France had exploded a nuclear device in the atmosphere over its Mururoa site Aug. 3. The test, described as of medium strength, was the 3d in a series begun July 7.

The French Polynesian Territorial Assembly voted Aug. 9 to ban further French nuclear testing in the Pacific area. The resolution opposed "the stockpiling, or dispersion into the atmosphere, ocean or earth, of all radioactive materials." (The Assembly had advisory powers *vis-a-vis* the French government.) Following the Aug. 24 explosion, Australia filed a formal protest with the French ambassador.

The French Armed Forces Ministry had announced July 4 the successful testing in France of 2 new long-range ballistic missiles. The first missile, a sea-to-ground, 2-stage, remote-controlled rocket with a 1,550-mile range, was launched July 2 in the Landes area. The 2d, fired July 3 from an underground silo, was a 2-stage, ground-to-ground weapon with a 1,864-mile range.

French Foreign Min. Michel Debre announced June 14 that the development of the French nuclear armed force, the *"force de frappe,"* would undergo a 1-2-year delay as a consequence of economic problems resulting from the month-long national strike. Debre said "certain financial difficulties" would "naturally hamper the build-up of France's nuclear striking force," and "certain goals we were scheduled to reach in a year or 2 will be reached one or 2 years later."

Land Mines Debated

NATO's 7-member Nuclear Planning Group met in The Hague Apr. 18—19 and announced unanimously at the end of the meeting that "present circumstances did not justify the deployment of an anti-ballistic missile system in Europe." The attending defense ministers agreed, however, that "it was necessary to keep the development in this field under constant review." The possibility of deploying such a system in Europe had been discussed at the group's last prevous meeting, held in Ankara, Turkey Apr. 6–7, 1967.

In their final communique the ministers reaffirmed "their hope that progress could be made in discussions with the Soviet Union toward a limitation of the strategic arms race, and welcomed the intention of the United States government to consult fully with its allies on new developments in this direction." The communique added that the ministers had discussed the possibility of emplacing nuclear land mines—known as atomic demolition munitions—along the borders of certain NATO members and that the question would remain under study.

The *N.Y. Times* reported Apr. 28 that Turkey, which had sought the emplacement of nuclear land mines along its border with the Soviet Union, had cooled to the idea, while Greece had urged at the Apr. 18–19 meeting that such weapons be emplaced along its northern border with Bulgaria. Turkey's waning enthusiasm reportedly stemmed in part from apprehensions that the U.S. would not approve the firing of the weapons early enough to forestall a Soviet advance.

U. S. Presidential Campaign

McCarthy's Position

In a position paper on missile policy made public in Washington July 10, Sen. Eugene McCarthy urged that the deployment of the Sentinel missile defense system and the Poseidon and Minuteman-3 offensive missiles be delayed. Neither the Chinese nuclear threat nor Soviet anti-ballistic missile program were "moving ahead perceptibly," and the delay would promote agreement with the Soviet Union on the limitation of strategic armaments, McCarthy declared. He advocated an effort to gain an immediate moratorium on strategic weaponry and a prohibition on weapons deployment and testing. This would be followed by negotiations on reduction of nuclear arsenals.

In a statement in Washington Aug. 9 McCarthy said that the U.S. should postpone the scheduled testing of multiple warheads. "Such testing would seriously jeopardize the success of future arms control negotiations," he asserted. "Postponement at this time, however, would not pose any threat to our security."

Democratic Platform

The Democratic Party platform adopted Aug. 28, stated in regard to nuclear arms and disarmament:

"While we have a significant lead in military strength and in all vital areas of military technology, yet Moscow has steadily increased its strategic nuclear arsenal, its missile-firing nuclear submarine fleet, and its anti-missile defenses. Communist China is providing political and military support for so-called wars of national liberation. A growing neclear power, Peking has disdained all arms control efforts. "We must and will maintain a strong and balsnced defense establishment adequate to the task of security and peace. There must be no doubt about our strategic nuclear capability, our capacity to meet limited challenges, and our willingness to act when our vital interests are threatened....

"We must recognize that vigilance calls for the twin disciplines of defense and arms control. Defense measures and arms control measures must go hand in hand, each serving national security and the larger interests of peace.

"We must also recognize that the Soviet Union and the United States still have a common interest in avoiding nuclear war and preventing the spread of nuclear weapons. We also share a common interest in reducing the cost of national defense. We must continue to work together. We will press for further arms control agreements, insisting on collective safeguards against violations.

"For almost a quarter of a century America's pre-eminent military strength, combined with our political restraint, has deterred nuclear war. This great accomplishment has confounded the prophets of doom.

"8 years ago the Democratic Party pledged new efforts to control nuclear weapons. We have fulfilled that pledge. The new Arms Control & Disarmament Agency has undertaken and coordinated important research. The sustained initiatives of Pres. Kennedy and Pres. Johnson have resulted in the 'hot line' between the White House and the Kremlin, the limited Nuclear Test Ban Treaty, the Non-Proliferation Treaty and the treaty barring the orbiting of weapons of mass destruction.

"Even in the present tense atmosphere, we strongly support Pres. Johnson's effort to secure an agreement with the Soviet Union under which both states would refrain from deploying anti-missile systems. Such a treaty would result in the saving of billions of dollars and would create a climate for further arms control measures. We support concurrent efforts to freeze the present level of strategic weapons and delivery systems, and to achieve a balanced and verified reduction of all nuclear and conventional arms."

Nixon & Humphrey Differ

The international treaty banning the spread of nuclear weapons, then before the Senate for ratification, was injected into the Presidential campaign Sept. 8. At a news conference in Pittsburgh, Pa., Republican candidate Richard M. Nixon said that he favored "the principle of non-proliferation" of atomic weapons and the negotiation of such a treaty but was "concerned" about some of the pact's provisions. Democratic candidate Hubert H. Humphrey, in a TV interview the same day, called the nuclear treaty "one of the most important peace projects that we have had since World War II."

In Charlotte, N.C. Sept. 11, Nixon told newsmen that his concern over the treaty lay in its provision for a U.S. commitment to aid non-nuclear countries threatened by nuclear attack and its lack of a provision permitting the transfer of "defensive nuclear weapons," such as mines or anti-ballistic systems, to non-nuclear powers. In a statement earlier Sept. 11, Nixon had said he favored the treaty but believed "it should be implemented at a future time." Asserting that the Soviet invasion of Czechoslovakia had "seriously damaged the prospects for early ratification" of the treaty, Nixon advocated delaying U.S. ratification until "the posture and intentions of the Soviet Union" could be "reassessed at a later time."

Humphrey, in a taped TV discussion with student interrogators in Houston, Tex. Sept. 11, said the doubts Nixon had expressed about the treaty "are going to injure" its chances for Senate approval. Nixon's criticism was "not an act of peace," he said, and it "aggravates the international situation" and "precipitates greater danger in the world situation."

Humphrey reiterated his views on the issue in a speech at ceremonies dedicating the 2d span of the Delaware River Memorial Bridge on the Delaware side of the river Sept. 12. He urged immediate Senate ratification of the treaty, which he described as "our child, our dream, our proposal." Although the Soviet invasion of Czechoslovakia had created "greater tension among the superpowers," he said, it made more necessary an agreement on arms control. Delay of the pact's approval, he said, "delay in setting into place this great building block of peace in the cathedral of peace, I say, is to deny our greatness and, in a very serious way, to prove that we are unworthy of trust." "We must serve notice on our adversary," he said, "that there is far more to be gained from peaceful engagement and work and the relaxation of tensions than from the reversion to the Cold War."

During a day of relaxation on the beach at Seaside Park, N.J. Sept. 13, Humphrey told newsmen that the treaty had nothing to do "with the Czechoslovak crisis except to warn us that the more nuclear weapons you have spread around, the more dangerous the world." The treaty was "to our advantage" and "in our national interest," he said, "but Mr. Nixon has sacrificed national interest for political demagoguery or for political tactics.... It's one thing to say you ought to firm up your defenses, which I surely believe in but I don't think you firm up your defenses by spreading nuclear weapons around to every country in the world."

Humphrey Sept. 18 urged immediate Senate ratification of the non-proliferation treaty. "Failure to act this year could mean killing this treaty forever," he said. He called Nixon "evasive" on the issue—"for the treaty but against ratifying it now." As for the argument that the ratification should be delayed in the light of the Soviet invasion of Czechoslovakia, Humphrey said the treaty "does not weaken our defenses" nor "deny this country the protection of our own nuclear arsenal."

Opposing early ratification of the treaty, Nixon said Sept. 24 in Sioux Falls, S.D. that "a decent interval" should pass between the Soviet "act of aggression" in Czechoslovakia and "the conclusion of a new agreement with the aggressors." "We can have peace," he said. "We must and shall negotiate, but where the Soviet Union is concerned, talking peace and acting weak does not promote peace."

In an address at a UPI conference in Washington Oct. 8 Humphrey reiterated his call for prompt ratification of the treaty and urged negotiation of "a halt in the nuclear arms race."

Nixon charged Oct. 24 that the Democratic administrations of Presidents Kennedy and Johnson had fostered "a gravely serious security gap." Since 1960, he said, the U.S. had followed "policies which now threaten to make America 2d best both in numbers and quality of major weapons." Nixon rejected the "parity" theory of defense, the contention that the U.S. need no more than to keep pace with possible adversaries. "If we let those who threaten world peace outpace us," he warned, "in time we will generate tensions which could lead to war—first, by our display of physical weakness and flabby will, and 2d, by tempting an aggressor to take risks that would compel us to respond."

On a TV panel show broadcast over an 8-state area and the District of Columbia Oct. 25, Nixon said he was not advocating a weapon-by-weapon arms race with the Soviet Union. He favored improving the "over-all strength" of the U.S. on a short-term basis in order to provide "the kind of superiority which will enable us to convince them [the USSR and Communist China] that the time has now come for the great powers—on a controlled, inspected basis—to reduce this tremendous expenditure for armaments. The major objective of my Administration will be to initiate that kind of negotiations."

Humphrey charged in Los Angeles Oct. 25 that Nixon was "playing politics with national security." At a Pentagon news conference Oct. 25, Defense Secy. Clark Clifford said the U.S. had a "substantial military superiority" over the Soviet Union. This superiority included a more than 3-1 margin in total deliverable warheads (4,206-1,200), Clifford asserted. He gave "as-of-today" figures showing U.S. leads over the Soviet Union in ICBMs (1,054 to 900), long-range bombers (646 to 150-155) and submarine missiles (656 to 75-80).

In a nationwide radio address Oct. 26, Nixon pledged, if elected, to seek "meaningful arms control agreements with our adversaries." Nixon said: "The vast resources of the industrialized nations must be diverted from the non-productive and wasteful channels of war-making capabilities and harnessed to a full-scale attack on the age-old problems of hunger, disease and poverty." He said he would seek "meaningful arms control agreements with our adversaries," ratification of the nonproliferation treaty, arms control through existing machinery and the UN, continued negotiations on arms reduction with the Soviet Union and development of new inspection systems. "We must move away from confrontation in this nuclear age into a new era—the era of negotiation," he declared.

On NBC's "Meet the Press" program Oct. 27, Humphrey attacked Nixon for pledging "superiority" in weaponry. Security depended on a balanced arsenal and arms control agreements, Humphrey contended. Besides, the U.S. had a "preponderance" in all major weapons systems and did not need to "pile on weapon after weapon." He said Nixon was "misleading" the public and was "really irresponsible" for not facing the economic consequences of his proposals. He estimated that the Nixon proposals would add $50 billion to defense costs.

In a New York speech Oct. 27, Pres. Johnson deplored Nixon's "ugly and unfair charges...about our security gap and...about our attempts to win peace in the world."

Wallace-LeMay Campaign

George C. Wallace announced Oct. 3 that Gen. Curtis E. LeMay, 61, ex-Air Force chief of staff, would run on his American Independent Party ticket as Vice Presidential candidate. Appearing with Wallace at a nationally televised news conference in Pittsburgh, Pa., LeMay immediately expressed a controversial view on the use of nuclear weapons. LeMay said he "would use anything that we could dream up, including nuclear weapons, if it was necessary," to fight the Vietnamese war. But he added that "I don't think it's necessary in this case or this war to use" nuclear arms.

Wallace, questioned by newsmen about LeMay's remark, explained that all LeMay had said was "that if the security of the country depended on the use of any weapon in the future he would use it."

LeMay said he desired "not to use any weapons," but "once the time comes that you have to fight, I would use any weapon . . . in the arsenal that is necessary." While he did not believe nuclear weapons were "necessary in Vietnam," LeMay said, he was "certainly not going to . . . tell our enemies that I advocate that under all circumstances I'm not going to use nuclear weapons."

NEW INITIATIVES

Kosygin & Gromyko Propose Arms Control

A 9-point disarmament and arms control plan was announced in Moscow July 1 by Soviet Premier Aleksei N. Kosygin. The plan, which Kosygin disclosed had been distributed as a memo to all of the world's governments, was made public during signing ceremonies for the nuclear non-proliferation treaty. Kosygin said the Soviet Union attached "exclusively great importance" to the proposals and felt that their "simultaneous or stage-by-stage implementation . . . would be a serious contribution to the struggle for the cessation of the arms race and for a radical solution of the disarmament problem." He urged "comprehensive discussion" of the proposals when the 18-Nation Disarmament Committee (ENDC) resumed its meetings in Geneva.

The Soviet proposals:

●The "conclusion of an international agreement banning the use of nuclear weapons."
●An "end to the manufacture of nuclear weapons, the reduction of stockpiles and the subsequent total ban on and liquidation of nuclear weapons under appropriate international control."
●The "mutual limitation and subsequent reduction of strategic means of delivery of nuclear weapons."
●A ban "without delay" on "flights of bombers, carrying nuclear weapons, beyond the boundaries of national frontiers" and an "end to the patrolling by submarines, carrying nuclear missiles, within missile-striking range of the borders of the contracting sides."
●The "banning of underground tests of nuclear weapons on the basis of using national means of detection to control this ban."
●A study by the ENDC of "ways and means of securing observance by all states of the Geneva protocol on a ban on the use of chemical and bacteriological weapons."
●The urgent examination by the ENDC of the "liquidation of foreign military bases."
●The establishment of "denuclearized zones in various parts of the world" and the "implementation of measures for regional disarmament and for the reduction of armaments in various regions of the world, including the Middle East." (The memo added: "The question of such measures for slackening the arms race in the Middle East, of course, could be considered only in conditions of elimination of the consequences of the Israeli aggression against the Arab countries and, above all, the full evacuation of the Israeli forces from the territories of Arab countries occupied by them.")
●The opening of talks by the ENDC on the "use of the sea bed beyond the limits of existing territorial waters exclusively for peaceful purposes."

In the UN General Assembly's general debate Oct. 3, Soviet Foreign Min. Andrei A. Gromyko said that the USSR had placed a disarmament memo on the Assembly's agenda. It contained these proposals: (1) a "ban on the use of nuclear weapons"; (2) the start on negotiations by all nuclear powers "to halt the production of nuclear weapons, to reduce their stockpiles and subsequently to prohibit and eliminate nuclear weapons completely, under appropriate international control";(3) "agreement on concrete steps in the field of the limitation and subsequent reduction of strategic nuclear-weapon delivery vehicles," including antimissile weapons; (4) "an immediate end to all tests of nuclear weapons"; (5) adherence to the 1925 Geneva Protocol prohibiting the use of chemical and bacteriological weapons. Gromyko declared that the USSR continued to be a "convinced advocate of finding possibilities of cooperation or even of joint action with the governments of bourgeois countries for the common purpose of preventing a new world war."

U.S. & USSR Plan Talks

Pres. Johnson announced in Washington July 1 that the U.S. and Soviet Union had agreed to begin talks "in the nearest future" on means of limiting and reducing their arsenals of offensive and defensive nuclear weapons. Mr. Johnson made the annoucement at the White House during signing ceremonies for the nuclear non-proliferation treaty. The President said the new talks would concern the "limitation and the reduction of both offensive strategic nuclear weapons delivery systems and systems of defense against ballistic missiles." He conceded that the discussion of this "most complex subject" would not be "easy" and that the U.S. did not underestimate the "difficulties that may lie ahead." But he expressed the belief that the "same spirit of accommodation" reflected in the conclusion of the non-proliferation treaty could "bring us to a good and fruitful result."

Mr. Johnson had proposed talks on the missile issue in Jan. 1967, and he had announced Mar. 2, 1967 that Premier Kosygin had confirmed the USSR's willingness to discuss the question. No further progress was reported in the following 18 months, in part because of the priority both countries had accorded to the nuclear non-proliferation negotiations in Geneva.

The President had renewed his plea in speeches at Glassboro, N.J. June 4, at UN headquarters June 12 and in Washington June 13. An article in *Izvestia,* the Soviet government newspaper, charged June 13, however, that the President had ignored the question of the Vietnamese war in his June 12 speech and that U.S.-Soviet cooperation was impossible as long as the war continued. *Izvestia* and *Pravda,* the Soviet Communist Party daily, reiterated this complaint June 19.

The first indication of a change in the USSR's position came June 27, when Foreign Min. Gromyko, in a wide-ranging foreign policy address to the Supreme Soviet, announced that the USSR was "ready for an exchange of opinion" on the question of a "mutual restriction and subsequent reduction of strategic vehicles for the delivery of nuclear weapons—offensive and defensive—including anti-missile." Gromyko declared that the Soviet Union was ready to sign "immediately" and international convention prohibiting the use of nuclear weapons and, as in the past, to implement "a program of general and complete disarmament." He said the USSR favored immediate discontinuance of underground nuclear testing. Referring to the problem of policing such a ban, he asserted that "the necessity of some control" was "unfounded and far-fetched" since "no one can explode nuclear weapons underground in secret without being detected."

In a speech in Nashville, Tenn. June 29, Pres. Johnson responded to the Gromyko statement by asserting that, with the non-proliferation treaty concluded, it was time to "turn to a task at least equally complex and difficult: to bring under control the nuclear arms race—in offensive and defensive weapons—in ways which do not endanger the security of the U.S., our allies or others."

The Soviet invasion of Czechoslovakia Aug. 21 destroyed the chances for an early opening of U.S.-Soviet talks on arms limitation. Republican Presidential candidate Richard M. Nixon favored postponement of the talks. In the introduction to his annual report to the UN General Assembly, UN Secy. Gen. U Thant Sept. 26 urged the Eastern and Western blocs not to use Czechoslovakia "as grounds for an intensified build-up of nuclear and thermonuclear weapons." He said that either side would attack only because of a "pervading fear by one side of a pre-emptive strike by the other." He warned that "this fear is fed by, and grows proportionately with, the increase in the offensive military power of the 2 superstates." Thant said that "a treaty banning nuclear weapon tests in all environments would be a most desirable step following the conclusion of the treaty on the non-proliferation of nuclear weapons." Concern over nuclear weapons overshadowed the dangers brought about by new developments in biological and chemical weapons, he declared.

On the Soviet side, Premier Aleksei Kosygin Nov. 19 urged U.S.-Soviet negotiations on the limitation of missile and anti-missile systems and American action to ratify the non-proliferation treaty. But Kosygin said that peaceful coexistence could not be achieved as long as one country demanded military superiority. (Kosygin's statement was regarded as an indirect criticism of Nixon's campaign demands for U.S. military superiority over the USSR.) Kosygin had expressed disappointment at press reports indicating that the Nov. 14–16 NATO ministerial meeting had concluded that U.S.-Soviet arms control talks could not take place because of the situation created by the Czechoslovak invasion.

The UN General Assembly Dec. 20 voted 180–0 (7 abstentions), to urge the Soviet Union and the U.S. "to enter at an early date into bilateral discussions on the limitation of offensive strategic nuclear weapon delivery systems and systems of defense against ballistic missiles." The resolution had been recommended Dec. 17 by the First Committee.

New Session of Geneva Conference

The UN's 18-Nation Disarmament Committee (ENDC) reconvened in Geneva July 16 for a session that lasted until Aug. 28. The committee had been in recess since Mar. 14 when it had concluded discussions about the final draft of the non-proliferation treaty.

In a message read to the conference by William C. Foster, chief U.S. delegate and co-chairman (with the USSR) of the conference, Pres. Johnson disclosed that the U.S. and Soviet Union would "shortly" decide on the time and place for their talks on limiting offensive and defensive ballistic missiles. The President said the U.S. was "prepared to consider reductions of existing systems" if agreement could be achieved on limiting them. In such a way, Mr. Johnson said,"we would cut back effectively—and for the first time—on the vast potentials for destruction which each side possesses." Mr. Johnson called on the conferees to "begin to define those factors vital to a workable, verifiable and effective international agreement" that would bar the use of the seabed for the "emplacement of weapons of mass destruction." The President also stressed the need for regional arms control measures and affirmed that the U.S. would support "any reasonable measures affecting the activities of the major weapons-producers that would make a regional agreement more effective." He suggested that one such provision could be a requirement that suppliers "publicize or register their arms shipments to a particular region."

Soviet delegate Aleksei A. Roshchin submitted to the ENDC the 9-point disarmament plan that Soviet Premier Kosygin had made public July 1.

British delegate Fred W. Mulley submitted a number of proposals designed to facilitate agreement between the U.S. and USSR on prohibiting underground nuclear tests. Noting past Soviet objections to the U.S. demand that such a ban be corroborated through on-site inspections, Mulley suggested that "arrangements could be made by which on-site inspection could only take place if there was strong seismological or other evidence that the treaty had been infringed." For this purpose Mulley proposed the formation of a 7-member committee, consisting of 3 nuclear-weapon states, 3 non-nuclear-weapon states and a representative of either the UN International Atomic Energy Agency to determine whether a particular earth tremor deemed suspicious by one side should be investigated through on-site inspection. According to the plan, such inspection would be authorized if the committee decided "by a majority of 5 to 2 that a *prima facie* case had been made out in support of the complaint." Mulley also proposed that there be an "agreed annual quota of underground weapons test explosions" with the objective of reducing them to zero over a period of perhaps "4 to 5 years."

In a separate message to the conference read by Mulley, British Prime Min. Harold Wilson lauded the successful conclusion of the non-proliferation treaty and said it represented a "tremendous opportunity which must be exploited to the full" in terms of further arms control measures.

UN Secy. Gen. U Thant said in a message to the conferees July 16 that the ENDC's "prime function" should be to discuss those items that were considered "most important and most amendable to early agreement."

The major event of the July 16-Aug. 28 session was the adoption of a report to the General Assembly calling for a study of chemical and biological warfare. The report was adopted unanimously, though objections by India and Brazil had forced the U.S. and the Soviet Union to give up their support of a clause that endorsed the non-proliferation treaty; India and Brazil opposed the treaty and protested a clause in the report that asserted that the treaty would aid in "halting the nuclear arms race and [in] the solution of disarmament problems." The conference report was an outgrowth of British proposals calling for a treaty "to ban and proscribe the use for hostile purposes of microbiological agents causing death or disease by infection in man, other animals or crops." In introducing the draft treaty Aug. 6, British delegate Mulley had called on governments to "declare that use of microbiological methods of warfare of any kind and in any circumstances should be treated as contrary to international law and a crime against humanity." The final report, drafted by the U.S. and USSR, asked the General Assembly to approve the establishment of an expert group "to study the effects of possible use of chemical and bacteriological means of warfare."

Among other events at the conference:

• The 8 nonaligned nations at the conference Aug. 27 denounced France and Communist China for carrying out atmospheric nuclear tests.

• The Soviet Union Aug. 13 accused the U.S. of violating existing international law by using chemicals in the Vietnamese war.

• The USSR put before the conference Aug. 20 an East German memo accusing West Germany of preparing to manufacture nuclear weapons alone or in cooperation with South Africa and Israel. The U.S. delegate, George Bunn, called the charges unfounded.

• Czechoslovakia July 23 stressed the importance of setting up a nuclear-free zone in Central Europe, thus increasing the possibilities for a reduction in conventional armaments.

OTHER DEVELOPMENTS

H-Bombs Lost in Crash off Greenland

A U.S. Air Force B-52 jet bomber with 4 unarmed hydrogen bombs aboard crashed and burned Jan. 22 on the ice of North Star Bay, 7-1/2 miles southwest of the U.S. Air Force base at Thule, Greenland. The H-bombs apparently were destroyed in the crash, and searchers found only fragments of them. The accident was the 13th involving nuclear weapons-carrying planes to be disclosed by the Defense Department since 1958 and the first to occur since a nuclear-armed B-52 crashed near Palomares, Spain in Jan. 1966.

About 150 Danes demonstrated outside the U.S. embassy in Copenhagen Jan. 22 in protest against the sending of a plane carrying nuclear weapons over Greenland, and some members of parliament demanded an investigation. Under the terms of agreements between the U.S. and Denmark, the U.S. was not to fly nuclear-armed planes over Danish soil; Greenland was a Danish possession. Danish Premier Jens Otto Krag Jan. 22 requested a full explanation of the incident and re-affirmed his government's policy of barring nuclear weapons from Danish soil. "This applies to Greenland as well," he said, "and consequently no airplane carrying atom bombs can pass over Greenland territory." He added, however, that "an American airplane in case of emergency might make a landing in Greenland."

The U.S. Defense Department announced Jan. 22 that, since the weapons were "unarmed," there was "no danger of a nuclear explosion at the crash site." Subsequent investigation revealed, however, that the conventional (TNT) explosive wrappers around the nuclear material in the bombs had apparently detonated. As a result, the bomb casings had fractured, and plutonium (the fissionable material used to trigger the hydrogen explosion) had been released. While the Pentagon did not disclose the size of hydrogen weapons aboard the plane, it was generally reported that they were of the 1.1 megaton class, *i.e.,* equal in explosive power to the force that would be created by the explosion of 1,100,000 tons of TNT.

The ill-fated B-52, based at Plattsburgh, N.Y., had been flying the Arctic Circle route on an airborne alert flight for the Strategic Air Command (SAC) when a fire broke out in the navigator's compartment. The pilot, Capt. John M. Haug, 36, headed for an emergency landing at the Thule Air Force base but ordered the crew to bail out when the cockpit filled with smoke and made navigation impossible. 5 of the 7 crewmen were picked up by dogsled almost immediately; the 6th, Capt.

Curtis R. Criss Jr., 43, the navigator, was rescued about 24 hours later and was hospitalized with a broken shoulder and frostbite. The 7th crew member, Capt. Leonard Svitenko, 36, the co-pilot, was killed while bailing out. Besides Haug and Criss, the survivors were: Maj. Frank F. Hopkins, 35, radar navigator; Maj. Alfred J. d'Amario Jr., 38, instructor pilot; Capt. Richard E. Marks, 29, electronic-warfare officer; Staff Sgt. Calvin W. Snapp, 29, gunner.

When the burning plane crashed, it skidded along the ice for about 1,500 feet and then exploded. The fire and explosion scattered parts of the plane and armament over a wide area, but it also melted the 7-to-9-foot ice cover sufficiently to allow part of the wreckage to sink to the bottom of the bay, which was 800-900 feet deep at the crash site; the hole was then covered with newly frozen ice. The Pentagon said Jan. 22 that "some of the wreckage is no longer visible and may have burned into or through the ice, but some has been observed on the surface of the ice by helicopters." Investigation was hampered by high winds, swirling snow, subzero temperatures and the Arctic winter, which provided only 4 hours of twilight every 24 hours.

An investigating team of about 70 Air Force and civilian specialists arrived in Thule Jan. 23 under the command of Maj. Gen. Richard O. Hunziker, SAC deputy chief of staff for material. Officials announced later Jan. 23 that low levels of alpha-particle radiation had been detected in an area 22 feet wide by 1,800 feet long that roughly conformed to the path left by the plane as it skidded across the ice. The Pentagon said Jan. 24 that the level of radiation was "well below that considered to be hazardous even on prolonged contact." After disclosing Jan. 24 that "pieces of weapons-associated hardware" had been found at the scene of the crash, SAC officials announced Jan. 28 that fragments from all 4 of the hydrogen bombs had been found. They also announced that the alpha radiation was confined to an area about 300 yards to either side of the skid path left by the plane and that their alpha oscillation counters had measured the radiation level at 2 million counts per minute, the maximum amount capable of being recorded by the instruments. (The alpha count reportedly was much higher but was not revealed because this would indicate how much plutonium had been used in the bombs.)

It was reported Feb. 28 that the U.S. had canceled all nuclear-armed airborne alert flights by the SAC's B-52 bombers as a result of the crash. Informed sources in Washington disclosed that Defense Secy. Robert S. McNamara had ordered the nuclear weapons taken off such flights a day or 2 after the crash. The airborne alert flights had first been announced by the U.S. in 1961 as part of its effort to maintain a retaliatory capability in the event of a Soviet nuclear attack on the U.S. But as the ICBM program developed in the following years, missiles superseded bombers as the U.S.' main deterrent force, and the number of airborne alert flights was consequently reduced. It was disclosed in May 1966 that the Defense Department had curtailed all such flights except those required for "training" missions. The number of nuclear-armed bombers kept aloft at any one time under this reduced program was reported to be less than 6. As a result of the latest Pentagon directive, such training flights would continue but without nuclear weapons aboard. The change had been preceded by protests lodged by the Soviet Union against the U.S. for maintaining the flights of nuclear-armed aircraft.

At the Geneva disarmament conference Feb. 1, the USSR proposed an international agreement to prohibit nuclear-armed aircraft from flying beyond their national borders. Soviet delegate Aleksei A. Roshchin said that the crash of the B-52 in Greenland "convincingly underscored" the need for such an accord.

The Soviet Union Feb. 10 filed a note with the State Department in Washington in protest against the "dangerous and even provocative flights" of U.S. nuclear-armed bombers near Soviet borders. The note asserted that such flights were "senseless" from a military viewpoint because of the development of missiles. It warned that an accident involving a bomber could produce "a whole chain of irreversible events dangerous to all mankind." The U.S., rejecting the note Feb. 12, asserted that "world tensions make necessary the carrying out of such flights in the interest of collective security against the threat posed by Soviet nuclear forces."

At the Geneva disarmament conference Feb. 13, the USSR again protested the U.S. flights. With the support of the Bulgarian, Czech and Polish delegates, Soviet delegate Roshchin read a statement charging that such flights "over many countries of our planet" increased international tension and violated international law, including the 1958 convention barring radioactive pollution of the seas. Roshchin also charged that the B-52 crash in Greenland had violated the 1963 limited test-ban treaty by releasing radioactive material. Roshchin asked: "Who can guarantee that the next crash involving a United States aircraft carrying nuclear bombs will not occur in a densely populated region?" U. S. delegate Samuel DePalma, assistant director of the Arms Control & Disarmament Agency, said that the crash had not produced a nuclear explosion and thus had not violated the test-ban treaty. He accused Roshchin of "gross exaggeration" in order "to inspire fear among those who do not have full knowledge of the facts."

(The U.S. Defense Department disclosed Feb. 16 that U.S. jet fighters had intercepted 2 Soviet bombers Feb. 9 50-70 miles off the coast of Newfoundland but that the planes had "evidenced no hostile intentions" and that the interception had been conduced "solely for the purpose of identification." The Pentagon also disclosed that 3 Soviet bombers had flown about 80 miles off the coast of Alaska Feb. 12 and 13. Officials said they believed the flights were training missions.)

Latin American Nuclear-Free Zone

Pres. Johnson announced Feb. 14 that the U.S. would sign, "with an appropriate statement," the protocol attached to the Latin American A-ban treaty calling on the world's 5 nuclear powers—the U.S., USSR, Britain, France and Communist China—to respect the provisions of the treaty. The treaty, concluded at Tlatelolco, Mexico, Feb. 14, 1967, barred nuclear weapons on the territory of signatories.

According to the *N.Y. Times* (Feb. 15), the U.S. statement was to make these reservations: (1) "The United States takes note of the view of the drafters of the treaty that it does not alter the traditional transit, berthing and landing rights of United States warships and planes." (2) "The United States interprets the treaty as allowing the Latin American signatories to request nuclear explosions for peaceful purposes under international safeguards." (3) "The United States will feel free of all obligations under the treaty if any signatory engages in armed attack with the assistance—of any kind—of a nuclear power."

Britain had indicated its readiness to sign the protocol. The Soviet Union, France and Communist China had not yet revealed their intentions. The treaty had already been signed by these 21 states: Argentina, Bolivia, Brazil, Chile, Colombia, Costa Rica, Dominican Republic, Ecuador, Guatemala, Haiti, Honduras, Jamaica, Mexico, Nicaragua, Panama, Paraguay, Peru, Salvador, Trinidad & Tobago, Uruguay and Venezuela. Cuba had indicated its refusal to sign the treaty. The signatures of Barbados and Guyana had been held up for what was described as technical reasons.

It was also reported Feb. 14 that the U.S. would not sign the treaty's protocol calling on the 4 states—the U.S., Britain, France and the Netherlands—with possessions in the Latin American and Caribbean area to permit the provisions of the treaty to be applied in these areas as well.

Sakharov Warning

A warning about the threat of nuclear war was given by Prof. Andrei Dmitrievich Sakharov, 47, a prominent Russian nuclear physicist, in his unofficial essay, entitled *Thoughts About Progress, Peaceful Co-existence and Intellectual Freedom,* which was first published by the *N.Y. Times* July 22. Sakharov wrote:

"3 technical aspects of thermonuclear weapons have made thermonuclear war a peril to the very existence of humanity. These aspects are: the enormous destructive power of a thermonuclear explosion, the relative cheapness of rocket-thermonuclear weapons and the practical impossibility of an effective defense against a massive rocket-nuclear attack.

"A complete destruction of cities, industry, transport and systems of education, a poisoning of fields, water and air by radioactivity, a physical destruction of the larger part of mankind, poverty, barbarism, a return to savagery and a genetic degeneracy of the survivors under the impact of radiation, a destruction of the material and information basis of civilization—this is a measure of the peril that threatens the world as a result of the estrangement of the world's two superpowers.

"Every rational creature, finding itself on the brink of a disaster, first tries to get away from the brink and only then does it think about the satisfaction of its other needs. If mankind is to get away from the brink, it must overcome its divisions. A vital step would be a review of the traditional method of international affairs, which may be termed 'empirical-competitive.' In the simplest definition, this is a method aiming at maximum improvement of one's position everywhere possible and, simultaneously, a method of causing maximum unpleasantness to opposing forces without consideration of common welfare and common interests."

1968's NUCLEAR TESTS

U.S. Explosions

All U.S. tests conducted during 1968 were underground. The dates, force and sites of the tests:

Date	Force	Site
Jan. 18	Low yield	Nevada test site
Jan. 19	1 megaton	Nevada test site
Jan. 26*	Low yield	Nevada test site
Feb. 21	Low-intermediate	Nevada test site
Feb. 29	Low yield	Nevada test site
Mar. 12	Low yield	Nevada test site
Mar. 14	Low yield	Nevada test site
Mar. 22	Low-intermediate	Nevada test site
Apr. 10	Low-intermediate	Nevada test site
Apr. 18	Low-intermediate	Nevada test site
Apr. 23**	Low yield	Nevada test site
Apr. 26†	Intermediate	Nevada test site
May 17	Low-intermediate	Nevada test site
June 6	Low yield	Nevada test site
June 15	Low-intermediate	Nevada test site
June 28	Low-intermediate	Nevada test site
July 30	Low-intermediate	Nevada test site
Aug. 27	20 kiloton	Nevada test site
Aug. 29	Low-intermediate	Nevada test site
Sept. 6	Low-intermediate	Nevada test site
Sept. 12	Low yield	Nevada test site
Sept. 17	Low-intermediate	Nevada test site
Sept. 24	Low yield	Nevada test site
Oct. 3—Nov. 24	4 Low yield	Nevada test site
Nov. 4	Low yield	Nevada test site
Dec. 8*	35 kiloton	Nevada test site
Dec. 12	Low yield	Nevada test site
Dec. 19	1 megaton	Nevada test site

* Part of Plowshare Program to develop peaceful uses of nuclear explosives.
** Part of Defense Department's Vela Program "to improve methods of detecting, identifying and locating underground nuclear detonations."
† Largest test ever conducted either underground or in atmosphere by the U.S. It was generally assumed that developmental warhead for the Sentinel anti-ballistic-missile defense system had been the device tested.

Date	Force	Site

Soviet Explosions

Date	Force	Site
Jan. 7***		Semipalatinsk
Apr. 24***	Low yield	Semipalatinsk
June 11***	Low yield	
July 1***	Low-intermediate	Caspian Sea Area (Soviet Union)
Sept. 5***	Low-intermediate	Semipalatinsk
Dec. 18***	Low yield	Semipalatinsk

French Explosions

Date	Force	Site
July 7★	"Moderate strength"	Muruora Atoll
July 15★	Medium	Muruora Atoll
Aug. 3★	Medium	Muruora Atoll
Aug. 24★‡	2 megaton	Muruora Atoll
Sept. 8★‡		Muruora Atoll

Chinese Explosion

Date	Force	Site
Dec. 27★‡	3 megaton	Lob Nor

*** Underground test.
‡ Hydrogen (thermonuclear) bomb tested.
★ Atmospheric test.

1969

Disarmament efforts appeared to suffer a partial setback during 1969 because of the expanded deployment of limited antiballistic missiles by the USSR and because of the decision of the U.S.' Nixon Administration to proceed with an ABM "Safeguard" program, which was authorized by Congress Nov. 6. The U.S.' missile superiority was reduced, and USSR efforts to establish its own superiority were reported. Yet some significant progress toward an arms control agreement was made. The U.S. and USSR signed the non-proliferation treaty Nov. 24 after ratifications by their respective legislative bodies; 22 of the 43 nations whose ratification was needed for the treaty to become effective had already adhered to the document. West Germany signed after its new Brandt administration had dropped the objections raised by its predecessor. During the Geneva UN Disarmament Committee meetings, held Mar. 6-May 24 and July 3-Oct. 30, the U.S. and USSR presented a draft treaty to prohibit the placement of weapons of mass destruction on the seabed and ocean floor. After repeated delays, the 2 superpowers finally held preliminary strategic arms limitation talks (SALT) in Helsinki Nov. 17-Dec. 22. They agreed to begin full-scale talks in Vienna Apr. 16, 1970.

U.S. ABM Policy Debated

Nixon Regime Continues Policy

Control of the U.S. government was transferred by the outgoing Johnson Administration to the new Nixon Administration Jan. 20, but little significant change was made in the policy that had been developed for creating an ABM (anti-ballistic missile) missile defense against Communist missiles.

In his final report to Congress, outgoing Defense Secy. Clark M. Clifford had requested Jan. 18 the continuation of the $6 billion Sentinel ABM system, which he described as "both prudent and feasible." Although the construction of anti-missile sites around Moscow had slowed during 1968, Clifford said, the development of ABM missiles continued in the USSR "at a high rate of activity." (Clifford had been named by Pres. Johnson Jan. 19, 1968 to succeed Robert S. McNamara as U.S. Defense Secretary.)

Senate Foreign Relations Committee hearings were focused Feb. 18 and 20 on U.S. plans to deploy an ABM system. Committee critics of the ABM plans questioned Nixon Administration witnesses about a disagreement within the Administration over whether the Sentinel System should be delayed until the U.S. held arms control talks with the Soviet Union.

William P. Rogers, the new U.S. State Secretary, told the committee Feb. 18 that he hoped arms-control negotiations with the USSR could begin within 6 months and before a decision on deploying the Sentinel system. (Deployment of the Sentinel was being held up by the Nixon Administration pending a review of the Johnson Administration's decision to buy sites and begin to build a "thin" protective net against "unsophisticated" missiles such as could be used by Communist China.)

An opposing view was expressed by Melvin R. Laird, the Nixon Administration's new Defense Secretary, who told the committee Feb. 20: "I would not be for delaying construction of an ABM system pending the outcome or convening of talks with the Soviet Union."

Committee members questioned the witnesses about the non-proliferation treaty's Article VI, which said: "Each of the parties to the treaty undertakes to pursue negotiations in good faith on effective measures relating to cessation of the nuclear arms race at an early date and to nuclear disarmament, and on a treaty on general and complete disarmament under strict and effective international control."

Committee chairman J. William Fulbright asked Rogers Feb. 18 whether there was not "a little inconsistency" in calling for ratification of the non-proliferation treaty while simultaneously deploying an ABM system and thus speeding up the arms race. Rogers denied any inconsistency and referred by implication to the Soviet Union's deployment of a missile defense system around Moscow. "Realism requires that there be a certain mutuality, and that is what we are hoping for," he said.

Questioned by Sen. Albert Gore (D., Tenn.) on the commitment entailed by Article VI, Rogers offered these arguments: (a) The treaty dealt with proliferation of atomic weapons to non-nuclear nations; (b) the article itself represented a hope that the nuclear powers might enter arms talks sometime in the future; (c) the article did not focus on negotiations over missile defense systems but on nuclear arms talks. Gore pointed out that the USSR had declared its willingness to enter into talks to curb ABM deployment. He asked whether U.S. ratification of the treaty would not commit the U.S. to participate in such talks. Rogers replied, "Yes sir."

Laird conceded Feb. 20 that ratification of the non-proliferation treaty would entail an obligation to begin arms-control talks with the Soviet Union, and he expressed hope they could start early. Laird insisted that U.S. national security probably required an ABM system for use against Soviet as well as Chinese missiles. He said the USSR had been moving at a "high rate" in developing new offensive and defensive weapons by: (a) shooting a nuclear-armed ABM at an incoming missile (this took place in 1962 and was not duplicated by any other nation); (b) "going forward with tests of a new, sophisticated ABM system"; (c) spending more than 3 times as much as the U.S. was spending on strategic defensive and offensive weapons; (d) making more ICBMs than the U.S. made (U.S. total: 1,054); (e) undertaking a "crash program" to overtake the U.S. in atomic submarines by 1974-5; (f) deploying a fractional orbital bombardment system capable of launching nuclear warheads from space. Although he indicated that it would be necessary to revamp the U.S. ABM system to give it some capability not only against Chinese missiles but also against Soviet missiles, Laird also suggested the possibility of working out an arms-control agreement with the Soviet Union that would limit each country to a "thin" anti-Chinese ABM system. He said he was "leaning" toward deployment of the Sentinel system.

(On the NBC-TV "Today" broadcast Feb. 13, Laird had said he was "more concerned" about defense against the Chinese threat than "about any other kind of defense at the present time." He reported that U.S. intelligence experts expected Communist China to test its first ICBM within 18 months and then to build at least 18-20 operational ICBMs. "I believe that we do not want to become hostages of the Chinese," he declared. He also expressed interest in deploying an ABM system in order to develop "the knowledge and the ability which the Russians have developed." At a news conference Feb. 18, Laird and Deputy Defense Secy. David Packard indicated that their planning was not directed so much toward whether or not an ABM system should be deployed as toward what kind of system should be deployed. They told newsmen they expected to propose a better deployment plan for the Sentinel system than that proposed by the Johnson Administration.)

U.S. Adopts ABM Plan

Pres. Nixon announced Mar. 14 that he had decided to proceed with a revised missile defense system. The decision, announced at a televised news conference, came in the midst of an intensifying debate in Congress over the advisability of deploying a Sentinel system. The President said he expected "a very spirited debate and a very close vote" in Congress on the request for appropriations for his ABM plan. Mr. Nixon had delayed his decision in the face of intense maneuvering against it. After his return from Europe, he had announced Mar. 4 that he would announce his decision "the first of next week." But his press secretary, Ronald L. Ziegler, said Mar. 11 that the President was giving the matter more consideration and in particular wanted to consult with Defense Secy. Laird after the latter's return from Vietnam Mar. 12. He discussed the project with Congressional leaders of both parties Mar. 14 prior to the press conference at which he announced his decision.

The ABM system recommended by Mr. Nixon would consist of 12 sites emplaced to defend the nation's missile retaliatory capacity. Each site would be equipped with both long- and short-range missiles. The system, to be operative in the mid-1970s, would cost an estimated $6-$7 billion. The Sentinel ABM system proposed by the Johnson Administration would have consisted of 15-20 antimissile sites near large urban centers. Mr. Johnson had requested $1.7 billion for fiscal 1970 to start work on it. Mr. Nixon planned to request $800-$900 million in fiscal 1970 for (a) continued research, (b) acquisition of sites and (c) initial work on the first 2 sites to protect Minuteman missile wings at Malmstrom Air Force Base in Montana and Grand Forks Air Force Base in North Dakota.

Mr. Nixon stressed that his plan was flexible and would be reviewed at every phase "to insure that we are doing as much as necessary but no more than that required by the threat existing at that time." He called his proposed system "truly a 'Safeguard' system, a defensive system only." He said: "It safeguards our deterrent and under those circumstances can in no way...delay the progress which I hope will continue to be made toward arms talks." "The imperative that our nuclear deterrent remain secure beyond any possible doubt requires that the U.S. must take steps now to insure that our strategic retaliatory forces will not become vulnerable to a Soviet attack." The modified ABM plan would safeguard against "any attack by the Chinese Communists that we can foresee over the next 10 years" and against "any irrational or accidental attack" from the Soviet Union.

Explaining the shift from defending the cities to defending the nuclear deterrent, Mr. Nixon said: "There is no way that we can adequately defend our cities without an unacceptable loss of life. The only way that I have concluded that we can save lives—which is the primary purpose of our defense system—is to prevent war. And that is why the emphasis of this system is on protecting our deterrent, which is the best preventive for war."

Mr. Nixon discounted arguments that the initiation of a U.S. ABM system would escalate the arms race or jeopardize arms-control talks with the USSR. His program was "not provocative," he said, and "the Soviet retaliatory capacity is not affected by our decision. The capability for surprise attack against our strategic forces is reduced. In other words, our program provides an incentive for a responsible Soviet weapons policy and for the avoidance of spiraling U.S. and Soviet strategic arms budgets." As for arms talks, Mr. Nixon pointed out that the Soviet Union had agreed to talks only 4 days after the Johnson Administration decision to deploy a Sentinel ABM system. Under his own plan, Mr. Nixon said, the USSR would have "even less reason to view our defense effort as an obstacle to talks."

This viewpoint had been expressed Mar. 6 by Gerard C. Smith, new director of the Arms Control & Disarmament Agency, before the Senate Foreign Relations Subcommittee on Disarmament, which was holding "educational" hearings on the foreign policy implications of an ABM system. Smith said he did not think deployment of the Sentinel system would "prejudice the prospects for strategic arms limitation talks," nor, he added, did he believe that a revision of the Sentinel system toward protection of strategic bases would evoke any significant Soviet reaction against arms talks.

3 scientific witnesses called before the subcommittee Mar. 6 tended to corroborate the need to protect strategic bases against Soviet missiles. But the scientists—Dr. Daniel Fink of General Electric, Dr. John P. Ruina of MIT and Dr. Hans A. Bethe of Cornell University—agreed that the Sentinel decision could wait one or 2 years since the Soviet Union did not currently have the capability of knocking out the U.S. retaliatory force.

3 other scientists appeared before the subcommittee Mar. 11 and testified that deployment of an ABM would endanger U.S. security by accelerating the nuclear arms race. They also pointed to a danger that the decision to trigger the complex ABM might pass from the President to a computer or junior military officer. Their testimony was considered so "impressive" by Sen. Clifford P. Case (R., N.J.) that he arranged for the scientists—Dr. James R. Killian Jr., MIT board chairman, Dr. George B. Kistiakowsky of Harvard and Dr. Herbert F. York of the University of California—to meet that afternoon with the President's national security aide, Henry A. Kissinger. During the hearing: York contended that, in "the inexorable logic of the arms race," deployment of the Sentinel would incite an increase in the potential adversary's offensive power, and "then you are actually worse off if the defense system doesn't work perfectly"; Kistiakowsky said the flash of the 2-megaton warhead on the long-range Sentinel interceptor (the Spartan)

could cause blindness if observed; Killian suggested a comprehensive review of the entire situation by an independent citizens group.

Sen. Edward M. Kennedy (D., Mass.) joined the opposition by warning Mar. 11 that ABM deployment "would hardly increase our own security and certainly would contribute to international tensions." "We and the Soviets have an unparalleled opportunity to begin preliminary discussions," Kennedy said. "This is one reason I believe it unwise to deploy the Sentinel anti-ballistic missile system. It signals to the Soviets that we are less interested in beginning talks than we are in deploying new weapons systems."

The Disarmament Subcommittee, headed by Sen. Albert Gore, heard additional scientific and academic testimony against ABM deployment Mar. 13. Dr. Donald F. Hornig, a science adviser to Pres. Johnson, warned in a telegram that such deployment "would impair the security of the United States and retard progress toward a stable, peaceful world." Similar warnings were voiced in person before the panel by Prof. Marshall Shulman, director of the Russian Institute at Columbia University; Dr. Carl Kaysen, director of the Institute for Advanced Study in Princeton, N.J. and a former National Security Council aide in the Kennedy and Johnson Administration, and Prof. Allen Whiting, professor of Chinese studies at the University of Michigan and former top intelligence analyst on Chinese affairs at the State Department.

Other Senators made known their objections to ABM deployment. A letter urging delay of deployment as a step to advance the "cause of peace" was sent to the President Mar. 13 by 4 freshman Republican Senators—Marlow W. Cook (Ky.), Richard S. Schweiker (Pa.), William B. Saxbe (O.) and Charles McC. Mathias Jr. (Md.). They expressed "grave doubt that the Sentinel could function effectively against increasingly complex weapons systems and amidst the chaos and confusion of a nuclear attack." (Cook had reported to the Senate Mar. 12 that, according to an unnamed Sentinel subcontractor, the Sentinel system was technically so unreliable that it "should not be deployed.")

On the Senate floor Mar. 7, Senate Democratic leader Mike Mansfield (Mont.) had warned that a decision to proceed with Sentinel deployment represented "a movement of the nation's leadership in the wrong direction and at the wrong time." He said the problem involved in its larger context "the basic direction of public leadership for a decade or more." "If we decide to go ahead with this project," he said, "the decision can only be seen as a continuance of both the practices and the priorities of the past.... Having spoken so long and so loudly of a distant danger, we are not able to hear the rising voice of need at hand.... Yet it is these inner difficulties, in my judgment, which present the nation with the clearest and most imminent danger. The multi-billion-dollar Sentinel system does not meet these difficulties anymore than Vietnam has met them. On the contrary, it, too, may well act to intensify them."

During the Mar. 7 session, 3 GOP Senators—John Sherman Cooper (Ky.), Jacob K. Javits (N.Y.) and Charles H. Percy (Ill.)—went to the White House to press their anti-deployment argument at a meeting with Kissinger.

The Senate Foreign Relations Committee Mar. 7 urged delay of the ABM pending negotiations with the USSR for strategic arms control.

Safeguard Controversy

Defense Secy. Laird, in public testimony before 2 Senate committees Mar. 20-21, cited the growing Soviet missile threat as the compelling reason for deploying the ABM system—currently being called Safeguard—recommended by Pres. Nixon. (The Sentinel ABM system as modified by the Nixon Administration to "safeguard" the U.S. deterrent strength was officially renamed the Safeguard system Mar. 20.) Laird presented his testimony—some of it heretofore classified information normally discussed with Congressional committees only in secret session—before the largely "hawkish" Senate Armed Services Committee Mar. 20 and before the Disarmament Subcommittee of the largely "dovish" Senate Foreign Relations Committee Mar. 21. Both appearances were televised. They highlighted a dispute between the 2 panels on whether or not to deploy an ABM system.

Laird told the Armed Services Committee that "the Soviet Union today is building at a rapid rate the kinds of weapons which could be used to erode our essential deterrent force." Accompanied by Deputy Defense Secy. Packard, Gen. Earle G. Wheeler, chairman of the Joint Chiefs of Staff, and Dr. John S. Foster, director of defense research and engineering, Laird buttressed his appeal for Safeguard by revealing previously classified details about the Soviet Union's SS-9 intercontinental ballistic missile: "They are installing many" SS-9s (estimated at more than 200 already deployed, nearly 500 scheduled for deployment by 1975); SS-9s were capable of carrying 20-25-megaton warheads (much larger than any the U.S. had), and they were "accurate" (Packard put their accuracy at about .6 mile).

Using other previously undisclosed data, Laird cited "evidence" that the Soviets had gone into mass production (about one a month) of their Polaris-like submarine and were deploying 7 of them a year. He warned that "new things that have taken place" had thrown into doubt the ability of the U.S. Polaris fleet to remain "very free from attack" after 1972. Packard estimated that the Soviet Union could achieve parity with the U.S. in the number of submarine-based missiles by 1971-4. Laird warned about the Soviet Union's fractional orbital bombardment system. "We cannot assume that the FOBS which have been launched or deployed do not carry nuclear warheads," he said.

Laird indicated that unless the U.S. took steps to defend its deterrent, the Soviet Union could acquire, by the mid 1970s, a first-strike capability of such magnitude that it could knock out the U.S. retaliatory strength. This situation would unbalance the nuclear-threat stalemate of the past decade. Laird held that Safeguard would not escalate the arms race and would be not a "stumbling block" to arms-control talks but "a building block to peace."

Laird's testimony was received sympathetically by most Armed Services Committee members. An exception was Sen. Stuart Symington (D., Mo.), who argued that the deployment of Safeguard would be a "grave mistake." He questioned the witnesses about the fact that the Soviet threat was being cited to justify Safeguard, although Safeguard had been brought forward as protection primarily against "a possible emerging Chinese ICBM capability." Laird and Packard admitted that their justification for Safeguard was based on construction of the full 12-site system. As such, it would provide an umbrella against the Chinese threat, which, Packard said, "is not much farther along today than it was 3 years ago." Laird reported that the Defense Department was reserving the "option" of adding 2 more ABM sites in Hawaii and Alaska (this would raise the cost of the program an estimated $300 million more than the 12-site system).

In his confrontation with the Senate Disarmament Subcommittee Mar. 21, Laird presented the same arguments—that "the Soviets are going for a first-strike capability, and there is no question about it," that the SS-9 "can only be aimed at destroying our retaliatory force," that "if the Soviet threat turns out to be, as the evidence now indicates, an attempt to erode our deterrent capability," then the U.S. had "no alternative" but to begin protecting its Minuteman bases with the Safeguard system.

Sen. J. W. Fulbright, chairman of the subcommittee's parent Foreign Relations Committee, accused Laird of employing "the technique of fear" to justify Safeguard. "Suddenly the Russians are becoming 8 feet tall," he said, "and they are about to overwhelm us." Subcommittee chairman Albert Gore contended that Safeguard deployment would "endanger our security" and "make an armaments limitation agreement more difficult, if not impossible, to attain and thus ultimately could degrade our deterrent." Gore questioned the adequacy of the initial 2-site deployment plan. This would cover only 1/3 of the Minuteman force and, if bombers and Polaris strength were counted, only 10% of the U.S. deterrent. Laird replied that even 10% protection could be "pretty important." (He revealed that the U.S. was targeting 2 warheads on each Soviet ABM missile.)

Subcommittee member Claiborne Pell (D., R.I.) questioned an apparent conflict in policy between developing a 2-megaton warhead and supporting a comprehensive nuclear-test ban. Foster had testified that the warhead for the Spartan missile, the long-range interceptor for

Safeguard, would not be "satisfactorily developed" until 1973. It was being developed in underground tests in Nevada. Under an "adequately verified" test ban, Pell pointed out, all underground testing would be prohibited. Laird replied that national security had priority over a test-ban agreement. He said the U.S. would not delay— it would be done "in the not too distant future"—deployment of multiple warheads on missiles.

The effect of ABM deployment, with the missile interception planned over Canadian territory, on the U.S.-Canadian relations, was also broached. Laird said the Johnson Administration had reached an "understanding" on the matter with the Canadian government, and he opposed giving Canada a "veto power" over the U.S. decision.

The Pentagon's ABM plans were attacked in the Senate Mar. 24 by Senate Democratic leader Mike Mansfield, who said the Defense Department was playing "one-upmanship" on Pres. Nixon while trying to sell Safeguard to Congress. Mansfield said: The President had stressed the limited 2-site AMB plan and had told Congressional leaders in White House briefings that he was hopeful negotiations with the USSR might make even this limited deployment unnecessary. Mr. Nixon had "specifically reserved until a later review any decision for elaboration of the proposed system beyong the initial 2-site installation." The Defense Department's testimony, however, left the "strong impression that the 2-site installations are just the beginning of a vast program to convert the entire nation into a missile Maginot." "It is as if future reviews of the international situation, which the President has stressed he would make prior to any further elaboration of the system, will be nothing more than some sort of charade for the benefit of those who have had grave concern about the entire enterprise from the outset." The Pentagon had requested authority to buy land for all 12 ABM sites; such purchases "would have no purpose other than to set in motion an elaboration which Pres. Nixon presumably has not yet decided."

In an addition to the defense posture statement before the House Armed Services Committee, Laird contended Mar. 27 that his proposed defense program "reinforces with actions the expressed desire of the United States for [arms control] negotiations." He cited the President's revision of the preceding Administration's missile defense system and the slowdown in the Minuteman-3 program, which, he conceded, was also "dictated by testing requirements." "It remains to be seen," he said, "whether our potential adversaries will similarly indicate with actions that they too are serious about desiring meaningful arms limitation talks."

Talking with European newsmen Apr. 7, Laird clarified an earlier remark by saying he was not "talking about intentions" in reference to the SS-9 but about "capability.... I've always made it clear that I do not believe the Soviet Union would be foolish enough ... to go forward with a first strike." State Secy. Rogers said Apr. 7 that while he did not believe the SS-9 deployment was based on "the intention of actually having a first strike" at the U.S., "one of the first questions we want to raise with them [at the forthcoming arms talks] is: Why would you have a 25-megaton missile?" Rogers reported Apr. 21 that Russia had test-fired the SS-9 in the Pacific. Acting Asst. Defense Secy. Daniel Z. Henkin confirmed Apr. 22 that the test-firing had occurred the previous week and said the missile had traveled 5,500 miles in its first long-distance test with a multiple warhead. Pentagon spokesmen said Russia had 200 of the missiles deployed, and "deployment is continuing."

Vice Pres. Spiro T. Agnew, addressing the Bureau of Advertising of the American Newspaper Publishers Association in New York Apr. 22, spoke of the Safeguard plan as a bargaining point for the U.S. at a time when the Soviet Union was "substantially increasing the potential thrust of its missile attack." He cited the SS-9, its capacity of up to 25 megatons, its "impressive accuracy," the Soviet Union's "testing and developing mid-air proliferation of nuclear warheads," intelligence reports "that the Soviet Union is building Polaris-type submarines at a rapid rate."

Laird, speaking before newspaper editors in Panama City, Fla. Apr. 25, said that "the Soviet Union has the capability of achieving by the mid-1970s a superiority over the presently authorized and pro-grammed forces of the United States in all areas—offensive strategic forces, defensive forces and conventional forces." He asserted that the Safeguard system was "the minimal step necessary at this time to insure that the safety and security of the American people will be preserved if arms limitations talks are not successful in the coming months and years." The argument that Russia would not maintain its current level of defense activity "could lead to a major and irretrievable mis-calculation if our judgment on intentions proves faulty," he declared. "We cannot gamble on estimates of Soviet intentions," he said, "If the Soviet Union is developing a capability that could endanger this nation, we must be prepared to counteract it." Laird reported that the USSR had 1,000 long-range missiles in "hardened" silos and 140 older missiles on launch pads. He said that at their current deployment rate of about 250 missiles a year, the Russians could have 2,500 missiles by 1975, compared with 1,054 deployed by the U.S., which was not planning to increase its force within the next 5 years.

Republican House leader Gerald R. Ford, following a meeting of GOP Congressional leaders with Pres. Nixon Apr. 29, suggested that opponents of the antiballistic missile defense system were bringing up the question of unilateral disarmament by America "in the face of a serious threat from the Soviet Union."

The Senate Armed Services Committee held public hearings on the issue Apr. 22-23. At the televised Apr. 22 session, Dr. Herbert F. York, ex-director of defense research and engineering at the Pentagon, and

Dr. Wolfgang K. H. Panovsky of Stanford University presented arguments against an ABM system; ex-Deputy Defense Secy. Paul H. Nitze and Dr. William G. McMillan of the University of California, Los Angeles, testified in favor of the ABM. The hearings revealed a division within the committee of possibly 1/3 against and 2/3 for deployment of Safeguard. Chairman John Stennis (D., Miss.), while backing Safeguard Apr. 22 as "the best horse we have in the stable" and favoring deployment, indicated to colleagues a possible inclination toward some modification of the Safeguard plan.

Louis Harris took a poll on the question: "Do you tend to approve or disapprove of the decision to go ahead with the anti-missile missile system?" He reported Apr. 28 that 47% of those interviewed approved, 26% disapproved, 27% were "not sure."

A study (reported in the Apr. 9 *N.Y. Times*) prepared for ABM opponents in the Senate by scientist Ralph E. Lapp, a critic of the missile program, concluded that even on the basis of the most pessimistic Pentagon assumptions, the USSR would not acquire a first-strike capability with its SS-9 missile.

A report issued in London Apr. 10 by the Institute for Strategic Studies predicted that by mid-1969 the Soviet Union would have more ICBMs deployed than the U.S. would have. The report said the U.S. would retain "a lead in total numbers of nuclear weapons" because of its superiority in delivery systems by planes and submarines.

Arthur J. Goldberg, former Supreme Court Justice and former U.S. ambassador to the UN, and Roswell Gilpatric, ex-Deputy Defense Secretary, announced in Washington Apr. 17 the formation of a national citizens committee to oppose Pres. Nixon's Safeguard plan. The committee's name: National Citizens Committee Concerned About Deployment of the ABM. Among its members: Dr. York; Whitney Young Jr., director of the Urban League; Vice Chairman Arjay Miller of the Ford Motor Co.; W. Averell Harriman, ex-ambassador to the USSR; Dr. Donald Hornig, science adviser to ex-Pres. Johnson; theologian Reinhold Niebuhr.

The formation of a National Religious Committee Opposing AMB was announced in New York Apr. 29. The announcement was signed by 26 churchmen, including 5 Protestant bishops and 2 Roman Catholic auxiliary bishops.

Nixon Presses Safeguard Program

Pres. Nixon said June 19 that his Administration was considering the possibility of offering a moratorium on tests of multiple-warhead missiles as part of an arms control agreement with the USSR. The President, speaking at a news conference, said the U.S. would not agree to unilaterally suspend such tests. Mr. Nixon reiterated his support for the Safeguard system, which he called "even more important" than ever.

He cited recent intelligence data that indicated Soviet progress in the development of multiple-warhead missiles and the targeting of these missiles "to fall in somewhat the precise area" in which the U.S. Minuteman missile silos were located. The President said 80% of the Minuteman force would be "in danger" from such Soviet missiles by 1973, and "ABM is needed particularly in order to meet that eventuality."

Defense Secy. Laird said June 23 that the USSR was testing its SS-9 with a 3-part multiple warhead that fell in a variable triangular pattern similar to the pattern of deployment of Minuteman silos. Laird made the point at a Pentagon news conference following a 5-hour closed session with the Senate Foreign Relations Committee, where he reportedly softened his previous testimony that the Soviet Union was "going for a first-strike capability ... no question." Laird modified his assessment, saying that the USSR was developing a first-strike weapon, the SS-9, aimed at only one part of the U.S. retaliatory force, the Minuteman. Laird was accompanied in his appearance before the committee by Richard Helms, director of the Central Intelligence Agency (CIA).

Reports had circulated June 18 that the U.S. intelligence community had reached a consensus that the Soviet Union was trying not for a first-strike nuclear capability against the U.S. but for simply more than parity in missile strength. The consensus was said to have been reached the previous week at meetings of the U.S. Intelligence Board, presided over by Helms, and several civilian and service intelligence agencies.

At a press conference in Washington Oct. 9, Prof. Pyotr L. Kapitsa, a leading Soviet physicist, assailed the development of ABM systems as costly as and ineffective. He added that if the system was deployed in the U.S., "it will only increase the number of missiles in the Soviet Union."

U.S. ABM System Authorized

A compromise $20.7 billion U.S. military authorization bill that provided for the initial authorization for the Safeguard system was cleared by Congress Nov. 6 and sent to the President. The bill had been approved by House voice vote Nov. 5 and by a 58-9 Senate vote Nov. 6. Although the Senate had subjected the bill to protracted debate and serious attack earlier in the year during a spate of defense-spending criticism, Chairman John C. Stennis (D., Miss.) of the Senate Armed Services Committee commented Nov. 4 after approval of the final bill by his joint conference committee that "there is no major weapon that's left out of this bill and none that's severely restricted."

The bill's authorization for fiscal 1970 defense procurement totaled $20,723,202,000. This was $721,616,000 more than approved by the Senate Sept. 18, $624,658,000 less than approved by the House Oct. 3, $1,240,458,000 less than requested by the Administration and some $900 million less than authorized in the previous fiscal year.

During the Senate consideration of the bill Nov. 6, Chairman J. W. Fulbright of the Senate Foreign Relations Committee objected to a $28 million authorization for research and development of a "free-world fighter" plane for U.S. allies. "Providing a subsidy to private companies for development of an aircraft suitable only for use by foreign countries—poor ones at that—involves many grave questions of foreign policy," Fulbright said. He obtained a pledge from Stennis that none of the planes would be supplied to countries outside Southeast Asia (which came within the jurisdiction of the Defense Department and hence the bill's authorization) without the approval of Fulbright's committee. The Senate version of the original bill had not included funds for the plane, and such funds were not specifically requested by the Administration. The House had approved a $52 million authorization for the plane, a favorite project of Chairman L. Mendel Rivers (D., S.C.) of the House Armed Services Committee.

The Senators who voted against the bill Nov. 6 were Fulbright, Philip A. Hart (D., Mich.), Eugene J. McCarthy (D., Minn.), George S. McGovern (D., S.D.), Gaylord Nelson (D., Wis.), Stephen M. Young (D., O.), Mark O. Hatfield (R., Ore.), Robert W. Packwood (R., Ore.) and Jacob K. Javits (R., N.Y.).

Many restrictive Senate amendments were dropped from the bill in conference. Among those eliminated: Several curbs on the use of biological and chemical warfare agents (the conferees imposed a requirement for safe shipment of such materials and reports on spending for them); a requirement of independent audits of major defense weapons contracts; curbs on the use of military assistance to Laos and Thailand for the support of combat operations.

Among restrictive Senate amendments modified: A 20% reduction in the Pentagon's independent research funds was reduced to a 7% cut; a proposed review by the controller general of defense profits was weakened; he would have no subpoena power except through the Congressional armed services committees and would have authority for only limited requisitioning of data contractors.

Among the items included in the authorization: $759 million for ABM research and initial deployment; $2.98 billion for Navy shipbuilding, or $352 million more than the Defense Department had requested (the House had approved $1 billion more for shipbuilding than had the Senate; the conferees compromised by adding $415 million to the Senate figure); $86 million for 170 Cozra helicopter gunships; $104 million for the Navy version of the A-7 subsonic attack plane and $374.7 million for the purchase of an Air Force version; $16 million to buy A-

37s; funds for 23 C-5As plus $52 million to buy some long-lead-time items if the Pentagon decided to buy an additional 20 C-5As; $20.4 million to buy the air-to-ground short-range attack missile (SRAM), plus $75 million for its continued development; $100 million for TOW antitank missiles; $20 million toward production of the main battle tank (MBT-70), plus $30 million for continued development; $60 million for research on the SAM-D surface-to-air missile; $66 million for research on the E2C command and control aircraft and $140 million for research on the S3A antisubmarine warfare aircraft.

Before passing its original version of the bill by 311-44 vote Oct. 3, the House Oct. 2 had defeated, by non-record 219-105 vote, a proposal to eliminate the $345.5 million for ABM procurement. The House bill was then sent to joint conference committee to be reconciled with the version originally passed by the Senate. The acrimonious 3-day House debate, contrasting with the earlier 8-week debate in the Senate over the Senate measure, was marked Oct. 3 by cries of "gag rule" when the House allotted only 1/2 hour to debate. Individual speeches were limited to 45 seconds, and the House rejected a series of efforts to reduce the authorization by about $2 billion. The rejected amendments would have reduced or deleted funds for a manned bomber, the airborne warning and control system, naval shipbuilding, procurement of helicopters and the C-5A cargo transport plane and the SRAM ground-to-air missile. A proposal to require periodic Defense Department reports on major defense systems was defeated by 100-97 vote. The support for the Safeguard and other defense programs was led by Rivers. House Speaker John W. McCormack (D., Mass.) also spoke in favor of the ABM funds. The effort to bar the ABM and trim other military items was led by 5 members of Rivers' committee—Reps. Otis G. Pike (D., N.Y.), Lucien N. Nedzi (D., Mich.), Robert L. Leggett (D., Calif.), Charles Whalen (R., O.) and Robert T. Stafford (R., Vt.).

The defense appropriations bill for fiscal 1970, totaling $69,640,568,000, was passed by voice votes of both houses of Congress Dec. 18 and was signed by Pres. Nixon Dec. 30. The total was $5,637,632,000 less than the final Nixon Administration requests. This was the biggest reduction in defense spending requests since 1953. This was also the first reduction in the defense budget in 5 years and an $8 billion reduction in the defense request of the outgoing Johnson Administration. Major projects funded by the bill included the Safeguard system, the C-5A transport plane, new generations of Navy and Air Force fighter planes and conversion of four Polaris submarines to carry the Poseidon multiple warhead missile. House-Senate conferees agreed to eliminate proposed funds for the Navy F-14 fighter and provide more funds for research aircraft. The conferees also deleted $10 million for the MBT-70 Main battle tank and approved $10 million for the SRAM missile and funds for the TOW Army missile. The bill carried appropriations of $22,268,634,000 for the Air Force,

$22,134,020,000 for the Army and $20,802,248,000 for the Navy. By military mission, the breakdown was: military personnel $20,834,800,000; operation and maintenance $20,860,100,000; research and development $7,368,820,000; and procurement $17,841,848,000. The latter included $4.3 billion for Army equipment and missiles, $2.6 billion for Navy aircraft and missiles, $2.5 billion for Navy shipbuilding, $3.4 billion for Air Force aircraft and $1.5 billion for Air Force missiles.

Non--Proliferation Treaty

West Germany Drops Reservations, Signs Pact

West Germany continued its opposition to the non-proliferation treaty until a new government headed by Willy Brandt succeeded the Kurt Georg Kiesinger regime in October. Bonn signed the treaty Nov. 28. During a visit to Bonn, British Prime Min. Harold Wilson had commented Feb. 13 on the Kiesinger regime's position. He said: "All of us in Europe know that the security of Germany, and equally of all of us, depends on NATO, and not whether one country or another signs or does not sign the non-proliferation treaty." Wilson expressed confidence that West Germany would not seek nuclear weapons. West German Chancellor Kiesinger reportedly had explained to Wilson Feb. 12 his government's hesitation to sign the treaty until it was further clarified.

(Wilson Feb. 13 expressed strong support for continued work on a British-German-Dutch project to perfect the gas centrifuge process for producing enriched uranium fuel at considerably less cost than current conventional methods. The project, viewed by Bonn as an important step into the non-military nuclear club, had been assailed by the USSR. *Pravda* had charged Feb. 6 that the project would violate the non-proliferation treaty because "West Germany will receive a screen behind which West German scientists, engineers and military personnel will be able to prepare for the production of their own nuclear arms.")

The West German Social Democratic Party (SDP) congress at Bad Godesberg Apr. 16-18 urged that Bonn sign the non-proliferation treaty and that it renounce nuclear, biological and chemical weapons. Bruno Heck, secretary general of the ruling Christian Democratic Union deplored SDP's statement and asserted that in calling for the signing of the non-proliferation treaty, the SDP had stabbed Chancellor Kiesinger in the back.

Kiesinger said in Tokyo May 20 that his government still feared that ratification of the non-proliferation treaty would lead to Soviet interference in West Germany's development of atomic energy for peaceful purposes. Kiesinger, indirectly responding to a *Pravda* charge May 19 that "the military group in West Germany favors a nuclear arms program and that his [Kiesinger's]... visit [in Tokyo] marks an attempt to form a new Berlin-Tokyo axis," emphasized Bonn's reluctance to ratify the treaty without a companion treaty requiring Soviet participation in international inspection procedures. The Soviet Union reportedly had offered West Germany a number of "positive" concessions Feb. 6 to encourage it to ratify the treaty. They were believed to include assurances that West Germany would enjoy the right to engage in peaceful atomic energy developments and that the USSR would view its differences with Bonn as ultimately subject to UN authority.

According to sources in Bonn Apr. 22, the U.S. had not deposited its treaty ratification documents in Moscow, London and Washington as a concession to West German concern over the Soviet stand. State Department spokesman Robert J. McCloskey confirmed Apr. 23 that the U.S. had proposed to Moscow simultaneous final ratification in early April but that Washington had not received a response to the offer.

Following the Bundestag elections in West Germany in September and assumption of power by a new coalition headed by Willy Brandt as chancellor, Brandt told the Bundestag Nov. 12 that his government had received assurances from the U.S. and the USSR that overrode objections to signing the non-proliferation treaty. West Germany's agreement to sign the treaty would constitute "an element of equalization of rights" rather than discrimination against the country, Brandt said. "It is not a question of whether we sign, but when we sign." Foreign Min. Walter Scheel told the deputies that Bonn Nov. 9 had received a Soviet note asserting that the USSR would not hinder West Germany's development of atomic power for peaceful uses. Similarly, he said, the U.S. had told Bonn that it would not hinder the delivery of fissionable materials to West Germany and to Euratom.

Bonn signed the non-proliferation treaty Nov. 28. At a press conference following the cabinet's unanimous approval, Brandt said that before the government ratified the treaty, agreement would have to be worked out on development, research and control with the International Atomic Energy Agency and Euratom. (Sources in Bonn said that it might be a year before ratification was completed.) The West German ambassadors in Moscow, London and Washington were instructed to sign the treaty on behalf of their government. The signing of the treaty ended almost 3 years of controversy within West Germany. Ex-Chancellor Konrad Adenauer and ex-Finance Min. Franz Josef Strauss had assailed the pact as an "unequal treaty." Ex-Chancellor Kiesinger had denounced the "atomic confederacy" between the U.S. and the Soviet Union. At a news conference Nov. 26, West German government spokesman Conrad Ahlers had said that Bonn intended to sign the treaty with the understanding that NATO's nuclear capability of the North Atlantic Treaty Organization would not be impaired and that Bonn would not be relinquishing the right to participate in a future European nuclear federation.

U.S. Ratification, U.S. & Soviet Signatures

The U.S. ratified the non-proliferation treaty in March, and it was signed by the U.S. and USSR Nov. 4.

In his State-of-the-Union message Jan. 14, outgoing Pres. Johnson had recommended early Senate approval of the treaty. Vice Pres. Hubert H. Humphrey Jan. 17 condemned the Senate's "unpardonable delay."

In his inaugural address Jan. 20, incoming Pres. Nixon did not mention the new Administration's policy in regard to the treaty's ratification. But at his first news conference Jan. 27, he said: "I favor the non-proliferation treaty" and "will urge its ratification at an appropriate time and I would hope an early time." Nixon urged the Senate Feb. 5 to give "prompt consideration and positive action" to ratification of the treaty. In a statement addressed to the Senate, he said he had concluded that early ratification would "serve the national interest" and "advance this Administration's policy of negotiation rather than confrontation with the USSR."

The Senate Foreign Relations Committee Feb. 25 approved the treaty by 14-0 vote. In its Mar. 7 report, the committee called the treaty "an important beginning in controlling the further spread of nuclear weapons." It noted in its report its finding that the treaty "in no way" affected U.S. rights to station nuclear weapons on allied soil.

Senate consent to ratification came Mar. 13 after 4 days of debate. Several proposed reservations to the pact were rejected during the debate. One was a statement, proposed by Sen. Sam J. Ervin Jr. (D., N.C.), that the treaty did not commit the U.S. to defend non-nuclear signatories against aggression. Foreign Relations Committee Chairman Fulbright, urging against the proposal, said the treaty did not "in any way extend our commitments to the use of our armed forces." The proposal was defeated by 61-30 vote Mar. 11. Also rejected were proposed reservations or understandings: (a) that the treaty would not be interpreted as barring the provision of nuclear weapons to regional organizations for defense (proposed by Sen. John G. Tower [R., Tex.], rejected Mar. 12 by 75-17 vote); (b) that the pact would be abrogated in the event of military attack by one of the signatories against another (proposed by Sen. Thomas J. Dodd [D., Conn.], rejected by 81-15 vote Mar. 13); (c) that the U.S. retained the right to deploy nuclear weapons in Europe and to plan nuclear defenses with its NATO allies (offered by Sen. Strom Thurmond [R., S.C.], rejected by 77-17 vote Mar. 13); (d) that the treaty would not compel the U.S. to defend a victim of nuclear attack and did not affect U.S. obligations under the UN Charter or other treaties (proposed by Ervin, rejected by 69-25 vote Mar. 13).

Pres. Nixon and Soviet Pres. Nikolai V. Podgorny signed the treaty Nov. 24. At ceremonies in Washington, Mr. Nixon lauded the actions by both governments and said: "It is my earnest hope that ratification of the treaty by the necessary number of additional states will soon occur so that it may enter into force at an early time.... This Administration seeks equitable and meaningful commitments to limit armaments and to resolve the dangerous conflicts that threaten peace and security. In this act of ratification today, this commitment is demonstrated anew."

In Moscow, Podgorny signed the treaty after it had been ratified by the Supreme Soviet. He said: "There is no doubt that the quickest effectuation of this treaty would create favorable preconditions for progress in the direction of stopping the armament race as well as disarmament and, from its side, the Soviet Union is doing all that is possible for the achievement of this noble aim."

The final step in the ratification process was to come when the 2 countries deposited the instruments of ratification with the 3 depositary governments—Britain, the USSR and the U.S. The treaty would become effective when 43 nations, including the depositary states, had deposited the instruments of ratification. As of Nov. 24, 22 nations had taken this action: Austria, Botswana, Britain, Bulgaria, Cameroon, Canada, Czechoslovakia, Denmark, Ecuador, Finland, Hungary, Iceland, Iraq, Ireland, Mauritius, Mexico, Mongolia, New Zealand, Nigeria, Norway, Poland and Syria. Switzerland became the 92d country to sign the treaty when Amb. Felix Schnyder signed the pact in Washington Nov. 27.

(The Executive Council of Japan's Liberal Democratic Party had ruled Nov. 14 that Japan would not sign the treaty until "further careful study." Disadvantage to non-nuclear powers, the security problem and inequality of inspection measures were given as the reasons. The council's decision was binding on Premier Eisaku Sato.)

GENEVA MEETINGS

Debate on Seabed A-Ban

The problem of outlawing the emplacement of nuclear weapons on the floors of the oceans was taken up by the UN's 18-Nation Disarmament Committee (ENDC) when it reconvened in Geneva Mar. 18 after a 7-month recess. The sessions continued through May 24.

Pres. Nixon explained the U.S. position in a message read at the conference Mar. 18 by Gerard C. Smith, director of the U.S. Arms Control & Disarmament Agency and head of the American delegation. The message said:

●The U.S. was interested in working out an international agreement that would prohibit emplacement of nuclear or other weapons of mass destruction on the seabed.

●The U.S. "supports conclusion of a comprehensive test ban adequately verified."

●Washington "will continue to press for an agreement to cut off the production of fissionable materials for weapons purposes."

●Actual reduction of armaments, and not merely limiting their growth or spread, remained a U.S. goal.

●With respect to proposed talks between the U.S. and Russia on the limitation of strategic arms, the U.S. hoped that the international political situation would evolve in a way that would permit the talks to begin in the near future.

Soviet Premier Aleksei N. Kosygin, in a message read at the reconvened conference, urged action on a new Soviet draft of an international convention for the prohibition of nuclear weapons and military installations of any kind on the ocean floor outside the 12-mile territorial limit. Kosygin also called for an agreement on non-use of nuclear weapons, a halt in their manufacture and the destruction of stockpiles. The Soviet draft treaty, submitted at the conference Mar. 18, would not prohibit missile-firing submarines but would bar from the ocean floor radar and other navigational devices for military uses, along with seabed missile-launching devices, which were reported to be under development. Text of the "Draft Treaty on the Prohibition of the Use for Military Purposes of the Seabed & the Ocean Floor & the Subsoil thereof":

The states parties to this treaty,

Noting that the developing technology makes the seabed and the ocean floor, and the subsoil thereof, accessible and suitable for military uses,

Considering that the prohibition of the use of the seabed and the ocean floor for military purposes serves the interests of maintaining world peace and reducing the arms race, and promotes a relaxation of international tensions and strengthening the confidence among states,

Being convinced that this treaty will contribute to the realization of the principles and purposes of the United Nations,

Have agreed as follows:

Article I. The use for military purposes of the seabed and the ocean floor, and the subsoil thereof, beyond the 12-mile maritime zone of coastal states, shall be prohibited.

It shall be prohibited to place on the seabed and the ocean floor, and the subsoil thereof, objects with nuclear weapons or any other types of weapons of mass destruction, to set up military bases, structures, installations, fortifications and other objects of military nature.

Article II. All installations and structures on the seabed and the ocean floor, and the subsoil thereof, shall be open on the basis of reciprocity for representatives of other states parties to this treaty for the purposes of verification of the fulfillment by the states, which have placed there such objects, of the obligations assumed under this treaty.

Article III. The outer limit of the 12-mile maritime zone established for the purposes of this treaty shall be measured from the same baselines which are used in defining the limits of the territorial waters of coastal states.

Article IV. 1. This treaty shall be open for signature to all states. Any state, which does not sign the treaty before its entry into force in accordance with paragraph 3 of this article, may accede to it at any time.

2. This treaty shall be subject to ratification by signatory states. Instruments of ratification and instruments of accession shall be deposited with the governments of . . . , which are hereby designated the depositary governments.

3. This treaty shall enter into force after the deposit of instruments of ratification by five governments, including the governments designated as depositary governments.

4. For states whose instruments of ratification or accession are deposited subsequent to the entry into force of this treaty it shall enter into force on the date of the deposit of their instruments of ratification or accession.

5. Each party shall in exercising its national sovereignty have the right to withdraw from this treaty if it decides that extraordinary events, related to the subject matter of this treaty, have jeopardized the supreme interests of its country. It shall give notice of such withdrawal to all parties to the treaty and to the United Nations Security Council three months in advance. Such notice shall include a statement of the extraordinary events it regards as having jeopardized its supreme interests.

6. The depositary governments shall promptly inform all signatory and acceding states of the date of each signature, the date of deposit of each instrument of ratification or of accession, the date of the entry into force of this treaty, and the receipt of other notices.

7. This treaty shall be registered by the depositary governments pursuant to Article 102 of the Charter of the United Nations.

The U.S. delegation rejected the Soviet proposal Mar. 25 with the assertion that it would be "simply unworkable and probably harmful." Smith said the ban on underwater conventional weapons "would raise insuperable verification problems." But he accepted the reciprocal inspection provision in the Soviet draft, which provided that each party to the ocean-floor treaty would have the right to verify compliance by others.

After the session, Soviet representative Aleksei A. Roshchin, said the U.S. reacted much as he had expected.

Statements at the conference by Britain, Canada and Nigeria Mar. 20 and by Sweden and Italy Mar. 25 indicated dissatisfaction with the priority given by Washington and Moscow to the ocean-floor question. The Nigerian delegate, Sule Kolo, said a prerequisite for halting the nuclear arms race was the elimination of possibilities for developing more sophisticated weapons. Kolo supported a British proposal for a phased approach to banning underground nuclear tests. Under this approach, there would be an annual quota of underground explosions, which would end entirely within a few years. Ivor Porter of Britain emphasized the urgency of bilateral talks on missiles and said the Soviet seabed treaty seemed to go too far in seeking to keep the seabed clear of all installations. Mrs. Alva Myrdal of Sweden and Mario Zagari of Italy insisted Mar. 25 that negotiations on a prohibition of underground nuclear tests and a cutoff in production of nuclear weapons were more important. The question of the ocean floor, Mrs. Myrdal said, should be left until the end of the current session.

Mrs. Myrdal Apr. 1 submitted Sweden's preliminary version of a treaty to prohibit underground nuclear tests. She presented the draft as an inducement to Washington and Moscow to make clear to the conference whether they were willing to make the "political decision" to ban underground tests.

The Soviet Union assured other conferees Apr. 3 that its proposal for demilitarizing the ocean floor was not as all-embracing as the U.S. had charged. Roshchin said his government's draft treaty did not presuppose restrictions on means of communication and on beacons or similar devices. He also maintained that it would not preclude military personnel from working with civilians in underwater research.

The U.S., in what an American spokesman described as a "major shift in . . . inspection policy," proposed Apr. 8 that the UN International Atomic Energy Agency (IAEA) take over sole responsibility for verifying a cut-off in production of nuclear weapons materials. Under previous U.S. proposals the U.S. and Soviet Union would have been primarily responsible for checking each other on compliance. The elements of the new proposal, submitted by Adrian S. Fisher: (a) From an agreed date, nuclear-weapons states would halt all production of fissionable materials for use in weapons; (b) the production of fissionable material would be permitted for non-weapons purposes, such as power and propulsion reactors and nuclear explosives for peaceful uses; (c) the IAEA would be asked to check the nuclear materials used in each country's peaceful nuclear activities. Fisher emphasized that the U.S. was not abandoning its insistence on inspection of a ban on underground nuclear tests. The U.S., he said, remained convinced that adequate verification of such an agreement necessitated on-the-spot inspection.

The USSR rejected the U.S. proposal Apr. 10. Roshchin called the U.S. plan an old idea with "but one new point." Roshchin said the Soviet position remained that a production cutoff would not contribute to the reduction of existing arsenals of nuclear weapons.

At the Apr. 22 meeting, Mrs. Myrdal rejected the U.S. position that total demilitarization of the seabed would be unworkable. She said: "The [seabed] prohibition must encompass all military installations"; otherwise the ban would be "unwieldy, not to say impossible" to enforce.

Polish delegate Henryk Jaroszek said Apr. 24 that the Baltic Sea should be specifically provided for in the proposed seabed treaty. He added that the adoption of the treaty would lead to the Baltic's being proclaimed "a sea of peaceful relations among its coastal states."

Roshchin May 8 expressed hope for agreement on a seabed treaty. He again rejected the U.S. position that only nuclear weapons should be barred under the treaty. "Proposals have been made that defensive weapons should not be prohibited, he said. "We believe this would be wrong, since by making an exception for certain weapons deployed on the seabed we should not solve the task of preventing the arms race in this field." After the meeting, Roshchin told reporters that submarine listening devices should be banned by the pact.

At the May 22 meeting, the U.S. presented its version of a draft treaty to ban nuclear weapons and other weapons of mass destruction "on, within or beneath the seabed and the ocean floor." The proposal, submitted by U.S. representative Fisher, differed on 2 important points from the Soviet draft treaty submitted Mar. 18. The U.S. proposal called for a ban only on nuclear weapons and their emplacements, whereas the USSR had argued for the banning from the seabed of "all objects of a military nature." Fisher May 15 had restated the U.S. contention that total demilitarization "would raise insuperable verification problems" and "make it impossible for us to reach an agreement." The U.S. proposal also called for "observation" to determine whether the treaty was being adhered to, whereas the Soviet Union had proposed reciprocal inspection. The U.S. proposal also differed from the Soviet draft in calling for the area in question to extend within 3 miles of the coast. The USSR had called for a 12-mile limit. The U.S. draft included provisions for "consultations" if one party was suspected of violating the treaty and a review every 5 years to consider amendments, The Soviet draft had been silent on both these issues.

Soviet representative Roshchin said after the May 22 meeting that he was "disappointed but not surprised" by the U.S. proposal. Fisher May 24 said he had strong hopes that progress could be made on the treaty during the summer because there was a "disposition on both sides to try to reach agreement."

Among other developments:

● In a joint statement May 23, the U.S. and USSR proposed the admission of Japan and the Mongolian People's Republic to ENDC membership. Reacting indignantly to the proposal, Rumanian representative Nicolae Ecobesco said it would have been "in conformity with the principles which should guide our activity if all delegations had been kept informed and consulted on this question in advance."

● Fisher May 23 invited foreign nations to attend an underground nuclear explosion scheduled for September in Colorado. The invitation reportedly was extended to underscore the U.S. contention that there was no way except on-site inspection to enforce bans on underground testing.

● In an attempt to reach a compromise between the U.S. and the Soviet positions on a seabed treaty, Canada May 13 proposed a seabed ban not only on nuclear weapons and weapons of mass destruction and their emplacement but in addition on "all other weapons, military activities, undersea bases, or fortifications from which military action could be undertaken against the territory, territorial sea or air space of another state." Canadian representative George Ignatieff said, however, that the treaty should allow a nation to provide coastal defenses against submarines and other means of underwater attack. He rejected the Soviet proposal for complete demilitarization outside a 12-mile coastal zone. Instead he proposed that a defense zone be permitted to extend 200 miles off a state's coast. Limited defense activities would be allowed in this zone as provided in the proposed treaty.

Britain Proposes Germ War Ban

The ENDC conference reconvened in Geneva July 3. At the July 10 meeting, Britain introduced a draft agreement to prohibit the development, production or use of biological weapons "in any circumstances." The proposal would also require current stocks of biological weapons to be destroyed or diverted to peaceful uses within 3 months after the agreement became effective. British State Min. Fred Mulley, who submitted the 10-article proposal, said the pact was designed to strengthen and supplement the 1925 Geneva Protocol, which prohibited the use of biological weapons but not their production and possession. (The U.S. had signed the protocol, but it had not been ratified by the U.S. Senate.)

The British proposal did not contain provisions for inspection machinery, since, as Mulley said, weapons could be produced "clandestinely in a building the size of a small house or garage." Should germ warfare be used against a signatory party, Mulley said, it could appeal to the UN secretary general, who would have "standing authority from the Security Council to investigate immediately and report to the council." Other, less serious complaints would be addressed directly to the council, which could then authorize the secretary general to investigate and report on the complaint. The only council action suggested by Mulley was assistance to a nation that had been a victim of biological attack.

Mulley said Britain's proposal did not apply to chemical weapons since a ban on these weapons presented greater problems of international agreement. A ban on biological weapons was more urgent because they were more destructive, he said.

In a message to the reconvening ENDC July 3, Pres. Nixon said the U.S. was ready to discuss approaches to controlling chemical and biological warfare. A sentence from Mr. Nixon's message, which stated that "the specter of chemical and bacteriological warfare arouses horror and revulsion throughout the world," had been deleted, however. A revised text of the message was read at the conference July 30. According to sources in Geneva, the omission represented the latest struggle between the U.S. Defense Department and other government agencies over the prohibition of chemical and biological weapons. Defense Secy. Melvin R. Laird had said July 28 that the U.S. needed to maintain its stocks of biological and chemical weapons as a deterrent against their use by other nations.

The USSR and Poland criticized the British proposal July 22. They insisted that the ban should cover chemical weapons. Soviet representative Roshchin said the "question arises whether the prohibition of biological weapons alone will not accelerate the chemical arms race." He held that separating the question of banning chemical and biological weapons would undermine the Geneva Protocol. Polish representative Anton Czarkowski urged all states to abide by the protocol.

Mexican representative Jorge Castaneda Aug. 7 indorsed the Soviet proposal for the demilitarization of the seabed and rejected the U.S. argument that the American proposal for seabed control would be easier to verify. Castaneda, however, agreed with the U.S. recommendation of a 3-mile coastal exemption limit rather than the Soviet proposal of a 12-mile limit.

Swedish delegate Alva Myrdal July 24 recommended a compromise version of the Soviet seabed proposal. She suggested that only nuclear and other weapons of mass destruction and their launching platforms be barred from the area between 3 and 12 miles from the coasts and that all military weapons be banned beyond the 12-mile limit. She added that a coastal nation should have the right to install defensive weapons inside its 12-mile limit.

Polish delegate Czarkowski accused the U.S. Aug. 14 of advocating a nuclear and chemical-bacteriological "balance of fear" and assailed Washington for stockpiling nerve gas in West Germany and Okinawa. The U.S. declined to comment on Czarkowski's statement.

(The Disarmament Committee, formerly called the 18-Nation Disarmament Committee, changed its name Aug. 21 to the Conference of the Committee on Disarmament. The committee had been enlarged to 26 nations Aug. 7 after the U.S. and USSR July 31 formally invited Argentina, Hungary, Morocco, the Netherlands, Pakistan and Yugoslavia to join. Japan and Mongolia had joined July 3.)

U.S. & USSR Offer Seabed Draft

A joint U.S.-Soviet draft treaty to ban nuclear weapons from the ocean floors was submitted in October to the Geneva disarmament conferees after both sides had signalled a willingness to compromise. Communist sources at the UN Disarmament Committee conference had said Aug. 22 that the USSR was ready to retreat from its original demand for a complete demilitarization of the seabed and to accept the U.S. proposal to ban only nuclear weapons and other weapons of mass destruction. The U.S. delegates at the conference reportedly indicated a U.S. willingness to accept the Soviet proposal that the ban apply outside a 12-mile coastal limit, rather than the 3-mile limit proposed earlier by the U.S. (The U.S. State Department and Arms Control & Disarmament Agency were reported Sept. 10 to have agreed to accept the 12-mile limit.)

The U.S. and the USSR submitted their joint draft at the conference Oct. 7. The main articles of the draft treaty, which represented concessions on both sides, provided for a ban on nuclear weapons and other weapons of mass destruction outside the 12-mile coastal limit as defined in the 1958 Geneva Convention on the Territorial Sea. U.S. representative James F. Leonard said the proposal prohibited nuclear mines anchored on the seabed, but it did not apply to submarines resting on or anchored to the seabed.

At the final 1969 meeting of the conference, the U.S. and the Soviet Union Oct. 30 presented a revised version of the seabed treaty. The new draft contained 4 revisions: (1) The U.S. and the USSR agreed to renounce their veto power to amendments to the treaty; only a majority of the signers would be needed to approve amendments. (2) The 2 nations agreed to a review conference in Geneva 5 years after the treaty took effect. (3) Any party could appeal to the UN Security Council if there was a "serious question" of violation." (4) The provision of the 12-mile "maximum contiguous zone" was further clarified. Several countries criticized the revised draft treaty; they protested the lack of time to study the document and the lack of controls and verification procedures.

Text of the "Draft Treaty on the Prohibition of the Emplacement of Nuclear Weapons & Other Weapons of Mass Destruction on the Seabed & the Ocean Floor and in the Subsoil Thereof."

The states parties to this treaty. Recognizing the common interest of mankind in the progress of the exploration and use of the seabed and the ocean floor for peaceful purposes,

Considering that the prevention of a nuclear arms race on the seabed and the ocean floor serves the interests of maintaining world peace, reduces international tensions, and strengthens friendly relations among states,

Convinced that this treaty constitutes a step towards the exclusion of the seabed, the ocean floor and the subsoil thereof from the arms race and determined to continue negotiations concerning further measures leading to this end,

Convinced that this treaty constitutes a step towards a treaty on general and complete disarmament under strict and effective international control, and determined to continue negotiations to this end,

Convinced that this treaty will further the purposes and principles of the Charter of the United Nations, in a manner consistent with the principles of international law and without infringing the freedoms of the high seas,

Have agreed as follows:

Article I. 1. The states parties to this treaty undertake not to emplant or emplace on the seabed and the ocean floor and in the subsoil thereof beyond the maximum contiguous zone provided for in the 1958 Geneva Convention on the Territorial Sea & the Contiguous Zone any objects with nuclear weapons or any other types of weapons of mass destruction, as well as structures, launching installations or any other facilities specifically designed for storing, testing or using such weapons.

2. The states parties to this treaty undertake not to assist, encourage or induce any state to commit actions prohibited by this treaty and not to participate in any other way in such actions.

Article II. 1. For the purpose of this treaty the outer limit of the contiguous zone referred to in Article I shall be measured in accordance with the provisions of Section II of the 1958 Geneva Convention on the Territorial Sea & the Contiguous Zone and in accordance with international law.

2. Nothing in this treaty shall be interpreted as supporting or prejudicing the position of any state party with respect to rights or claims which such state party may assert, or with respect to recognition or non-recognition of rights or claims asserted by any other state, related to waters off its coasts, or to the seabed and the ocean floor.

Article III. 1. In order to promote the objectives and ensure the observance of the provisions of this treaty, the states parties to the treaty shall have the right to verify the activities of other states parties to the treaty on the seabed and the ocean floor and in the subsoil thereof beyond the maximum contiguous zone, referred to in Article II, if these activities raise doubts concerning the fulfillment of the obligations assumed under this treaty, without interfering with such activities or otherwise infringing rights recognized under international law, including the freedoms of the high seas.

2. The right of verification recognized by the states parties in paragraph 1 of this article may be exercised by any state party using its own means or with the assistance of any other state party.

3. The states parties to the treaty undertake to consult and to cooperate with a view to removing doubts concerning the fulfillment of the obligations assumed under this treaty.

Article IV. Any state party to the treaty may propose amendments to this treaty. Amendments must be approved by a majority of the votes of all the states parties to the treaty, including those of all the states parties to this treaty possessing nuclear weapons, and shall enter into force for each state party to the treaty accepting such amendments upon their acceptance by a majority of the states parties to the treaty, including states which possess nuclear weapons and are parties to this treaty. Thereafter the amendments shall enter into force for any other party to the treaty after it has accepted such amendments.

Article V. Each party to this treaty shall in exercising its national sovereignty have the right to withdraw from this treaty if it decides that extraordinary events related to the subject matter of this treaty have jeopardized the supreme interests of its country. It shall give notice of such withdrawal to all other parties to the treaty and to the United Nations Security Council 3 months in advance. Such notice shall include a statement of the extraordinary events it considers to have jeopardized its supreme interests.

Article VI. 1. This treaty shall be open for signature to all states. Any state which does not sign the treaty before its entry into force in accordance with paragraph 3 of this article may accede to it at any time.

2. This treaty shall be subject to ratification by signatory states. Instruments of ratification and of accession shall be deposited with the governments of—, which are hereby designated the depositary governments.

3. This treaty shall enter into force after the deposit of instruments of ratification by 22 governments, including the governments designated as depositary governments of this treaty.

4. For states whose instruments of ratification or accession are deposited after the entry into force of this treaty it shall enter into force on the date of the deposit of their instruments of ratification or accession.

5. The depositary governments shall forthwith notify the governments of all states signatory and acceding to this treaty of the date of each signature, of the date of deposit of each instrument of ratification or of accession, of the date of the entry into force of this treaty, and of the receipt of other notices.

6. This treaty shall be registered by the depositary governments pursuant to Article 102 of the Charter of the United Nations.

Article VII. This treaty, the English, Russian, French, Spanish and Chinese texts of which are equally authentic, shall be deposited in the archives of the depositary governments. Duly certified copies of this treaty shall be transmitted by the depositary governments to the governments of the states signatory and acceding thereto.

In witness whereof the undersigned, being duly authorized thereto, have signed this treaty.

PREPARATIONS FOR STRATEGIC ARMS TALKS

U.S. & USSR Favor Negotiations

In his State-of-the-Union message Jan. 14 outgoing Pres. Johnson urged the resumption of talks with the USSR on limiting offensive and defensive nuclear missiles. He said the U.S. must "seek areas of agreement" with the Soviet Union "where the interests of world peace are properly served." This should be done, he said, despite "the strained relationship" between the countries, "especially in the light of the brutal invasion of Czechoslovakia." "Totalitarianism is no less odious to us because we are able to reach some accommodation that reduces the danger of world catastrophe," he said. "What we do, we do in the interest of peace in the world, and we earnestly hope that time will bring a Russia that is less afraid of adversity and individual freedom." Mr. Johnson added: "European and international security cannot be safeguarded through the arms race or inflated war preparations—they can be safeguarded on the basis of peaceful cooperation, a genuine relaxation of tensions and the solution of existing international problems by peaceful means at the table of negotiations."

Asserting that the "arms race is the greatest single danger facing humanity," Vice Pres. Humphrey Jan. 17 urged the Nixon Administration to move immediately to begin missile talks with the USSR.

The Soviet government declared Jan. 20 that it was prepared to begin talks with the U.S. on the control of nuclear-armed missiles. The statement, read to a news conference at the Foreign Ministry in Moscow by Leonid M. Zamyatin, ministry press chief, and Kirill V. Novikov, director of the ministry's International Organizations Department, reviewed the Soviet disarmament plan presented by Foreign Min. Andrei A. Gromyko at the UN General Assembly Oct. 2, 1968 and affirmed: "The problem of limiting the nuclear arms race is, in the opinion of the Soviet government, a practically realizable, though not an easy, undertaking." Questioned about the coincidence of the Soviet statement with the inaugural of Richard M. Nixon, Zamyatin denied that it was deliberate.

The Soviet statement said: "Of great importance for strengthening peace and international security is the treaty on the non-proliferation of nuclear weapons, the entry into force of which would create favorable prerequisites for further efforts to stop the arms race." "The Soviet government has proposed that all nuclear powers immediately enter into negotiations on the cessation of nuclear weapon production and the reduction of nuclear stockpiles followed by complete prohibition and elimination of nuclear weapons. The Soviet government has also proposed that agreement be reached on a mutual limitation and subsequent reduction of strategic means of delivery of nuclear weapons."

At his first press conference as President, Mr. Nixon said Jan. 27 that he favored strategic arms talks with the Soviet Union, and "the context of those talks" was "vitally important." "What I want to do," he declared, "is to see to it that we have strategic arms talks in a way and at a time that will promote, if possible, progress on outstanding political problems ... in which the United States and the Soviet Union acting together can serve the cause of peace." Mr. Nixon was asked about "the need for superiority over the Soviet Union" in nuclear weapons, a point "stressed, quite hard" by Mr. Nixon and Defense Secy. Laird. He was asked to "distinguish between the validity of that stance and the argument of Dr. [Henry A.] Kissinger [Mr. Nixon's special assist-ant for national security affairs] for what he calls 'sufficiency.'" Mr. Nixon replied: Kissinger's "suggestion of sufficiency" "would meet, certainly, my guideline—and I think Secy. Laird's guideline—with regard to superiority." "I think sufficiency is a better term, actually, than either superiority or parity." Parity opened the possibility for each side to believe "it has a chance to win" a war and, "therefore, parity does not necessarily assure that a war may not occur." Superiority "may have a detrimental effect on the other side, in putting it in an inferior position and, therefore, giving great impetus to its own arms race."

Pres. Nixon reported to the American people Mar. 4 after a trip to Western Europe. He said: The interests of the Soviet Union and the U.S. "would not be served by simply going down the road on strategic-arms talks without at the same time making progress on resolving these political differences that could explode." All European leaders he had talked to on his trip "recognize that most wars have come, not from arms races...but...from political explosions. Therefore, they want progress, for example, on Berlin; they want progress in the Mideast; they want progress on Vietnam, at the same time that they want progress on strategic arms talks. So our attitude toward the Soviet is not a highhanded one of trying to tell them that you do this or we won't talk. Our attitude is very conciliatory, and...in our talks with the Soviet ambassador, I think that they are thinking along this line now, too. If they are, we can make progress on several roads toward a mutual objective."

Ultimately, the 2 sides tacitly agreed that they should meet before long in serious Strategic Arms Limitation Talks (or SALT, as the pro-posed negotiation were soon called).

USSR Proposes Phased Disarmament

The Soviet Union announced Apr. 22 that it was prepared to nego-tiate global disarmament on a step-by-step basis instead of insisting on one inclusive agreement. The Soviet delegate to the Geneva meetings of the UN Disarmament Committee, Aleksei A. Roshchin, said that the USSR was ready to deal separately on each item in the Soviet Union's original 3-proposal package plan. Roshchin enumerated the 3 parts as (1) "limitation and further reduction of means of delivery of strategic weapons, (2) prohibition of flights beyond national borders of bombers carrying nuclear weapons and (3) limitation of navigation zones for rocket-carrying submarines [and] elimination of foreign military bases."

U.S. officials said the latest Soviet proposal for general dis-armament was the same as the one rejected by the U.S. 7 years previous-ly. (The U.S. had repeatedly rejected the Soviet proposals because they made no provision for inspection or for controls to insure against secret stockpiling of nuclear weapons.)

The U.S. representative at the Geneva meeting, Gerard C. Smith, indicated Mar. 25 that the Nixon Administration was not prepared to begin bilateral talks with the USSR on limiting anti-ballistic missile systems. Smith said the new administration needed "the passage of some time" to thoroughly prepare itself for negotiations. He added that even then, talks might be delayed until a favorable political situation existed.

SALT Advances

Pres. Nixon said at his press conference June 13 that both multiple-warhead missiles and ABM systems would be on the agenda at forthcoming arms control talks with the Soviet Union. He mentioned July 31 as the "target date" for beginning such talks, and he said that negotiations, barring complications, would start between then and Aug. 15. A Soviet reply on this matter was being awaited, he said.

In a wide-ranging foreign policy statement before the Supreme Soviet in Moscow July 10, Soviet Foreign Min. Andrei A. Gromyko stressed that halting the strategic arms race was "one of the most acute problems facing humanity." He said Moscow was prepared for strategic arms negotiations with Washington and he indicated interest in Pres. Nixon's proposal for a "well-prepared" summit meeting. Agreements to stop the production of nuclear weapons could be reached only if all nuclear powers participated, Gromyko said. He called on the Western powers not to complicate the issue of a total nuclear test ban with "unjustified conditions which extend beyond the framework of the tasks of banning nuclear weapons tests." A nuclear arms-free zone covering the Mediterranean was "more vital today than ever before," Gromyko said.

U.S. State Secy. William P. Rogers July 11 praised the "positive tone" of Gromyko's speech, but he asserted that the U.S. was still awaiting word from Moscow on the time and place of the talks.

(In contrast to the relatively conciliatory tone of the Gromyko speech, Soviet Marshal Nikolai I. Krylov charged Aug. 30 that the U.S. was preparing a surprise nuclear attack on the USSR. In an article in the Russian [RSFSR] newspaper *Sovetskaya Rossiya*, Krylov, commander of the Soviet strategic missile forces and deputy defense minister, said: "Preparing for a surprise attack on the Soviet Union and other Socialist countries,...the U.S. some time ago created a special 'department of strategic planning' which is working out plans for a massive nuclear-rocket blow against targets on the territory of our country and other Socialist countries." Krylov implied that it was necessary to maintain a powerful Soviet nuclear arsenal to deter the U.S. The article had been written to commemorate the 30th anniversary of World War II, Sept. 1.)

Gromyko informed Rogers Sept. 22 that Moscow was not yet prepared to begin talks on limiting strategic arms. Gromyko reportedly promised Rogers only that the USSR would soon propose a date and place for "preliminary" arms talks. Asked after the meeting whether the 2 countries had reached "agreement" on any points, Gromyko replied, "I would not use that word."

At his Sept. 26 press conference Pres. Nixon said that he expected an answer from the Soviet Union "in the near future," and "it is likely to be a positive answer," on the U.S. proposal for strategic arms negotiations.

SALT Opening Scheduled

The U.S. and the USSR announced jointly Oct. 25 that they had agreed to send representatives to Helsinki, Finland Nov. 17 for "preliminary discussion" on curbing the strategic arms race. At a White House briefing, Presidential Press Secy. Ronald Ziegler said that Soviet Amb.-to-U.S. Anatoly F. Dobrynin had proposed the place and date of the meeting to Pres. Nixon during an unreported meeting Oct. 20 and that Mr. Nixon had accepted immediately. The President then asked Dobrynin to work out the details with State Secy. Rogers. This he did Oct. 22. Gerard C. Smith, director of the Arms Control & Disarmament Agency, was to lead the U.S. delegation.

At a news conference shortly after the announcement, Rogers explained that the preliminary SALT discussions would cover procedural matters such as the agenda, size of the delgation and working rules, a permanent site for later talks, and which weapons would be discussed. Rogers said the U.S. preferred Vienna as the site of the talks but was not adamant about the location. Characterizing the forthcoming talks as "one of the most important that we ... ever undertook with the Soviet Union," Rogers expressed the belief that both sides were serious about the talks but he warned against over-optimism. Asked whether MIRV (multiple independently targeted re-entry vehicles) would be an issue, Rogers replied "that will be one of the subjects that will be considered when we start these talks." He declined to say whether ABM systems would be discussed.

Soviet Pres. Nikolai V. Podgorny said in a Bolshevik anniversary address Nov. 6 that "a positive outcome of these [SALT] talks would undoubtedly help improve Soviet-U.S. relations and preserve and strengthen the peace. The Soviet Union is striving to achieve precisely such results." Referring to U.S. intentions to proceed with missile developments, Podgorny warned, however, that "We have never allowed and will not allow anybody to talk to the Soviet Union from a position of strength." (An article in the Soviet magazine *New Times* Nov. 13 said the USSR was "full of determination to attain positive results" at the Helsinki talks.)

Communist China had accused the U.S. and the USSR Nov. 5 of using the Helsinki talks to maintain their "nuclear collusion." Peking said the 2 countries were cooperating with each other "in their big conspiracy to further the nuclear military alliance between the 2 countries so as to maintain their already bankrupt nuclear monopoly."

State Department spokesman Robert J. McCloskey Nov. 6 denied rumors that the Nixon Administration was attempting to link the arms talks with European security problems. Asserting there were no conditions to the talks, McCloskey said: "We do not believe there should be a linkage between [European and other political questions] or the arms talks and any other subject . . . Secretary of State [Rogers] stated administration policy [Oct. 25] when he said we enter the arms talks without conditions."

Rogers urged the USSR Nov. 13 to recognize that both the U.S. and the USSR would benefit from a limitation on the arms race despite certain risks. Declaring that both sides could effectively destroy the other side no matter who struck first, Rogers said, "The risks in seeking an agreement seem to be manageable, insurable and reasonable ones to run. They seem less dangerous than the risks of open-ended arms competition—risks about which we perhaps have become somewhat callous." Without mentioning any specific proposals that the Administration might make at SALT, Rogers asserted that "competitive accumulation of more sophisticated weapons would not add to the basic security of either side." He listed 3 U.S. objectives at the Helsinki talks: (1) to raise international security "by maintaining a stable U.S.-Soviet strategic relationship through limitations on the deployment of strategic armaments"; (2) to "halt the upward spiral" of the arms race and thus avoid uncertainties, tensions and costs, and (3) to decrease the risk of nuclear war "through a dialogue about issues arising from the strategic situation."

In an unusual appearance before the Senate Nov. 13, Pres. Nixon cautioned Senators against public statements on the arms talks. He said: "It is vital that we recognize that the position of our negotiators not be weakened or compromised by discussions that might take place here."

In an article in the October issue of *Foreign Affairs* (published Sept. 17), McGeorge Bundy, former special assistant to the President for national security affairs, had said the next year or 2 would give the USSR and the U.S. the best opportunity to limit the strategic arms contest. Bundy said: "The neglected truth about the present strategic arms race between the U.S. and the Soviet Union is that in terms of international political behavior that race has now become almost completely irrelevant. The new weapons systems being developed by each of the 2 great powers will provide neither protection nor opportunity in any serious political sense. Politically the strategic nuclear arms race is in a stalemate." The article, entitled "To Cap the Volcano," argued that in political terms, as distinct from technical ones, the idea of nuclear "superiority" was totally incorrect. Bundy said: "In sane politics...there is no level of superiority which will make a strategic first strike between the 2 great states anything but an act of folly.... Sufficiency is what we both have now, in ample measure, and no superiority worth having can be achieved." Bundy praised Pres. Nixon for recognizing that the need was for "sufficiency" not "superiority." He said that "if the President is hesitant about arms limitation, it is... because he does not yet see any solid political base, here at home, for relatively low-keyed, low-cost parity."

In an interview in *Der Spiegel* magazine Nov. 10, West German Defense Min. Helmut Schmidt urged the U.S. to avoid any agreement with the Soviet Union that would exclude the 700 Soviet medium-range missiles (MRBMs) targeted at Europe. He said: "I would oppose any proposal... which reduced all the conventional armaments of East and West Europe to a very low level, but left everything in the nuclear field the way it is today, including the 700 Soviet MRBMs." (Most of these missiles were located in the western USSR and had ranges varying from 1,100 to 2,000 miles.)

U.S. officials in Washington disclosed Nov. 14 that State Undersecy. Elliot L. Richardson had proposed at a NATO meeting in Brussels Nov. 5 that NATO invite Warsaw Pact members to negotiations on reducing conventional forces in Europe. The NATO-Warsaw Pact talks, according to the sources, could begin after the preliminary talks in Helsinki were completed.

Helsinki Talks

The U.S. and the USSR opened their preliminary SALT (strategic arms limitation talks) discussions in Helsinki, Finland Nov. 17. In an atmosphere of cordiality, both sides pledged to avoid any agreement that would place the other side at a military disadvantage.

Deputy Foreign Min. Vladimir S. Semenov, chief of the Soviet delegation, said the USSR attached great significance to curbing the arms race. He declared: "Given genuine desire on both sides to seek mutually acceptable agreement without prejudice to the security of our states and all other countries, it is possible and imperative to overcome obvious complexities and obstacles and to bring about reasonable solutions."

Gerard C. Smith, chief of the U.S. delegation, read a statement by Pres. Nixon, who asserted that the U.S. would be guided by the principle of maintaining "sufficiency in the forces required to protect ourselves and our allies." Mr. Nixon said he recognized that the USSR had similar defense responsibilities, but he affirmed: "I believe it is possible, however, that we can carry out our respective responsibilities under a mutually acceptable limitation and eventual reduction of our strategic arsenals." The President continued: "We are prepared to discuss limi-

tations on all offensive and defensive systems and to reach agreements in
which both sides can have confidence.... We seek no unilateral advantage. Nor do we seek arrangements which could be prejudicial to the
interests of 3d parties. We are prepared to engage in *bona fide* negotiations on concrete issues, avoiding polemics and extraneous matters."

In his welcoming address, Finnish Foreign Min. Ahti Karjalainen
emphasized the urgency for negotiations on the arms race. Calling the
meeting "a historic occasion," Karjalainen said: "By starting these discussions, the 2 powers which are in control of the major part of the nuclear arsenal of the world have on their part acknowledged their supreme responsibility for the peace and security."

The 30-minute formal opening ceremony was held in Smolna, the
Finnish state banquet hall, with the first full working session to be held
in the U.S. embassy Nov. 18. By prior agreement, there would be no
daily press briefings, only brief communiques issued from time to time.

The U.S. delegation was headed by Smith, director of the Arms
Control & Disarmament Agency. Other members included Philip
Farley, Smith agency deputy; Paul Nitze, former Deputy Defense
Secretary; Harold Brown, former Air Force Secretary; Llewellyn E.
Thompson, former ambassador to the Soviet Union, and Air Force Maj.
Gen. Royal B. Allison.

The Soviet delegation was led by Semenov, a former member of
the Soviet delegation to the UN and regarded as an expert on German
and European problems. Other members included Col. Gen. Nikolai V.
Ogarkov, a first deputy chief of the General Staff; Pyotr S. Pleshakov,
deputy minister of the radio industry; Aleksandr N. Shchukin, an aca-
demician; Col. Gen. Nikolai N. Alekseyev, and Georgi M. Korniyenko,
head of the Foreign Ministry's U.S. Department.

It was reported Dec. 4 that the 2 sides had agreed that the items
subject to SALT negotiations should include offensive and defensive
weapons, the relationship between the 2 and means of verifying any
agreement.

Pres. Nixon commenting at his Dec. 8 press conference on a U.S.
request for a cancellation of the scheduled 8th SALT session Dec. 8,
said: the postponement did not have "any longrange significance" but
had been proposed "for the purpose of developing the positions in a
proper way." He was encouraged by the talks because both sides were
serious and neither had attempted to use their positions for propaganda
purposes. "I believe that the progress to date has been good. The prospects are better than I anticipated they would be when the talks began."

In an 11th-hour compromise, the USSR and the U.S. agreed Dec.
22 to begin full-scale SALT talks in Vienna Apr. 16, 1970 with the
understanding that negotiations would be held again in Helsinki at a
later date. The U.S. had objected to the Soviet choice of Helsinki because of lack of room and privacy. The Soviet Union had objected to the
U.S. choice of Vienna because of Austrian criticism of the 1968

Czechoslovak invasion. The preliminary SALT sessions had been scheduled to end Dec. 19 but had been delayed because of the deadlock over the future site. In a joint communique issued Dec. 22, the conferees asserted that the 5 weeks of preliminary talks had been useful. The key passage of the communique read: "The preliminary exchange of views concerning the limitation of strategic arms which took place was useful to both sides. As a result of that exchange, each side was able to understand better the views of the other side in regard to the problems under consideration. An understanding was reached on the general range of questions which will be the subject of further Soviet-U.S. exchanges of opinions."

OTHER DEVELOPMENTS

Reports on Soviet & U.S. Arms

In his final report to Congress Jan. 18, outgoing U.S. Defense Secy. Clifford had asserted that the Soviet Union had significantly increased its intercontinental ballistic missile strength over the past 2-1/2 years. Clifford said that the Soviet ICBM force had grown from 250 in mid-1966 to 900 in Sept. 1968. (Other Washington sources had estimated the Soviet ICBM force at more than 1,000.) Clifford, however, held that the U.S. had retained its strategic missile superiority over the USSR and he predicted that the Soviet ICBM growth rate would be "considerably smaller over the next 2 to 3 years."

Other data revealed in Clifford's 165-page unclassified report; (a) The Soviet Union had begun to use solid-fuel ICBMs similar to the U.S. Minuteman missile, but most Soviet missiles still were of the liquid fuel type. (b) The Russians had begun to operate nuclearpowered submarines carrying missiles with a range of more than 1,500 miles; the submarines were similar to the U.S. Polaris type; but the U.S. had 656 operational submarine missiles, and the USSR had only 45. (c) Communist China's nuclear weapons program had slowed during 1968, but Peking was expected to have a "moderate" ICBM force by 1975.

In the report's section on U.S. defense, Clifford said: (a) A new early warning system to guard against incoming ICBMs was being developed. (b) A long-range aerial decoy called SCAD (subsonic cruise armed decoy) was being developed by the Air Force; the decoy, designed to look like bombers on radar scopes, would draw enemy fire away from planes; the missile would also carry a nuclear warhead in case it penetrated detection. (c) Minuteman silos would be strengthened against improved Soviet ICBMs. (d) An Underwater Long-range Missile System

(ULMS), designed to emplace ICBMs in the ocean, would be developed. (e) A $15 billion request for a new system of defense against Soviet bombers would be submitted to Congress. (f) The U.S. had canceled its plan to reduce its force of antisubmarine aircraft carriers from 6 to 5; plans to reduce the number of anti-submarine patrol aircraft also had been voided. (g) The number of U.S. nuclearpowered attack submarines would not be limited to 69 as earlier projected. (h) The Defense Department would ask Congress for the construction of 15 fast deployment logistics ships. (Congress twice before had vetoed the request for 30 such vessels.)

In connection with the opening of the SALT talks in Helsinki, these assessment of U.S. and Soviet strength in intercontinental ballistic missiles (ICBMs) and ballistic missile submarines were made:

●*Time* magazine (Nov. 21): U.S. land-based ICBMs totaled 1,054 compared with Soviet strength of about 1,350. The U.S. missiles were described as more accurate and the Soviet Union's larger. The U.S. had 41 Polaris submarines, each carrying 16 missiles, or a total of 656 sub-launched missiles. The USSR had only 9 such subs.

●*Newsweek* magazine (Nov. 24): U.S. ICBMs totaled 1,054, compared with about 1,300 Soviet ICBMs. The Soviet missiles were described as carrying larger warheads, so Moscow "holds an even greater lead in deliverable 'megatonnage.'" The U.S. had 41 Polaris subs equipped with intermediate range missiles (up to 2,800 miles). 31 Polaris subs were being converted to the Poseidon missile, which had a longer range and greater accuracy than the Polaris missile. The USSR had "about 8 'Yankee' subs that carry Polaris-type missiles" and were building 8-12 new Yankees every year. The USSR also had about 105 subs that fired short-range missiles (up to 700 miles).

●*N. Y. Times* (Nov. 18): U.S. ICBMs totaled 1,054, compared with about 1,350 Soviet ICBMs, "including some that are still being installed." The Soviet sub force "includes 28 nuclear-powered missile vessels, including a new type that resembles the American Polaris.... All told, this force mounts about 200 missiles."

● The *Economist* (Nov. 1): Soviet deployment of ICBMs was "beyond the 1,000 mark and on a par with the Americans." The Soviet Union was building its own Polaris-type sub for the first time.

● The London-based Institute for Strategic Studies (Sept. 11): U.S. ICBMs totaled 1,054, compared with 1,050 Soviet ICBMs. The USSR was expected to increase its ICBM strength to 1,150 by the end of 1969. The USSR had a total of 160 sub-launched missiles. The USSR was building Polaris-type subs at a rate of at least 4 a year.

In its annual report to Congress, published Jan. 31, the Atomic Energy Commission had said that it should complete expansion of 8 of its weapons plants by 1971 and be able to supply atomic materials and components needed for the Poseidon and Minuteman ballistic missiles and the Sentinel ABM system. The AEC asked Congress for $30 million in fiscal 1970 to complete the plant expansion. This would make a total of about $315 million spent on the plants in 3 years.

World's Military Spending

A study sponsored by the Stockholm International Peace Research Institute and published Nov. 19 found that the world's current annual military spending exceeded the total amount of goods and services produced in 1900. The 440-page study, compiled by a group headed by

Frank Blackaby, a British economist, showed that the world spent $159.3 billion for military purposes in 1968, using official Communist exchange rates, or $173.4 billion at rates adjusted for real buying power. The U.S. spent $79.3 billion, the USSR $39.8 billion (at the adjusted rate) and Communist China $7 billion according to the estimates. During the 1949-68 period, world military spending had increased 5.9% annually, but for the past 3 years the rise had jumped to 8.9%. The sharpest increase was in the Middle East with a 19.9% increase annually over the past 3 years.

The U.S. outlay increased from an average annual rise of 7.7% to 12% in recent years, with the USSR and its allies following this trend, the study reported. The U.S. and the USSR showed cumulative gains of 40% in military spending since 1965 and currently accounted for 70% of the total. In developing states, arms expenditures had increased at an annual rate of 7.5%. While world production had increased by 5 times in the last 50 years, military spending had multiplied about 10 times. The Soviet Union had caught up with the U.S. in supplying arms to the 3d world, mainly because of Soviet arms shipments to Arab states. (The estimate did not include shipments to North or South Vietnam.)

The study revealed that nuclear testing had increased since the 1963 treaty banning all but underground explosions. It said the number of tests had risen from 39.6 annually before the treaty to 46.2 tests a year since 1963.

U.S. MIRV Moratorium Urged

A resolution calling for a moratorium on the testing of MIRVs (multiple independently targeted reentry vehicles) was filed in the Senate June 17 by Sen. Edward W. Brooke (R., Mass.). It had 38 other co-sponsors, including the Democratic leader and assistant leader, Sens. Mike Mansfield and Edward M. Kennedy. Sen. Clifford P. Case (R., N.J.) June 16 introduced a resolution urging the President to suspend such testing as long as the USSR did the same. In the House June 16, Chairman John B. Anderson (R., Ill.) of the House Republican Conference had told members "the time has come to call a halt to this insane nuclear version of keeping up with the Joneses." He urged an "immediate and mutual moratorium" on multiple-warhead testing before "irrevocable" escalation of the arms race.

(The Senate Appropriations Committee June 13 had released testimony, taken at a closed session, in which Dr. John S. Foster Jr., chief of research and development for the Defense Department, reported that the U.S. was testing its Minuteman-3 and Poseidon missiles and that deployment of these MIRVs was planned after a "relatively short and orderly" testing program.)

Sen. Edmund S. Muskie (D., Me.) Oct. 21 proposed a unilateral move by the U.S. to postpone for 6 months its testing of MIRVs. The move should be accompanied, he said, by an announcement that the U.S. would not resume tests unless the Soviet Union tested its MIRV. Muskie advocated the moratorium as a way "to stimulate mutual efforts" by the 2 countries "to control the escalation of nuclear weapons systems before it is too late." Muskie's proposal was denounced by Vice Pres. Spiro T. Agnew Oct. 22 as a "classic example of confused thinking." "No responsible person would propose that the President play Russian roulette with U.S. security," he said, "yet that is what Sen. Muskie just did." Muskie, he said, "is not content with this nation keeping prudent pace. He wants it to slip backward." The exchange prompted Senate Democratic Leader Mike Mansfield Oct. 23 to recommend, in order "to get this matter out of the stage of semantics," that the Senate Foreign Relations Committee hold hearings "as soon as appropriately possible" on Brooke's resolution. The Administration position was to delay consideration of such a proposal until after the SALT talks had begun.

U.S. Curbs CBW, Renounces Germ War

Defense Secy. Melvin R. Laird was reported by the *N.Y. Times* Oct. 17 to have submitted to the National Security Council a secret memo urging that the U.S. halt production of biological agents for use in warfare. The *Times* reported that the 2-page document was offered to supplement an interagency report, on chemical and biological warfare (CBW) agents, that had also been given to the council.

Pres. Nixon Nov. 25 renounced the use of biological weapons and ordered the destruction of the U.S. germ warfare stocks. The White House emphasized, however, that Mr. Nixon would continue to authorize the Defense Department to deploy tear gas and chemical defoliants in Vietnam. The President pledged not to make any use of bacteriological weapons, even as a retaliatory striking force against an enemy attack. (This apparently cleared up a statement by Defense Secy. Laird July 28 that the U.S. might deploy chemical or biological weapons in retaliation to an enemy strike.) Mr. Nixon asked the Defense Department to draw up plans for the disposal of America's germ warfare stocks. Mr. Nixon described his action as "an initiative toward peace." "Mankind already carries in its own hands too many of the seeds of its own destruction," he said. "By the examples we set today, we hope to contribute to an atmosphere of peace and understanding between nations and among men."

The President expressed fear that a CBW attack might produce a global epidemic that could affect future generations. "Biological weapons have massive, unpredictable and potentially uncontrollable consequences," he warned. "They may produce global epidemics and impair the health of future generations."

Mr. Nixon extended the current U.S. policy against a first-strike use of CBW weapons to include the first use of "incapacitating weapons." White House sources said later that "incapacitating weapons" did not include tear gas, which the Administration classified as a "riot control weapon." The Army currently deployed tear gas in Vietnam. It was reported later however, that Mr. Nixon intended to tighten the restrictions on the use of tear gas by limiting the purposes for which it was used by American forces in Vietnam.

Mr. Nixon said the U.S. would "associate itself" with the British proposal made july 10 at the UN Disarmament Committee in Geneva. At the talks, Britain had introduced a proposal to prohibit the development, production or use of biological weapons "in any circumstances." The President cautioned, however, that the U.S. would "seek to clarify" provisions of Britain's draft proposal to "assure that necessary safeguards are included." (The U.S. was the 2d nation to indorse Britain's proposal. Canada had previously indicated support for the CBW ban.)

Mr. Nixon said that neither the decision to support the British proposal nor his decision to curtail the use of bacteriological weapons would "leave us vulnerable to surprise by an enemy who does not observe these rational restraints." "Our intelligence community will continue to watch carefully the nature and extent of the biological programs of others," he said.

Reaction to Pres. Nixon's decision to restrict the use of chemical and biological weapons was favorable, although some government officials in Western Europe felt the curbs did not go far enough. The Soviet government newspaper *Izvestia* Nov. 27 welcomed Mr. Nixon's move but expressed regret that he had not precluded the deployment of tear gas and other riot-control agents. *Pravda,* the USSR Communist Party newspaper, termed Mr. Nixon's action "a positive step" that came "as a result of pressure from peace-loving forces." The British Foreign Office said it "was naturally delighted" at Pres. Nixon's action, but some British officials said Mr. Nixon should have included tear gas in the ban. In Helsinki, where the U.S. and the USSR were engaged in talks on strategic arms limitations, officals said Mr. Nixon's move should serve to build confidence in the ability of the 2 countries to reach an accord halting further arms buildups.

West German officials expressed reservations over Mr. Nixon's announcement; although they supported his decision to destroy existing U.S. bacteriological stocks, they expressed dissatisfaction over what they termed Pres. Nixon's failure to explain what the U.S. would do about destroying or withdrawing chemical and biological weapons stored in West Germany.

The reaction of Congressional leaders of both parties was favorable. Chairman J. William Fulbright (D., Ark.) of the Senate Foreign Relations Committee said he was pleased with Mr. Nixon's decision.

Senate Democratic Leader Sen. Mike Mansfield (Mont.) said "he saw no reason" why the President's action to resubmit the Geneva Protocol of 1925 should ignite controversy. House Republican leader Gerald R. Ford (Mich.) said he saw in Pres. Nixon's announcement a "highly salutary impact" on the SALT talks in Helsinki.

(A Pentagon spokesman said Nov. 26 that it might take up to a year for the Defense Department to destroy the nation's existing bacteriological stores in accordance with Pres. Nixon's order. A Pentagon spokesman said destruction of the stores would require slow, careful handling to insure against an accident during the dismantling process.)

A House subcommittee Nov. 18 began the first Congressional consideration in more than 40 years of the Geneva Protocol of 1925 banning the deployment of CBW agents. The Subcommittee on National Security Policy & Scientific Developments immediately got into the most controversial issue connected with the 1925 accord—U.S. use of tear gas in Vietnam. The committee's 2d witness, Rep. John R. Dellenback (R., Ore.), called on the Administration to stop using the gas and to support ratification of the 1925 protocol. The subcommittee was considering resolutions, indorsed by more than 100 members of the House, urging the U.S. to ratify the 1925 agreement. The accord, ratified by 84 nations, had not been ratified by the U.S. Senate. In 1926 the Senate had not voted on a proposal to have the U.S. ratify the agreement.

Army Secy. Stanley R. Resor announced Oct. 17 that he had ordered the Edgewood Arsenal in Maryland to revise the procedure for open-air testing of chemical warfare agents after a civilian panel had recommended tighter testing regulations. The arsenal, 20 miles north of Baltimore, had been ordered to stop atmospheric tests after Sen. Charles McC. Mathias (R., Md.) had asked Defense Secy. Laird to review the testing procedures at the arsenal. Resor ordered the arsenal's commander to implement the changes before resuming the tests. The changes included more frequent monitoring, fencing off all test areas and submission of proposals for Defense Department approval before actual testing.

The civilian panel that recommended the changes at Edgewood also examined the testing procedures at Fort McClellan, Ala. and ruled that they posed no threat to base personnel or nearby civilians. Resor had ordered Fort McClellan July 16 to suspend all open-air testing of CBW agents.

The Pentagon had revealed Sept. 18 that the Army had conducted environmental testing of nerve gases in Hawaii on 4 occasions in 1966-7. The Pentagon's statement came after ranking Army officials had told a Honolulu newspaper that it had not tested CBW agents in Hawaii. A spokesman for the Pentagon said, however, that the Army's statement was true since the lethal gases were not tested in weapon form. Jerry Friedheim, a Defense Department spokesman, said the tests were trials of the gas' effectiveness in a jungle environment.

An Army spokesman had reported Oct. 11 that the U.S. was stock-piling chemical agents at 8 depots across the country, but he asserted that the munitions posed no threat to nearby communities. The agents were being stored at these sites: Edgewood Arsenal, Edgewood, Md.; Blue Grass Army Depot, Richmond, Ky.; Anniston Army Depot, Anniston, Ala.; Pine Bluff Arsenal, Pine Bluff, Ark.; Pueblo Army Depot, Avondale, Colo.; Rocky Mountain Arsenal, Denver; Tooele Army Depot, Tooele, Utah, and Umatilla Army Depot, Hemiston, Ore.

The House Government Operations Committee Nov. 13 accused the Army of "deception and disregard for the public interest" in its open-air testing of chemical and biological warfare agents. Its report called for more stringent restrictions on future atmospheric tests. 2 committee members, Reps. Gilbert Gude (R., Md.) and Paul N. McCloskey Jr. (R., Calif.), released a minority report urging a total ban on environmental testing of CBW agents. The committee issued its report after a year-long study of the 1968 gas-testing accident at Dugway (Utah) Proving Ground that killed 6,000 sheep. The Army had disclaimed any responsibility for the accident, but it conceded later that the wind had blown the gas over the rangeland where the sheep were grazing. The panel attacked what it called the Army's efforts to escape responsibility for the accident. The committee accused the Army of using "a web of secrecy, lack of candor, deception and disregard of the public interest in connection with the open air tests." The report concluded that the study "showed that the Army's testing procedures were unsafe and that future tests could result in catastrophic harm to people and animal life." (The Army evacuated more than 200 personnel from a munitions installation at the Dugway Proving Ground Dec. 12 after a container of a lethal nerve gas was damaged, causing a small leak. The Army reported "there were no casualties and there was no danger to anyone outside the immediate area." According to the Army, the area was decontaminated within 2 hours. The gas was identified as GB or Sarin, one of the most toxic agents in the Army's biological arsenal. A similar gas was responsible for the killing of the sheep in 1968.)

The Army Dec. 2 announced plans for the transfer of all its lethal chemical munitions from a U.S. depot on Okinawa to a storage site in Oregon. Army Secy. Resor said the shipments would be completed by the spring of 1970. Resor said the gases, a mustard gas known as HD and 2 types of nerve gas. GB and VX, would be moved by sea to a Navy depot at Bangor, Wash. and then by rail to the Army's Umatilla depot near Hemiston, Ore. But Oregon Gov. Thomas L. McCall asked Pres. Nixon Dec. 5 to halt the planned shipments of the lethal gases to Oregon. "To say that the citizens of Okinawa or Guam should not be subjected to the proximity of these inherently dangerous and frightening chemicals is an incredible statement," McCall declared, "when you go and say that it is all right for the citizens of Oregon to suffer the same proximity." McCall urged the President to order the detoxification of gas already stored at the Umatilla arsenal.

The *N.Y. Times* had reported Oct. 30 that the Army had produced and stockpiled more than 20,000 poison bullets in an arsenal in Arkansas. The bullets were believed treated with botulin, a toxin that produces a fatal disease of the nervous system. The *Times* reported that a secret memo prepared for Resor in 1966 by officers in the Army's Chemical Corps had said that thousands of the bullets had been produced and stockpiled at the Pine Bluff (Ark.) Arsenal.

Western European Defense

British Defense Min. Denis Healey called on the Nixon Administration Feb. 20 to reaffirm the U.S. commitment to defend Western Europe with nuclear weapons. Speaking at a news conference in London, Healey said: "I hope the credibility of the nuclear elements in NATO strategy will be maintained by present and future U.S. governments no less strongly than it has in the past." Healey cautioned against any U.S. policy that would place Western Europe in doubt about American nuclear intentions if the Soviet Union were to attack. He stressed that any U.S. hesitancy would result in Europeans demanding nuclear weapons under their own control.

Healey's remarks were a follow-up to a speech he had delivered to an international defense symposium in Munich Feb. 1. Healey had said then that "nuclear escalation" would be the only alternative to defeat in the event of a major Soviet attack in Europe. Citing defense figures published by the Institute for Strategic Studies in London, Healy emphasized that the Warsaw Pact's conventional forces were so superior "as to render doubtful any prospect NATO might have of putting up a successful conventional defense for more than a few days." Healey also argued that any reduction of U.S. forces in Europe "would mean a lowering of nuclear threshold in NATO strategy." (Earlier Feb. 1 Gen. Lyman L. Lemnitzer, supreme commander of NATO forces, had given a different appraisal of the current NATO military situation. Speaking at a news conference in Vilseck, Bavaria after observing NATO military exercises currently in progress, Lemnitzer said that the Czechoslovak invasion had not caused any revision of NATO plans for the defense of Western Europe. These plans, Lemnitzer stated, included the basing of U.S. troops committed to NATO both in Europe and the U.S.)

In an interview with the West German magazine *Der Spiegel* Feb. 10, Healey was quoted as saying that the entire Soviet Mediterranean fleet would be demolished in minutes in the event of war. Healey said that the Soviet fleet of 20 warships was not modern and that its vessels were "operating far from their home base and without any air cover." As long as NATO maintained air superiority in the Mediterranean, the Soviet fleet represented only a limited threat, he said. Healey asserted that Britain intended to enlarge its own Mediterranean fleet in March.

The foreign and defense ministers of the 15 North Atlantic Treaty nations met in Washington Apr. 10-11 to commemorate the 20th anniversary of the alliance. In an address at the metting Pres. Nixon said the "talks will be a test of the ability of the Western nations to shape a common strategy." He restated his Feb. 24 pledge that the U.S. would consult with its allies "both before and during any negotiations directly affecting their interests.

West German Finance Min. Franz Josef Strauss proposed in London May 19 that Britain and France pool their nuclear weapons as the first step toward a European defense organization allied to the U.S. within NATO. "There is no room in Europe today for a purely national defense policy," he said. He added that a European defense organization "is the only chance Western Europe has of becoming a potentially equal and autonomous military partner of the U.S. within the Atlantic alliance in the forseeable future." Strauss stressed, however, ". . . that this concept would not give Germany national control over nuclear weapons." (The London *Times* had reported Mar. 5 that Britain and West Germany had developed joint proposals for the use of nuclear arms in Europe without devastating the European countries.)

The West German magazine *Stern* reported Aug. 25 that it had received in the mail in June a photocopy of a top-secret U.S. document that included operational plans for deployment of chemical, biological and atomic weapons in Europe. A spokesman for the U.S. European Command in Stuttgart, West Germany refused to confirm or deny the authenticity of the document, but he said other publications had been sent the same or similar papers since 1968.

Stern said the document included tables on troop strength and weaponry and details on the deployment of atomic weapons and "chemical and biological munitions." The 33-page photocopied document also described preparations for psycholocical warfare and evasive and protective tactics in the event of a nuclear war. *Stern* said the document was mailed from Rome June 15. The plans, according to *Stern,* were drawn up by the headquarters of the U.S. Army in Europe, stationed in Heidelberg.

The document's purpose—described in a letter accompanying the plans, and signed by a Col. Boswell and a Col. Taylor—was to "prepare the leadership and to point out the responsibility for beginning and carrying through unconventional warfare in the area of the U.S. Command in Europe." (The U.S. European Command declined to confirm or deny the authenticity of the 2 names.) *Stern* said a typed, anonymous letter that accompanied the document had said that the sender was acting on a request of a friend of Maj. Gen. Horst Wentland, deputy chief of West Germany's top intelligence-gathering service, who had committed suicide in Oct. 1968. The magazine claimed that the letter suggested that Wentland had stolen the plans because he opposed the U.S. CBW depots in Europe, and then had passed the classified information on before killing himself in anguish over the threat of a war fought with chemically-armed weapons.

U.S. sources said the plans might have been forged and circulated by Communist espionage agents to undermine allied morale in Western Europe and cause dissension between Washington and Bonn. But a reporter for *Stern* said that he had shown the plans to an American officer stationed with the U.S. Army Command in Stutgart and that the officer had confirmed the authenticity of the information.

The NATO Nuclear Defense Affairs Committee Dec. 3 approved political guidelines for defensive tactical use of nuclear weapons. NATO Secy. Gen. Manlio Brosio stressed, however, that the guidelines did not change the alliance's basic strategy nor did they "contemplate in any way a hypothesis of the offensive of tactical nuclear weapons" but "are specifically intended to discipline their defensive use." The U.S. reportedly maintained 7,000 tactical nuclear weapons within NATO.

A 3-day meeting of the NATO Council of Ministers in Brussels was ended Dec. 5 with the issuance of a communique asserting that: The studies on mutual and balanced force reductions [between the East and West] have progressed sufficiently to permit the establishment of certain criteria which [in the ministers' view] such reductions should meet. Significant reductions under adequate verification and control would be envisaged under any agreement on mutual and balanced force reductions." "These ministers directed that further studies should be given to measures which could accompany or follow agreement on mutual and balanced force reductions. Such measures could include advance notification of military movements and maneuvers, exchange of observers and possibly the establishment of observation posts."

French Nuclear Policy

The French newspaper *Le Monde* reported Jan. 4 that influential French army officers had recommended that the U.S. be asked to help in developing France's atomic weapons. France's nuclear weapoms system had been delayed in recent years; Mirage-4 bombers armed with atomic bombs were to have been ready in 1966, but the planes and bombs were not delivered until May 1968. Informed souces also that the testing of intermediate nuclear missiles, scheduled for 1968, had only just begun. Under France's recent austerity program, the 1969 neclear test program had been cancelled.

Georges Pompidou, elected president of France June 15 after Charles de Gaulle's resignation said at his first presidential press conference July 10 that France would continue to develop an independent nuclear strike force. He said the government's attitude to the non-proliferation treaty and the Geneva disarmament talks remained "absolutely unchanged."

Japan Seeks A-Ban on Okinawa

Japanese Premier Eisaku Sato stated indirectly Mar. 10-11 that he would seek a nuclear weapons ban on Okinawa after the island was returned to Japanese control. Addressing the Budget Committee of the Diet's (parliament's) upper house, Sato proposed that U.S. bases on Okinawa be made subject to the same restrictions as American bases in Japan proper. Those restrictions, based on the U.S.-Japanese military security treaty, had been interpreted by Tokyo to bar the storage of nuclear weapons and use of the bases for purposes not directly related to Japan's defense without prior consultations. He proposed that Okinawa be returned to Japanese control within three to five years.

Ex-Premier Nobusuke Kishi, elder brother of Sato, said in an interview Mar. 26 that nuclear weapons should be banned from U.S. bases on Okinawa but that the U.S. should be allowed to continue to use the bases for combat operations outside Japan proper. Kishi's statement reversed his earlier position that the U.S. be allowed to use nuclear weapons on Okinawa.

Finance Min. Takeo Fukuda said in Washington Oct. 2 that Japan would not acquire nuclear weapons in the near future but would continue to depend on U.S. nuclear protection.

During a meeting with Pres. Nixon in Washington Nov. 19-21, Premier Sato emphasized his people's and government's sentiments against nuclear weapons. According to a joint communique, Mr. Nixon "expressed his deep understanding and assured [Sato] that, without prejudice to the position of the U.S. government with respect to the prior consultation system under the [security treaty], the reversion of Okinawa would be carried out in a manner consistent with the policy of the Japanese government as described by [Sato]." (Officials explained that nuclear weapons would be withdrawn from Okinawa but that they could be redeployed there with the consent of the Japanese government.)

The Nixon-Sato communique, issued Nov. 21 was greeted with skepticism and disappointment in Japan and Okinawa. A Tokyo radio broadcast said "the majority of the Japanese people may not be satisfied since the reintroduction of nuclear weapons is still possible after consultation with the U.S.... It is regrettable that the communique does not clearly guarantee a nuclear-free Okinawa." Chobyo Yara, chief executive of the Ryukyu Islands (Okinawa is the largest island in the chain), said he was disappointed because details concerning prior consultations and the removal of B-52 bombers and nuclear weapons had not been fully specified.

At a news conference on his return to Japan Nov. 26, Sato said that Japan would refuse the reintroduction of nuclear weapons on Okinawa after reversion was completed. He said that if the U.S. sought permission to reintroduce nuclear weapons, the government's response would be decided "on 3 non-nuclear principles"—non-possession, manufacture and introduction of nuclear weapons on Japanese soil.

Soviet Threat of Pre-Emptive Strike against China

The U.S. State Department acknowledged Aug. 28 that it had heard reports that the Soviet Union had sounded out other Communist parties in Eastern and Western Europe about a possible pre-emptive strike against China's nuclear installations, but the department said it did not expect the USSR to launch a nuclear attack on China. U.S. State Secy. Willaim P. Rogers had said Aug. 20 that "our best judgment is that border clashes and incidents will continue.... We are convinced that the hostility between them is deep." Rogers said, however, that he doubted the clashes would result in all-out war.

A spokesman for the Indian Foreign Ministry reported Sept. 10 that China had been moving its nuclear installations in the Lob Nor area of the Sinkiang Uighur Autonmuous Region to a "safer place" in northern Tibet, farther from the Soviet border. He said that a gaseous diffusion plant and a plant for the production of nuclear bombs had already been transferred and that the pace of transfer had accelerated in recent months.

Latin Nuclear-Free Zone

The first general meeting of the Organization for the Prohibition of Nuclear Arms in Latin America, created by the Latin denuclearization treaty signed in Mexico City in 1967, was held Sept. 2 in Mexico City. The 14 nations that had ratified the treaty participated. Speaking at the conference, UN Secy. Gen. U Thant hailed the treaty and expressed his conviction that "other nations, inspired by the Latin American model, would proceed in the near future to the creation of new denuclearized zones." He said that the Treaty of Tlatelolco (Mexico City) "shone like a beacon" in an atmosphere where disarmament actions were "few and far between." Describing the treaty as "the first multilateral nuclear disarmament treaty which foresees an institutionalized and rational system of control," International Atomic Energy Agency Director Sigvard Eklund offered his organization's help in promoting peaceful use of nuclear energy among the 14 nations.

Great Britain Dec. 11 ratified a protocol attached to the 1967 Treaty of Tlatelolco banning nuclear weapons from Latin America and thus pledged that it would not store or transport nuclear weapons in its possessions or territories in the hemisphere. The protocol, which stipulated that the treaty would be respected by the 4 nations with foreign possessions in the area (the U.S. Britain, France and the Netherlands), already had been ratified by the Netherlands.

1969's NUCLEAR TESTS

U.S. Explosions

All U.S. nuclear tests conducted during 1969 were underground. The dates, force and sites of the tests:

Date	Force	Site
Jan. 15	Low yield	Nevada test site
Jan. 15	Low-intermediate	Nevada test site
Jan. 30	Low-intermediate	Nevada test site
Feb. 12	Low yield	Nevada test site
Mar. 20	Low yield	Nevada test site
Mar. 21	Less than 100 kilotons	Nevada test site
Apr. 30		Nevada test site
Apr. 30		Nevada test site
May 7	Low-intermediate	Nevada test site
May 27	Low-intermediate	Nevada test site
June 12	Low yield	Nevada test site
July 16	Low-intermediate	Nevada test site
July 16	Low-intermediate	Nevada test site
Aug. 14	Low yield	Nevada test site
Aug. 27	Low yield	Nevada test site
Sept. 10*	40 kilotons	Battlement Mesa, Colo.
Sept. 12	Low yield	Nevada test site
Sept. 16	Intermediate	Nevada test site
Oct. 2	1.2 megaton	Amchitla Island
Oct. 8	Intermediate	Nevada test site
Oct. 30	Low yield	Nevada test site
Oct. 30	Low-intermediate	Nevada test site
Oct. 30	Low-intermediate	Nevada test site
Nov. 21	Low-intermediate	Nevada test site
Dec. 5	Low yield	Nevada test site
Dec. 17	Low yield	Nevada test site
Dec. 17	Low-intermediate	Nevada test site
Dec. 18	Low-intermediate	Nevada test site

Soviet Explosions

Date	Force	Site
May 7**	Low-intermediate	Semipalatinsk
May 16**	Low-intermediate	
May 31**	Low yield	
July 22**	Low-intermediate	
Sept. 8**	Low yield	Southern Urals
Sept. 11**	Low yield	Semipalatinsk
Sept. 26**	Low-intermediate	Volgograd
Oct. 1**		Semipalatinsk

---

*Part of Plowshare program for developing peaceful uses of nuclear explosives. The purpose of the test was to pulverize heavy Mesa Verde formations of shale and sand. The project was sponsored jointly by the AEC and Austral Oil Co. of Houston, Tex. It was the 2d joint industry-government nuclear test to free natural gas.
**Underground test.

Date	Force	Site
Oct. 14**	Intermediate	Novaya Zemlya
Nov. 30**	Intermediate	Semipalatinsk
Dec. 6**	Low-intermediate	Kazakh Desert
Dec. 28**	Low-intermediate	Semipalatinsk

Chinese Explosions

Sept. 22★	Low-intermediate	Lob Nor
Sept. 29★	3 megatons	Lob Nor

★Atmospheric test.

G

GABON—165

GALLEY, Robert—175

GAMBIA—165

GANDHI, Mrs. Indira—152, 162

GARBUZOV, Vasily F.—54

GARCIA Robles, Alfonso—84

GASBUGGY, Project—156

GENEVA Conferences—See DIS-
ARMAMENT Committee, etc.

GERMANY, Democratic Republic
of (East)—77. Disarmament &
nuclear weapons control—13-4,
108, 122. Military spending—155.
Nuclear non-proliferation — 172.
Troop withdrawal proposals—89

GERMANY, Federal Republic of
(West): Chemical & biological
warfare (CBW)—229. Military
spending—155. Nuclear energy
(peaceful use)—206. Nuclear non-
proliferation—71, 74, 126, 131-2,
134, 162-3, 171-2, 192, 206-8. Nuclear weapons & policy—13-4, 41,
58, 63, 66, 68-9, 104, 185. Strategic
arms limitation talks—223; see
also under 'S.' Troop withdrawal
proposals—89. U.S. relations—41

GHANA—165, 172

GILPATRIC, Roswell L.—42, 202

GILPATRIC Committee—87

GODLETTE, Dr. G. B.—45

GOLDBERG, Arthur J.—80-1, 84-5,
115, 118, 141, 150, 164, 169, 202

GOLDBLAT, Jozef—78

GOLDWATER, Sen. Barry (R.,
Ariz.)—3, 18, 20-2, 24-6, 36-7

GOMEZ Robledo, Antonio—110

GOMULKA, Wladyslaw—13-4

GORDON Walker, Patrick—38

GORE, Sen. Albert (D., Tenn.)—
194, 197, 199

GORE-Booth, Sir Paul—65

GREAT Britain—12, 15, 17-8, 30, 35.
Chemical & biological warfare
(CBW)—214, 229. Defense policy
& spending—59, 67, 106, 155. Inspection issue—113, 138. Latin
American nuclear-free zone—145,
189, 236. Nuclear-armed planes—
68. Nuclear non-proliferation —
24-5, 31, 38, 86, 88, 115, 140, 161,
164-5, 169-70, 172-3, 209. Nuclear
tests—47. Soviet relations—8, 45-6,
88. Space treaty banning nuclear
weapons—140-1. West European
defense—232. See also CARADON,
Lord; CHALFONT, Lord; WIL-
SON, Harold

GREECE—68, 165, 172, 176

GREENLAND: U.S. H-bombs lost—
186-8

GROMYKO, Andrei A.: Bomber &
missile destruction proposal—28.
British relations — 88. Disarmament—11, 81, 88, 115, 182, 218.
French relations—87-8. Nuclear
non-proliferation—81. Nuclear test
ban & extension—121, 183. Space
proposals — 118. Strategic arms
limitation talks (SALT)—183,
220-1. U.S. & NATO nuclear policy
—70. U.S. relations—115

GRONOUSKI, John A.—98

GUATEMALA—144, 165, 189

GUDE, Rep. Gilbert (R., Md.)—231

GUEST, Rear Adm. William S.—
121

GUINEA—165

GUTHRIE, John C.—10

GUYANA—165, 189

H

HAEKKERUP, Per—82

HAITI—144, 165, 172, 189

HARRIMAN, W(illiam) Averell—
72, 202

HARRIS, Louis—173, 202

HART, Sen. Philip A. (D., Mich.)
—174, 204

HASSAN, Abdel Fattah—16, 30

HATFIELD, Sen. Mark O. (R.,
Ore.)—204

HATONO, Brig. Gen.—77

HAUG, Capt. John M.—186-7

HAWAII—230

HEALEY, Denis—103, 154, 232

HECK, Bruno—206

HEIKAL, Mohammed Hassanein—
77

HELLYER, Paul—154

HELMS, Richard—151, 203

DISARMAMENT & NUCLEAR TESTS 1964-69

Contents:

FACTS ON FILE, 119 W. 57th St., NEW YORK, N.Y. 10019

INTERIM HISTORY

The Bridge Between Today's News and Tomorrow's History